THE GROUP
THERAPY
EXPERIENCE

THE GROUP THERAPY EXPERIENCE

From Theory to Practice

LOUIS R. ORMONT, PH.D.

ST. MARTIN'S PRESS
New York

Library of Congress Cataloging-in-Publication Data

Ormont, Louis R.
    The group therapy experience from theory to practice / Louis Ormont.
        p.   cm.
    Includes index.
    ISBN 0-312-07036-5
    1. Group psychotherapy.   I. Title.
    [DNLM: 1. Psychotherapy, Group.   WM 430 073g]
RC488.074   1992
616.89'152—dc20
DNLM/DLC
for Library of Congress   91-37184
                                                              CIP

10   9   8   7   6   5   4   3   2

To my friend George Weinberg

CONTENTS

ACKNOWLEDGMENTS

I would especially like to thank my wife, Joan Ormont, for her many psychological insights, her logic, and of course, her love, and my children, Marion and Michael, for their encouragement and patience.

Naturally, a great many people have provided encounters and experiences that found their way into this book: the members of my treatment groups and of my training groups over the years, fellow professionals, friends, teachers, literary figures. Though I cannot cite all of them, I would like to mention a few people who worked very directly on this book: Mary Evans, Cora Hook, Dianne Rowe, and Margaret Scal.

Of the numerous teachers and other professionals I worked with during my formative years, a few above the rest kept coming to mind while I was writing this book: Sender Abend, John Gustin, Azya Kadis, Joost Meerlo, Fritz Perls, Theodor Reik, Hyman Spotnitz, and Alexander Wolf.

Finally, I would like to thank the faculty and students of the Center for the Advancement of Group Studies. My involvement with this community, which is so enthusiastic about group therapy and so questioning, has helped sustain me over my many months of putting these ideas down on paper.

THE GROUP
THERAPY
EXPERIENCE

CHAPTER ONE

GROUP ANALYSIS

Group therapy has become a remarkably widespread and accepted form of treatment. Owing to the influence of movies, television, books, popular articles, and word of mouth, virtually everyone knows at least a little about what goes on.

People know, for instance, that a set of members come together in a room regularly, typically once a week; they sit in a circle and talk. Nearly always, a therapist, someone trained in the technique of working with groups of people, mediates in some way. To the extent that a group is successful, its members learn to cope with problems and to take more from life.

The majority of those who undertake group treatment are not acutely disturbed. Some are already highly accomplished in their chosen fields. Others are floundering because of the very personality difficulties that they hope to surmount as a result of their group experience.

It is a mistaken notion that the aim of group treatment is to help people socialize better. Group should accomplish this. Far more important, however, the group itself, when used effectively, is a vehicle for people to identify and deal with their own emotional blocks and limitations. The successful group member finishes not simply with a superior capacity to relate to others, but also with more inner comfort and with a far better ability to realize his or her own potential.

In short, effective group treatment should enable people to make inner adjustments, and to use themselves effectively on Earth—so that

1

they are better able to love and to work. This means even to work in solitude, if that is what they wish to do.

But these are general statements, and necessarily so. Exactly what can the participants expect to get out of a group? What does the therapist actually do?

Such questions are puzzling to the millions of people who have heard smatterings about group therapy—and indeed, even to most professionals. This book, though addressed to the practitioner, aims at describing the whole group process both to professionals and to anyone who is interested in group treatment.

Group therapy is almost a century old. Its earliest advocates spoke about their work apologetically. While maintaining that groups could help people learn skills in relating to others, they too readily succumbed to the argument that group therapy did little more than this, and that it was in a sense makeshift, inferior to one-on-one treatment, especially for the patient with a serious problem.

Opponents of group treatment argued that such a patient wouldn't have time or space enough to pay his tortured psyche the needed attention. They imagined a whole group spending its time investigating one person's slip of the tongue, much to the chagrin of the other group members who would derive nothing. At best, only one individual stood to profit from any segment of a session.

And indeed, in the 1940s this was precisely what often happened. Not surprisingly, during the first twenty years of group treatment, nearly all practitioners continued to advocate the deep-delving instrument of individual psychoanalysis.

For decades psychoanalytic institutes refused all alliance with group therapy; to the orthodox, it seemed that placing many patients together in a room could lead to nothing but chaos. Anyone attempting to treat a whole group at once was perceived as having a shaky grasp of technique. No one doubted that Freud himself, who often barred people from his inner circle for violating his tenets, would have disqualified group treatment as a form of true psychoanalysis. The story goes that Freud once, having walked into the office of a therapist who had two couches, remarked mockingly, "Ah-hah! Group therapy."

On the other hand, many contended that group therapeutic techniques deeply affected people—and not merely by teaching them how to act in company. An obvious benefit was that the patient could receive diverse reactions to his or her social behavior and could glean different opinions about it.

Another benefit, which became evident a bit more slowly, was that patients in group behaved in ways that were characteristic of them in the world but that might not surface in the presence of their therapist alone.

For instance, those who overreacted to slight irrationalities in others would have no chance to do this in the presence of a therapist, who was, ideally, rational himself and well analyzed. They would show their true problems only when provoked by the slight irrationality of fellow group members.

Also, there were those patients whose problems appeared in the presence of members of one sex but not the other: if their therapist was of the "wrong" sex, their real problems would not arise and so could not get resolved. Countering this, groups provide an ample supply of both men and women.

As time went by, other benefits of group therapy became apparent. In the group, people felt a curious freedom to express ideas that did not occur to them during their individual hours. Many who felt inhibited by the vaunted presence of someone they revered cut loose when they found themselves in a room with people they considered their equals or inferiors.

More recently, still subtler benefits of group therapy have been identified. Chief among them is that when a person speaks to *many* others and not just to one other individual, his own words echo in his or her mind more loudly. And finally, the very fact that many people vie for attention tends to elicit early childhood feelings of helplessness and competition among siblings, feelings that have influenced the person's life profoundly over the years and that can be resolved in group.

So the benefits of group therapy have become increasingly appreciated. Defenses of the technique have ceased, and many therapists now recommend group treatment in preference to individual treatment where both are equally available. Even among card-carrying psychoanalysts, the idea is disappearing that group therapy is off-course. In orthodox circles, therapists who run groups meet and discuss their work without the old stigma that it is not truly psychoanalysis.

Over the years, group therapists have begun to codify their work, qualifying it and adding to it. We in the field have created our own vocabulary for group therapy events, devising technical terms, giving us what the philosopher Carl Pearson has called a "conceptual shorthand." For instance, we have conceived of such notions as "shared resistance" and "subgrouping." These have application uniquely to our work, referring to events that arise exclusively in the group context and have meaning only there.

As our techniques evolved and their success became more evident, nonpsychoanalytic therapists have become attracted to our work. Today relatively few group therapists have classically traditional training. Indeed, not all who practice group therapy are professional psychologists; our ranks include social workers, nurses, and industrial organizers.

People with problems are realizing from their end too that group therapy may address their needs more directly than individual therapy does. Take someone whose failings are interpersonal. A man is fine when alone or with his wife, but suffers or behaves irrationally in social contexts. He may well need to explore his problems alone with a private therapist.

But actual immersion in a group also becomes helpful, possibly indispensable. To people with interpersonal difficulties, the group context serves as a *microcosm of reality* and is the ideal place to solve real problems. There is no substitute for experiencing one's worst moments in the lab before approaching them in life.

Fundamental to all group therapeutic treatment is a single truth. It is that people in their daily lives and as patients in group therapy always create their own impasses, and in virtually the same ways. Wittingly or unwittingly, they block themselves in their relationships with other group members, just as they block themselves with associates, friends, lovers, and relatives. People have ingrained mannerisms by which they handicap themselves, and group therapy is the arena in which we both evoke these mannerisms and help the patient recognize and overcome them.

A few words about the use of the group itself as an arena. We make the assumption that virtually everything that our group members do and experience in their outside lives, they also do and experience with the other group members. This means that the group itself may be used as a theater of study and change, rather than as merely a place for postmortems and dissections of what has taken place in people's lives during the week.

We encourage our members to respond to one another and to talk about their responses, to discuss how others make them feel. We rest everything on the premise that whatever their problems are in the outside world, they will be manifested in the group and can be resolved right in front of us.

The result is a great new immediacy, which marks so-called modern group analysis and distinguishes it from earlier methods. In modern analysis, the group experience becomes emotionally alive for all the members simultaneously, no matter who is actually speaking, and to whom.

It has been my good fortune to have been an early practitioner of group therapy, and, so far as I know, the first to make a practice exclusively of doing group work in the U.S. I began running groups back in the early fifties, during the pioneering days of the discipline. My training was originally in psychoanalysis, what we called "pure" analytic work. That meant that all my patients came to my office at least three times a week, lay down on a couch, and free-associated while I sought to decode the messages hidden in their communications.

Like all analysts, I sought to study my patients' resistances to forming relationships with me and to understand how they were unconsciously recreating their past lives. Ultimately, I would help them see how they were doing this, and where I succeeded, they could resume the emotional development that had been thwarted during their formative years.

My interest in the group process had evolved long before I became a psychoanalyst. Without my realizing it, a near-obsession of mine with what we now call "group dynamics" led me to study drama. As a boy, I read plays and acted. After college I went to Yale Drama School on a three-year scholarship as a playwright. My first career was as a writer of radio drama and of television plays, when that medium was in its infancy.

It now seems to me that I pursued group therapy rather than playwriting for a reason obscure to me back then. As playwright, one creates a universe. It is the writer's task to compose a world and to people it with characters—it is hoped fertile ones, but nevertheless with one's own creations.

On the other hand, to the therapist is given a real world—people who write their own scripts, who create their own inevitabilities. The group therapist has a ready-made population, intense and interactive. Every member of every group has a story to tell and has no choice *but* to tell that story. Group analysis, it seems to me, not only gives patients unique opportunities for self-expression, it also gives the group analyst an experience not forthcoming in any other way.

This book is about group analysis by a practitioner who has lived the experience for nearly forty years. In running groups and in teaching the intricacies of group analysis to others, I have seen many therapists succeed and fail. There are common pitfalls, and subtler ones; there are groups that stagnate and others that rush ahead too fast; there are groups that go out of control, like Phaethon with his chariot. There are others that never seem to start. Some therapists are only too well aware that trouble is brewing, and others, who think they are doing well, have their groups unexpectedly fall apart.

Very possibly, you, the reader, are either running a group already or will do so soon, or if not, you are a member of a group. Possibly, I am wrong in these assumptions, and you have come with me thus far out of sheer curiosity about how group therapy works. In every case, you are welcome.

CHAPTER TWO

HOW TO DO IT WRONG

As with all science, it is through trial and error that we learn the most *no;* about which techniques are effective. And perhaps half the mistakes *theory!* that group therapists make stem from a single misconception—namely that what works with an individual patient will work with a group. Therapists, without reflecting on the matter, simply assume that what they did successfully with a single patient lying on the couch they can do with ten or more of them sitting around in a circle. They mistakenly conceive of the group not as a unit with an identity and a life of its own, but as a collection of individuals who happen to be in the same room.

Certainly, much that therapists have learned about treating individual patients does give them a head start when it comes to treating a group. Their cultivation of empathy, of understanding, of ability to articulate, their lexicon of people's personalities will help them. But group treatment is far more than a simple extension of individual treatment, an enlargement from one to many. Our whole approach and purpose is different. We are not merely treating people individually, going from one to the other in rapid succession. We are literally *treating a group.*

The therapist who does nothing more than transfer to his or her group the techniques he evolved to a high level with individual patients lying on the couch is sure to have trouble—big trouble.

Witness the case of Reggie.

Reggie loved his mother, and she always understood him. He had a brother, much older, who had no time for him, and his father, reticent by nature, withdrew from him early. Growing up, Reggie had one friend at a time; he put himself through school, was effective but isolated. He was, in Tennyson's words, "always roaming with a hungry heart."

Perhaps in an effort to puzzle out his own problems, Reggie chose to become a psychologist, and in private practice he established solid and lasting relationships with both men and women. He was liked, even adored, by his patients. Only a sophisticated observer might have deplored Reggie's failure to have any patients who vented rage at him, who told him off.

After nine years of seeing patients individually, some lying on the couch and others sitting in front of him, Reggie decided to start a group. He put into that group people he liked and who relied heavily on him, but whose personal isolation baffled him and appeared to limit their progress. There was Claire, a librarian with a vast vocabulary but no social life. There was Martha, also isolated, who ran home at lunchtime to feed her cat; there was Eduardo, a computer repairman who spoke to very few; there was Ralph, a back-room lawyer at a big firm, who hit the books when others were out to lunch. And there were a handful of other isolates.

Reggie's first session was a smash. The members jumped at the chance to talk about themselves and their difficulties. They felt no longer alone. Several told Reggie at the door that daylight had come for them at last.

"I couldn't possibly have been in a group like this two years ago, the timing is perfect."

"You've been saving this up for us all along, haven't you, Reggie?"

Reggie continued to see a few of those same patients individually, and the sessions burst with new material: members recalled past social humiliations and years of being in private hell. For weeks, the new experience kept its hold. They felt bursts of energy at work, they could do dull tasks with grace, they were emboldened to talk to higher-ups. It all seemed too good to be true.

And it was.

The sixth week showed signs of reversion.

Claire became reticent and resorted to discussing only generic facts: political, geographical—even which celebrities had died that week and were mentioned on the obituary page. She was trying to offset her fear of looking stupid, but by using a mechanism that put people off.

Eduardo's device was to become absentminded when others spoke; he seemed constantly distracted. Martha seemed to suffer from malaise; she clutched her side, and from time to time popped a pill or two while someone else was talking.

In their own characteristic ways, the members had begun isolating themselves, using techniques they had employed all their lives. That is, they were resorting to their characteristic resistances, devices they had used to conceal from themselves what they were feeling. In using these resistances, they were pushing other people away. After all, what are other people if not stimuli that provoke feelings? And when our feelings are unwanted, so are those who induce them in us.

While all that was happening, Reggie, the therapist, felt some frustration but had no idea what was causing it. Naively, he assumed that whatever had beclouded the group in that session would pass. He dimly recognized that people were retracting into themselves, but that was all. He had no idea what to do, partly because he had no idea of how much material the group was actually giving him, even in that recalcitrant session.

Though Reggie didn't know it, the members were doing much more than retreating. They were engaging, each in his own way, in a *form of communication*, and a very meaningful one at that!

Claire's talking about dead celebrities was not only a retreat to an isolated topic but also a communication that the group was dying for her. Eduardo's absentmindedness was a form of dismissal. Martha's popping pills while other people spoke was both an avoidance of them and a statement that she would have to supply herself with energy because the group was offering her none.

Within a few weeks, real interaction came to a halt. Some of the members stopped talking altogether, as if waiting. Waiting for what? And those who did speak were very obviously only filling the void, reducing their own anxiety but not saying anything meaningful. They talked about the old and familiar, introducing nothing new. The group had become repetitive and felt stale.

Though no one said as much, everyone knew that it had lost its stuff. Whereas originally the sessions had been an oasis for the members, the group-room now became merely another place for them to conduct their sterile lives.

Reggie felt the tedium, but had no idea what to do next. Techniques that he'd used with patients he'd seen individually were of no avail. Alone in his office with a single person, when he'd been stymied, it had sufficed merely to bring the person out. Here something else was required—that he elicit an *interpersonal* flow. But Reggie did not even attempt this.

Ironically, the warmer Reggie was, the more inventive he was in dealing with any individual in the group, the more his other patients regretted having shared him in the first place! Some were sorry that they had sacrificed individual sessions with him to go into the group.

One patient after another told him, either after a session or over the phone, that they wanted out. Some denounced the group as superficial, others blamed themselves for not being up to the experience. The most sophisticated complaints sounded like compliments.

"Thank you," said Eduardo. "Putting me into this group showed me how isolated I really am. Now I've got to get down to basics, just you and me. I'll be stopping the group because what I really need is to see *you* more often."

Reggie didn't catch on to the implied criticism of him as a group leader. He threatened them, cajoled them, remonstrated with them to come back. But they were adamant. The group fell apart.

It need hardly be said that the members got little or nothing of durable value out of that group experience. They had utterly failed to derive the rich benefits that a successfully run group might have afforded them. If anything, as with bad therapy of any form, they felt they had tried it out and wanted no more of it. In that sense, they were worse off.

What Reggie had confronted was a shared refusal by the members to interact with one another. They wanted their cure, and their love, *from Reggie*—and they perceived what others had to offer as sorry substitutes. This had been the crux of their resistances; each was expressing a variant of his or her defensive pattern.

They had wanted something only from a figure they could adore. They had no idea that as a group working in harmony, they might have given one another ten times the insight and strength that Reggie or any other individual could have supplied them.

Reggie had failed to show them the power of the group. They had seen life itself, interactions with their peers, with friends, lovers, colleagues, as a poor substitute for what they really wanted—nurturance from a parent who wasn't there. In effect, they had disdained others like themselves and kept their relationships highly superficial.

When treating any resistance with a person on the couch, our aim is to identify the resistance and bring it to the person's attention. This

must be done repeatedly, and from many angles, before we can resolve the resistance.

Also, with groups we faced *shared resistances,* ways of resisting
communication that a set of members or a whole group used in common. A group may be stingy or overintellectualized or sadistic, for
example, and we must help the members reveal to themselves and to
each other what the precise nature of that resistance is. We cannot
possibly confront a group and do all the work ourselves.

Thus we see how and why Reggie failed. Far from analyzing the
shared resistance, Reggie had not even identified it.

Reggie had regarded himself as the sole force for change. It was he
who would help them, not they who would help one another. Yes,
they might have something to say to one another, but the ultimate
leverage would come from him: that was how Reggie saw it. For that
reason, and because essentially Reggie was untrained as a group therapist, as someone geared to *utilize the group as an instrument of cure,*
he defaulted in many ways.

Consider these examples of how Reggie botched the job, each bearing
an implication for what he might have done.

Often a member had helped another, as by naming the fellow member's feeling or by giving an interpretation or simply by expressing
warmth. Virtually as often, the recipient shrugged off the comment.

For instance, Eduardo had remarked to Claire that she would constantly correct people even when they wanted to help her. Claire had
responded automatically, "Well, I like things to be said politely, I can
hear them better that way. Otherwise I just tune out." In this way,
Claire used her inveterate criticality to defend her criticality—that is,
as a resistance.

Such moments might, ideally, have prompted Reggie to intervene,
to help Claire see that she was throwing away people's potentially
valuable contributions to her self-understanding. It is perhaps too
much to hope that Claire would have come to perceive her resistance
the first time it was noted, but the accumulation of such interpretations by Reggie might have afforded her insight.

If Reggie had broken in, those who could have been of benefit to
Claire might have pressed on. By even a few words pointing out
Claire's tactic of refusing help, Reggie might have encouraged others
to tell Claire how they experienced her. Eduardo, who in actuality fell

by the wayside when Claire rebuffed him, could have benefited Claire and himself by becoming even more explicit—with Reggie's support.

Reggie defaulted, too, on another occasion when one patient's potential contribution was refused by another. When Martha spoke about her sense of isolation and hopelessness, Maria, another woman in the group, responded empathetically, saying that she often felt just the way Martha did. But Martha, paying absolutely no attention to her, went on complaining as if no one had even heard her, much less sympathized with her. She acted as if Maria wasn't in the room. Thus Martha paraded in front of the group the very activity that, over a lifetime, was dooming her to her own sense of isolation.

Could one hope for more than that a patient in group would do the very thing that had been self-destructive elsewhere! However, here too Reggie had said nothing, thus allowing Martha to re-create the worst of all possible worlds for herself, without improving that world. In the process, Reggie had allowed Martha's potential rescuers to go on feeling unwanted; he virtually discouraged them from trying to rescue poor Martha.

These were two instances in which it might fairly be said that Reggie had, unknowingly, permitted people to resist intimacy in their customary ways, without helping them achieve any insight. It wasn't simply that he himself didn't confront them—a direct confrontation from Reggie might have been overwhelming. The members were far too reliant on his good opinion to have been anything but crushed by his public censure of them. However, he might have veered the group toward those loners. In each case, the *group's reactions* to the person who spoke could have been very helpful to that person and to others.

And, ideally, Reggie could have done much more. After all, the loners were more than victims of neglect, they were inflicting their own experiences of neglect on others. This means that Reggie could very profitably have brought in still other participants by asking them how they felt about those who had spoken. Having them talk about their own sense of being neglected would have been invaluable.

For instance, Claire was not merely a victim but had her own victims. Surely there were others in the group besides Eduardo who felt excluded when Claire told Eduardo to address her politely or not at all. And those "victims of her rebuffs" within the group, if appropriately brought in, might have helped Claire understand how she affected people—and even what she herself was feeling.

As it turned out, those who might have spoken to Claire must have

been discouraged by what happened to Eduardo. Instead of participating, they elected to remain a silent majority. Almost surely, if
Reggie had made an opening for them, at least one of them might have
told Claire that she was asking for too much. Later, others might have
joined in. Without Reggie's intervention, such potential agents of
change found it easier to defer, and the power of the group was lost.

A seasoned Reggie might have enjoined one or two of the silent majority to speak. By well-aimed questions, he could almost surely have
gotten them to help expose what was going on. After all, they too must
have felt walled off by Claire. For instance, Reggie might have asked
one woman, "Jane, how did you feel when Claire said that?"

Had Reggie done this, it might have astonished Claire to see that
she influenced more than one person by her unconscious rebuffs—
that there is a near universality of response to such behavior as hers.
To put it another way, it was not Eduardo's problem alone that made
him feel unwanted when Claire spoke to him as she did. Claire's
behavior by its very nature was destructive to intimacy. And Reggie
might have helped her see this, using the whole group.

All this may seem unduly complex, and in its presentation it certainly sounds that way. However, there are solid principles behind
these interventions. What must necessarily seem complex before one
gets accustomed to thinking about the orchestration of groups may
become second nature the more one thinks this way.

Once we appreciate that the aim of group analysis is to *utilize all the
members as players,* we see that a variety of techniques may further
our objective. Indeed, the very progress of group analysis as a science
and art may fairly be described as the unfolding discovery of methods
to accomplish this. Even members not directly involved in an emotional flow (such as those who sided neither with Claire nor with
those she rejected) become useful as observers. "Yes," one member
on the sidelines might have said when asked about the speaker, "you
are doing what they say, and this is how I feel about it."

The group analyst's task is to deal with the group as a whole, to
bring people in when needed. The analyst should always deem himself
or herself responsible to those members not talking as well as to those
who are.

A successful group moves forward as a whole. If the analyst does include all the members all the time, he will find to his delight that, before long, the group members themselves will assist the cohesiveness of the group. They are quick to feel any disturbance in its intactness. They are alert to stragglers, to those who are not contributing, and thus *every member becomes part of the organism that is a successful group*.

So far, I have meant merely to illustrate how patients create their own impasses, and why the analyst working alone has insufficient power to resolve those impasses. The most he or she can do is to help the group identify obstacles and to *use the group as a whole to resolve them*. However, that "most" should prove more than enough.

Exactly how, then, are we to get a group to work as a whole, as a creative unit?

Let's look next at the fundamental methods for uniting a group, for enabling the members to work together in a common enterprise. The methods by which we do this, taken collectively, I call techniques of *bridging*.

Let's consider now how we build bridges between the members, so that they have easy access to one another. Only as we bridge does a group develop a therapeutic force of its own.

CHAPTER THREE

INVOLVING THE PLAYERS—
The Technique of Bridging

For any group to succeed, it must go forward as a unit, as an organism. Ideally, every member would have reactions and attitudes toward every other member and would express them freely. But if this ideal were a reality, the members wouldn't need us; they might not need treatment of any kind. And so it is a safe assumption that such open expression is an end product if we are successful, and not a starting condition.

We've seen how therapists fail by trying to treat patients individually, one after the other, in the presence of others. The crisscross reactions of the members, one to the other, will do more to impede a group than to advance it, unless we get the members to say in no uncertain terms how they feel. On the other hand, if we get the members to express their reactions to one another, we are tapping a powerful resource for treatment. It matters less who is speaking than who is feeling the import of what is being said. Even silent members feel their participation and their progress.

Our primary task then in making our group function as an organism is to do what I have called *bridging* between the members. By "bridging," I mean any technique geared to evoke meaningful talk between group members, to develop emotional connections where they did not exist before.

In bridging we are uniting what sociologists call a "scattered community," namely an array of people who, despite similarities, do not ordinarily identify with one another. To the extent that we succeed, our group patients supply insights and support to one another and draw strength from the recognition that they are no longer alone.

Doubtless, most highly intuitive group therapists, regardless of their orientations, have at times felt the need for bridging. Even without having the word *bridging* in mind, these therapists have devised techniques of their own to link the members. But they do so only under certain conditions and in crude ways. When they create bridges, they do so intuitively, not as professionals who should have an explicit consciousness of their purpose and who are drawing from a corpus of knowledge. With a clear formulation of what bridging is, its purposes, and its values, group therapists will in the future have a lexicon of techniques to draw from and of indications concerning when and how to use these techniques.

In the future, the very word *bridging* should serve group therapists as a reminder to keep thinking about their groups as working units—and never to become diverted by the problems of individuals. Ideally, what is now only occasional practice will become the expected and near-universal procedure of the trained group therapist.

Helping the members build bridges to each other—that is, establishing meaningful communication—is not the same as bridging might be in an ordinary social gathering. "John, let me introduce you to Bill. You both went to Yale within three years of each other. I guess you had the same president. You must have a lot in common."

Such introductions do not establish *emotional communication*. By pointing up coincidences in the past histories of the members, we are, if anything, *stopping* them from conveying their personal experiences. Under the guise of giving them something to talk about, we are, to some degree, preventing their forming a real emotional bond. They are meeting under *our* premise on our terms, instead of on their own personal terms. For this reason, we should try not to make demographic introductions between members in group treatment.

Nor is bridging synonymous with establishing common interests or even warmth between two members. Once again, that would be insisting too much on our terms. Bridging is, pure and simple, a mode of getting people to *expose* their inner lives to one another, to reveal what in usual conversation they might not consider saying.

Bridging consists of bringing out *differences* as much as *similarities*. It is by bridging that we bring out the latent psychological energy of the group. No individual analyst has the energy necessary to sustain a group, but all groups contain more than enough energy themselves.

WHEN IS BRIDGING CALLED FOR?

Always we want our members to interact, for the sake of group fluidity, and there are times when unless they do, a group will absolutely fall apart. Let's start by looking at some of these extreme instances, when if we don't build bridges our group will self-destruct, before going on to discuss the technique of bridging more generally.

As implied, bridging is especially useful in the early stages of treating any group. Doubtless, all therapists with even a modicum of experience attempt to bridge members in the early sessions to get a group started. They feel a need to have the members talk about themselves, about each other, about *anything*. Where there is talk, there is life—this is the premise, and it has much to be said for it.

Also familiar is the need to bridge as a remedy when there are lulls in a group. Nearly all therapists recognize the potential dangers of prolonged silences. When a group is bogging down, the members feel this as keenly as the therapist does. They sit fidgeting and with bored expressions. They drift off into their private fantasies. We may see them peeking at their watches, and we ourselves wonder with them, "When will this session ever end?"

We can guess at such times that their experience is more one of captivity than of making progress, and at least some may be hatching plans to leave. Prolonged silence often signifies that they resent us, that they regard us as inept—and in a sense we are. The experience is deadly for them and for us.

It is not enough for us to surmise exactly what is on their minds, to foresee their disgruntlement before they express it. We must do something. And our choice of intervention will determine whether the group self-destructs or whether the members will convert the energy now used for defiance into the constructive energy that is needed to do creative work in the group.

An understandable first impulse might be to interpret how it is going wrong. "You people are using silence to express your annoyance and disappointment. You would be much better off talking."

Such a communication, however, could very well drive the members even further into silence, by making them feel helpless or guilty.

Indeed, nearly anything that we ourselves might say runs the risk of confirming the members' sense of inadequacy and their expectation that we, not they, will do the work.

This is where the technique of bridging becomes indispensable. By asking questions of the members, we pointedly release their pent-up energy, enabling them to express it in making contact with one another.

"George, how do you feel about Edna's opening and closing her pocketbook?"

"Jerry, why that look of impatience every time Marty starts whispering to Al?"

"Jack, when you stretch out and cross your legs and yawn, looking at the ceiling, does that imply that you'd rather be home in bed than here?"

Such questions are designed to bring the members into direct touch with what they are feeling and doing in the moment. It is this very consciousness of feeling that becomes an antidote to the silence and that helps the members use their energy in the new way.

And the right questions do more than start the members talking. They invite the members to discuss what is central to them, at the heart of their experience. Silence, as mentioned, has its own intensity. But by asking well-timed and well-placed questions of silent members, we can convert that into group intensity.

Another kind of impasse that requires us to do bridging may hide behind wordiness. I mean the impasse resulting from excessive self-preoccupation. A set of members, or perhaps the majority of them, blocks out the rest of the would-be participants and thinks only about itself. Or an individual may do this.

We are all painfully acquainted with the person whose every sentence begins with "I," and who constantly complains of being neglected. In his own convoluted way, he tells us over and over, "My boss bypasses me for opportunities," "My wife ignores me," "My mother ignored me too," "Everyone has it easier than I do."

In group, while complaining that the others neglect him, he tries to monopolize the total attention of those present. The other members get the message after a while and give up.

As group therapists, we may find ourselves facing a gallery of narcissists, who have come to air their grievances, and would use the group as their own private looking glass. These people resent any intervention we might make; they won't even sit still for a description of what they're doing or how it affects others. Our best recourse is to spot those in the group who seem most visibly affected by the narcissist's exclusion of them, and to use those impacted members to highlight what is going on.

For instance, we observe that while Nate raves on about himself and his misfortunes, Edith, another member, scowls and stops talking. After waiting for an opening to edge in her own few words, she has apparently given up in disgust.

We approach her. "Edith, why do you think that Nate won't give you any time to talk? What has he got against you?"

But Nate won't let us finish our question. "Look," he explains, "I can't listen to anybody until I get this out."

At best, Edith will follow our lead and say something indicating that she feels bullied. But, just as likely, Edith won't be the one to respond. After all, we've chosen Edith as our protagonist because her discomfort seemed most apparent to us. However, another member, anyone in the group feeling stifled by Nate, may be the one who speaks out against Nate. Our intervention, our bridge, was something we put there for anyone to cross who chose to.

Of the many other indications for bridging, one especially worth mentioning is the problem that arises when a subgroup dominates the room and would, if left to its own devices, deprive the silent majority of its chance to talk. For instance, four women in a group feel discontent with their husbands, who, they argue, tend to be taciturn and ungiving. It's as if these four women have decided that the theme of the session—of *every* session—is "How to Endure the Man Not in Touch with His Feelings."

As with all outside problems presented in group, the therapist's first task is to find their expression within the group and deal with that. To the extent that the problem is truly her patient's, she can always do this. That is, she must deal with the expression of the problem in group, instead of relying on what the members are merely reporting. She has far less leverage with events that took place in the past and with people not in the room with her. In effect, we want to keep the plot but use as players the group members rather than people we know only by hearsay. Here, addressing the collection of complaining women in the group, the therapist might ask, "Which men in this room are ungivers?"

Instantly, one or more of the plaintiffs will tell us. "I could walk in here in tears, with mascara all over my face, and Bill wouldn't notice it."

We turn to Bill, asking him, "Why do you think she has this idea about you? Why does she think you're so oblivious of her?"

Bill answers, "Believe me, if she had something sincere and honest to say, sure I'd respond, but I don't want to be manipulated like her husband. I'm no sucker."

Having heard him out, we might ask others if they feel the same way. They begin talking. Whether they are right or wrong is not the point. They are communicating, building bridges themselves.

Conceivably our very question, our attempt to start the bridge, will itself be ignored. The complainants are truly bent on blocking out those in the room and are concentrating on themselves. They are excluders, either by nature or because they have also had traumatic relationships with important men in their lives. Feeling helpless, they are resorting to shared complaints, acting out their aggression toward their husbands by cutting out the men in the room.

We might construct our bridge elsewhere, for instance, by asking some particular man in the room if he feels that he is being given ample time to talk. Very likely, he or someone else will take the lead by complaining that he doesn't feel that he's getting a fair chance. That person may go on to vent his anger at one or more of the women who treat him as if he's made out of stone.

For example, Eddie says, "I can't stand the way Maria talks to me. She talks to me just the way my brother did. She treats me as if I'm defective and there's no hope for me. All she ever does is cry about having to deal with me. Well, I have a terrific impulse to just walk out of the room. You know I left home when I was seventeen."

Not content with this, we may scan the room for other men likely to feel the same way. We see John also looking crushed and ask him, "Do you feel the way Eddie does?"

John concurs, and adds, "Yeah, every time I start to talk, they just listen and then go back to their standard complaint. About a month ago, I just gave up."

Now others, liberated by these two men, chime in, "I know. I felt that for a long time. No matter what we talk about, they always go back to themselves and their husbands. It's a big waste of time."

Accuracy of perception is not at issue here. Far more important is that the members are participating. Our aim when we bridge is not to do analysis but to involve people in the group with one another—to turn the group into a coherent whole.

METHODS OF BRIDGING

Open-ended Questioning

Since an open-ended question is one that can be answered in many ways, the very choice of answer the patient gives is hard to anticipate and therefore diagnostic. It is the kind of question most individual analysts ask, especially in the early states of treating someone.

In group treatment, our most usual open-ended questions are inquiries of one patient regarding what he or she imagines another patient is feeling. Open-ended questions become a powerful means of bridging because whatever "inference" a patient makes indicates her own feeling as well as that of the person she is discussing. Open-ended questions are a primary invitation for the member to establish a bridge to another by a demonstration of awareness of the other person.

For instance, we might ask Jane, "What do you think Leslie is actually feeling when she purses her lips?"

Jane answers resoundingly, "Disappointment!"

Jane, almost surely, has told us a little about herself as well as about Leslie. But more important, to the degree that she is accurate, she has built a bridge, one that others will cross.

Revelation breeds revelation. Jane's insight disposes others in the group to reveal themselves next, and a desire to be understood activates the whole group and not merely the two women. The members feel less isolated and more willing to extend themselves.

We might, if we wish, frame our question so that, in answering it, the member is describing himself as well as the other person. For instance, two men in a group are each inclined to react with great irritation when their suggestions go unheeded. We ask one of them what the other is feeling and doing while the second is on one of his rampages. He tells us, "Bill is battering Brook because he feels ignored and is willing to settle for any kind of attention." His is a twofold revelation, and both profit.

Directed Questioning

Another way of bridging is to design our question so that it sounds like an interpretation, asking it almost as if we were referring to a forgone conclusion. We ask Arthur, "I guess you're aware that Mickey feels injured by what you just said?"

In posing such a question, we are not merely bridging between Arthur and Mickey; we are alerting the others in the room to Mickey's inner state, converting potential adversaries of Mickey into sympathetic students of his condition.

However, when using such a technique, there is a caution. If the person about whom we make our conjecture tells us we are wrong, we must instantly retract and inquire of the person himself what he really feels. It is never our domain to be proprietary about anyone else's inner state. Always the person with the feeling is the ultimate judge—his assertion about how he feels must stand. Whether we are right or wrong becomes a trivial matter alongside his feeling that we are superimposing our conception over his regarding his own state of experience.

Much is gained by our speculations if they are timely and right, and if we are also flexible, we actually help the patient by allowing him to rebut us and "win." The patient must learn, if he or she does not know it already, that, no matter how insightful an expert we may be, each person is the ultimate judge of his own inner states.

Directed questioning is a powerful technique for bridging in group. The method enables us to form links that remain imprinted in the members' subconscious minds. However, we must remain mindful that all such interpretive questions are only *invitations* for the members to form their own liaisons—and to bond with one another as they will. If we attempt to make them more than that, they become less.

Questioning a Member About an Interaction
Taking Place Between Two Others

Sometimes we bridge by asking a critical question not of the two people engaged in an interaction but of a third member.

Pam, a woman of thirty-four, had been molested in childhood by her father; over the years he would make bawdy references in front of her and observe her reactions. Not surprisingly, Pam learned to play dumb when he did, and had trouble with men while growing up. Now in adulthood, Pam was unresponsive and overly suspicious of men, and virtually blind to an expression of genuine interest in her.

In treatment, Pam would resist even the most tentative suggestions of mine concerning how she might feel. Clearly I had taken on the role of lecherous father in her mind, and she would concede nothing to me beyond her presence in group.

I realized after a time that I would have to communicate with her through a *third person*—ideally, someone who could also profit.

In that group was Carlos, an ebullient youth given to overstatement. "What a wonderful day!" "You make me feel like Superman!" And to Pam he would often comment, "You look like an angel!"

In the face of such flowery prose, Pam would do her best to act unmoved. She sought to discourage Carlos by nonresponse, but one could detect the light of pleasure in her eyes. Even before Pam could acknowledge wanting a relationship with a man, she would have to see how she pushed men away. Her refusals of men mirrored her psychic refusal to accept the sense of delight that men gave her.

What better place to start than with Carlos! He meant no ill. And yet she routinely discouraged him, doing her best to appear utterly unmoved by him.

Though I wanted her to see what she was doing, and to recognize what she truly felt, for me to suggest these things seemed risky. I was, after all, a father figure to her—the last person whose references to sex, even oblique ones, Pam could accept. Even to imply anything about a man's interest in her, to broach the topic of sex or affection, I would run the risk of looking like a child molester, a derelict, or worst of all, like her father.

Therefore I scoured the group for someone to create a bridge between Pam and Carlos. Ideally it would be someone who understood Pam's reaction, who liked Pam, but who did not push men away so instinctively.

A woman, Judith, emerged as the best candidate. Judith had grown up in an unexpressive, overtly unemotional home—her parents loved each other but seemed always to take that love for granted. Both worked hard and created security in the home, but there were few overtly tender moments. Judith had wept at her mother's reaction of profound sadness when Judith's father had died the year before. "If only they had acknowledged each other and enjoyed each other while they lived."

During the previous year, Judith had succeeded in breaking through the pattern of nonreaction that she had acquired in her parents' home. She had freed herself to express warmth for the first time.

The more I thought about it, the more Judith seemed the perfect choice to bridge the gap between Carlos and Pam. Pam liked Judith, and was unafraid of her.

Carlos had just finished telling Pam how pretty she looked that day, and Pam had assumed her usual stoical aspect.

I asked Judith, "What feeling is Pam hiding from Carlos right now?"

Judith responded at once. "She's scared but delighted that he's attracted to her, and maybe she's sexually turned on."

Pam blushed. She looked down for a moment but then over at Judith and at Carlos. "You're right." She laughed.

Others in the group chimed in. Someone added that Pam always blushed when a man praised her. Pam didn't corroborate what they said but didn't refute them either.

After that, Pam often became much more responsive when men spoke to her. She seemed less threatened by affectionate gestures and had more access to her own positive feelings.

In this case, Judith did what I could not possibly have done alone. The very words, which would have sounded intrusive and gross coming from me, did not seem so coming from Judith. Quite the contrary, they lifted Pam's spirits and eventually helped her appreciate how she had fended men off, and why.

The use of a third person to bridge, more than any other tactic, taps potentialities that a working group has for unlocking inhibitions—potentialities that no single individual, no matter how talented, could possess all by himself or herself.

These modes of bridging are not exhaustive, though they are our first recourse. Beyond their own value, the discussion of them helps us appreciate the power—indeed, the necessity—of bridging when we conduct groups.

All techniques of bridging utilize the power of the group, the specialness of the group experience, and the leverage of having different people seeing the same problem and addressing it from different vantage points.

THE RIGHT AND THE WRONG TIME TO BRIDGE

Though the purpose of bridging is to open lines of communication, not all bridging accomplishes this. What may appear as a bridge can sometimes turn out to be an impediment between members. No technique is valuable apart from how we employ it, and bridging is no exception. For instance, few group therapists would hope to employ someone seething with aggression to interpret between two members straining to draw closer, to understand each other better. And there are less obvious contraindications.

With timid people, there is a special consideration. Though such people often benefit by acting as bridges, we must always consider risks in using them. In our attempts to draw them out, we may unwittingly drive such persons deeper into themselves. By calling on these people at the wrong times, we make the group a frightening place, rather than a sanctuary where they can learn to express their ideas and feelings. And such people, when mortified, may not reveal it, but rather they retreat.

The gingerly approach is best. "Have you any opinion about what's happening?" is a far better question than "What's your idea about what's going on?"

Whoever hesitates may cross our bridge or not as he chooses, and we spare him even the mildest comment about whichever choice he makes.

Also, it is especially important that when we address the timid person, we do so early in the session so that he or she has plenty of time to talk, to tell us his or her reaction to being spoken to. Even if we think it would benefit that person to serve as a bridge, we should never do so toward the very end of a session.

Though we are active and engaged, and words come easily to us, we must always remember that for the reticent member every word is a challenge. The patient who, when called on by us, gives his opinion but has no time to see its impact on the group may feel desperately unfulfilled. After participating only at the end of a session, unless there is a very full response from the group, such people are almost sure to leave the session feeling trivial and peripheral—even invisible.

And naturally, we should avoid introducing an outside person into an exchange when two members have just discovered each other and are communicating well.

Still another pitfall might best be described not as misusing a bridge but as mistaking a defensive tactic for bridging. It occurs most often when therapists, who have not explicitly formulated the notion of bridging, bring in outsiders to help them handle what they see as a dangerous uprising.

For instance, the therapist is under attack and worries that he or she is coming across badly. Instead of merely becoming quiet or coping directly with the attack, the therapist calls in an outside member. Such a call for help is not truly bridging. The mistake is that of turning for help rather than dealing with an assailant directly. Communication is not truly progressing. After all, the aim has not been progressive understanding, but self-defense.

As an example of this mistake, someone, who has been silent for a long time, accuses us in no uncertain terms of neglecting him. He lambastes us for our lack of compassion and announces that our professional degree is phony.

Actually, we never doubted what he could contribute, but were afraid that if brought into a discussion, he would seize the moment to dominate more timid members. But now we feel as if our back is to the wall.

At such a time we might indeed feel the impulse to call in the Marines. We have a cadre of highly educated, sympathetic men and women in our group who, though they are low-key, would put him in his place. A few of them have shown active dislike of him already.

However, any impulse we may feel to conscript an outside member as a mercenary in this skirmish, as by asking a hitherto silent ally what he or she thinks, should be resisted. Hiding behind a defender is never tantamount to constructing a useful bridge. On the contrary, such a tactic makes our assailant a scapegoat of the group and, before long, creates distance between him and the group, rather than bridging the gap between him and others.

Throughout this book, I will be mentioning a variety of bridges, often without identifying them as such. They range in complexity of design and in function, as real bridges range from the primitive rope bridge to the high-suspension bridges and high-tech cantilever bridges that are works of art as well as functional. Most important is that the therapist appreciate the necessity and value of bridges, the connecting of members, which is always far preferable to the analysis and interpretation of individuals in a group.

CHAPTER FOUR

HOW GROUP HELPS

I saw a man chasing the horizon.
Round and round they sped.
I said, "Sir, you can never."
"You lie," he said, and ran on.
—STEPHEN CRANE

Freud once observed that if a patient could simply lie down on the couch and say everything that came into his mind—report without scruple every feeling, impulse, misgiving, fantasy, and idea, he would not need therapy at all. We might or might not like the person, but he would be his own person. Whether he chose to be productive or destructive, liberal or illiberal, would be up to him. He would be someone who weighed his feelings, but was not actuated by them unthinkingly.

Whatever his life plan, this ideal patient would have the ultimate power over his destiny that we want for those who come to us. He would be the rare individual whom Hamlet described when he said, "Give me that man that is not passion's slave, and I will wear him in my heart's core." We like to think that such a person would use his powers for his own good and that of others. But that too would be up to him.

By analogy, in the ideal group our patients would work so cooperatively that they would have no need of us. They would comply with our contract, telling one another what they felt and why. Always they would put their thoughts into words, rather than express them in physical actions. They would keep confidentiality. They would, in effect, constantly rebuild those bridges that we helped them set down at the outset. In theory, such a group would run smoothly without us.

Naturally, none of us has seen this ideal group, but it is important to hold it in our minds, as a template against which we measure the failings and difficulties of the members who do come to us for help.

Ironically, we who chose to become group analysts would find "the perfect group" boring, unchallenging. Having dismissed the members with high praise, we would search for another group whose difficulties required our talents.

With this picture of the ideal group in mind, we may fairly ask, "How may we assist a group in moving toward this ideal state?" And next, more boldly, "What can group therapy accomplish even beyond what individual therapy can?"

THE SPECIAL BENEFITS OF GROUP TREATMENT

Ideally, all therapy imparts knowledge—it helps people see how they have been, unknowingly, thwarting their own best efforts to achieve what they say they want, and in many cases really do want. Doubtless, most patients start out with some confusion over whether they are repeatedly unlucky, cursed by certain hazards over which they have no control, or whether they themselves are engaging in behavior that thwarts them. Good therapy of any kind helps people appreciate the role that they themselves are playing in shaping their destiny.

Therapy, one on one, is geared to helping people explore in depth their personal histories, which, obviously, they would not have time enough to do in group. But though group analysis cannot give itself over to the same minute investigation of the past, it does see the past through a very special lens.

To appreciate this, consider that our every recollection of the past has an overlay: it is in part a screen memory. No patient ever tells the same incident exactly the same way twice, but adds colors that reflect his own development, his mood of the moment, and whom he is talking to. And those very colors, those additions, are themselves valuable sources of information.

For instance, one patient is not only telling a story but asking for sympathy. He is pleading. "Wasn't I terribly misunderstood?" A second, when talking about her past, is seeking acceptance; a third wants advice; a fourth exoneration for what he or she regards as a misdeed.

As pioneering psychiatrist Harry Stack Sullivan taught us, even repression is not a fixed phenomenon, but occurs in accordance with how the speaker feels about the listener. In an important respect, the past is always seen through the present. Even memories differ according to the listener and the atmosphere in which one reports them.

In group treatment, memories are used largely to elucidate why people act, how they feel, and how they react to one another, consciously and unconsciously. Interactions are primary. Even when a patient is talking about his or her own personal history, he is interacting. The memories one has in group are part of the chain of action, discovery, and interaction.

In this chapter, I want to be specific about five general classes of benefit group therapy has—five ways in which group treatment can benefit people even more effectively than individual treatment can.

1. *Groups elicit self-destructive behavior.* The group context elicits forms of behavior that the patient may well not engage in with his or her individual therapist. It is especially likely to elicit the very kinds of self-destructive patterns that the person engages in outside.

2. *Groups enable the members to see how others respond to them.* In group treatment, the patient has the advantage of having people respond to him freely, and without reservation, often in ways that his private therapist cannot—at least not until treatment has progressed very far.

3. *Groups afford patients diverse views of their behavior.* Group affords the patient the benefit of not one but a variety of reactions—including spontaneous reactions in the moment from people who do not always see him with the clarity and forgiveness that a loving parent or his therapist might extend toward him. Even the irrational responses to him, including overreactions if they are typical of those the person often evokes in key figures outside the group, prove beneficial to see and understand.

4. *Group treatment affords the opportunity for on-the-spot self-definition.* The patient gets a chance to find out how he looks, how he comes across, and to discover what he actually feels when he deals with people. Call this, if you will, the benefit of *in vivo* versus *in vitro* learning.

5. *Groups afford the chance to practice new behavior.* Finally, group treatment affords "life situations" in which the patient can try out new aspects of behavior; it offers a gradient along which he can work his way back to an identity that is truthful and that serves him. The patient can use the group to rehearse dealing with the outside world, whereas often such rehearsal is difficult or impossible with an indi-

vidual therapist. Traversing from the group-room to the world is a much shorter step than going from the individual therapist's office to the world.

Let's look more closely at the preferability of group treatment to individual treatment in each of these five respects.

Eliciting of Self-Destructive Behavior

For his long-term purposes, the private therapist sets out, from the very first session, to create an atmosphere of trust. Unless the patient feels comfortable enough in the sessions, he or she is very unlikely to reveal what is most essential. Trust is the stuff of which private therapy is made. Without supreme belief in his therapist, a patient could hardly be expected to report sexual failures, blunders on the job, mortifying disloyalties, both his and other people's, to him.

To achieve such trust, the individual therapist must proceed slowly, making few or no interpretations for a long time, so as not to inhibit the flow of what the patient is presenting. Certainly at the start, if not throughout treatment, the private therapist is mannerly, scientific, warm. But none of this elicits the patient's worst side.

True, good therapists are able to infer from small responses to them how the patient defeats himself. Subtle hints of negativism, egocentrism, or even doting on the therapist's words may suggest how the patient does this. The sensitive therapist imagines small traits magnified.

The therapist also draws conclusions from what a patient reports having done—from his description of his part in a relationship, for example. However, this may prove difficult, as when the patient remembers events in a biased way, or has been unobservant. Nearly always, the private practitioner draws his conclusions slowly; he must wait for the patient to defeat himself over and over again before being sure how it happened.

Paradoxically, the therapist's very reasonableness, the acceptance he or she must extend in the service of his inquiry, reduces the evidence that becomes available. A patient given to murderous sarcasm may restrain it in the presence of an expert, someone he needs and respects. Or if the therapist is a woman and the male patient is irrational only when with men, who evoke competitive feelings, the therapist won't see the problem firsthand. And one could go on and on.

The difficulty of seeing the problem is compounded by the fact that many patients tend to seek for their therapist someone they feel comfortable with. This means they seek the kind of person least likely to elicit their pathology, the self-destructive behavior they show with others.

Group treatment affords no such haven.

Every group is almost sure to have in it members who *invite the self-destructive behavior* of a patient. Once a person enters a group, he or she is likely to encounter his nemeses, to have his irrational reactions evoked, and quickly. One is reminded of a comment that heavyweight champion Joe Louis made in his heyday when he was asked about the speedy Billy Conn, whom he was to fight. Louis replied simply, "He can run, but he can't hide." In group, people with facades that protect them much of the time outside can similarly run, but they can't hide. Group sessions are circumscribed and repeated exposures, and the patient, whose concealed irrationality has repeatedly undone him in the outside world, finds that in group his worst is evoked, and soon.

In short, the group experience invites each member to engage in his characteristic self-destructive behavior. It affords stimuli that may not be present in his private hour. Sometimes these stimuli are not aversive but are loving. People who push away what they want most on Earth will show this tendency in group. We study how our members respond to warmth.

For instance, our patient is a man who automatically rebuffs a woman as soon as he finds himself attracted to her. He has sabotaged his love relationships so consistently that by now he feels almost convinced that he can never have one, that the women he wants will always let him down. Unless his private analyst is a woman whom he finds attractive, he may stay rational in private treatment, showing none of this, not engaging in his self-defeating patterns. He is in for a long haul, while both he and his therapist wait for him to meet new women, to report his experiences, to fail, to discover why he failed, and to resolve the problem.

However, in his group, almost surely there will be at least one woman who appeals to him, someone like the women he has had his trouble with. Predictably, before long he will go into his usual routine, but this time in plain view of all. He will treat this woman disdainfully; she will recoil from him; a vicious cycle will ensue, and his behavior will be there to be observed and analyzed.

This is the simplest kind of scenario. More often, the group members whose presence triggers a patient's self-defeating behavior bear only a partial resemblance to those in the past who have evoked that behavior. A trait or even the appearance of someone there will remind him of his mother or of his boss or of a person who mistreated him long ago. The stimulus might be a piece of behavior only coincidentally like that of the antecedent person—a smile, a hair color, a name, a job status. No matter. Whatever the stimulus, it invites our patient to do, on the spot, the very things he has done unwittingly that have defeated him. We welcome these repetitions. They afford a firsthand version of what the private therapist may have to wait a long time to see.

Sometimes it is not an individual but the group as a whole that induces feelings and impulses absent in private treatment. For instance, a fearful person cannot hide so readily in a group. He cannot seek shelter with a single supportive friend. He is almost surely, at times, forced to suffer interruptions, rebuttals, misunderstandings, indifference, callousness—the whole array of reactions from others that life itself subjects him to. Sooner or later, events that have exaggerated historical meaning to him touch his irrational zone, as if someone had put salt in wounds that have never truly healed.

For instance, a young man can easily cope with most forms of treatment but becomes wildly humiliated whenever an older man talks down to him. Or a usually self-possessed woman loses her perspective when a man she likes compliments her and is attentive. As if on command, she turns herself over to him, losing critical faculty, expecting him to take care of her.

These people, too, find their nemeses among the group members. They succumb to showing their least-evolved traits in response, and thus find group treatment ideal for uncovering their problems—and subsequently for helping them solve these problems.

Paradoxically, the very complaints that many patients make about group therapy, the reasons they give for preferring to remain with their private therapist, are often exactly the reasons why they should be in group. One woman says that her private therapist is the first man she has ever known who listens to her, who understands her. She has accomplished much with him—this is true and unarguable. But after two years of private treatment, she is unprepared when one evening her fiancé is grossly inattentive and unfair to her. As she had years ago with her husband, she overreacts, shouting her complaints before offering them more equably. Caught in his own anxiety, the man refuses to bend. Whereupon she goes berserk and walks out, only to feel terrible remorse later on. She once again has fantasies of marrying her analyst, who is truly sensitive and who understands her.

Two years of therapy have accorded her the invaluable experience of being understood. But they have not prepared her *for being misunderstood.* Such a woman needs not just a man who understands her but a man who doesn't! She needs the experience of being misunderstood, not once but over and over—misunderstood as her father misunderstood her. Nearly any group would have been likely to provide such a man, and the opportunity for her to put the experience in perspective.

It seems ironic that people's emotional deficiencies are useful in helping others learn to cope, but it is so. The very interruptiveness of the group experience often has value. As one psychotherapist pointed out, this interruptiveness, owing to the limitations of time that members have to talk, induces in all patients feelings of helplessness akin to those they must have experienced in childhood. To those who object to the harshness of group experiences, we answer, in Nietzsche's words, "What doesn't kill me makes me strong."

It need hardly be added that group therapy, which can evoke disquietude, has also as a prime value that it can be remarkably nutrient and supportive to individuals. To have a roomful of allies, even a roomful of listeners, is for the participants a dream come true. The seasoned therapist never lets a group become wanton or destructive but titrates its power. A group that cannot relent when it becomes too critical is not yet ready to be critical at all.

Enabling the Patients to See How Others Spontaneously Respond to Them

Patients in group treatment share the advantage of having people respond to them freely, and without reservation. True, they often speak for their own purposes and not just for their listeners, but even so they deliver spontaneous and often keen observations. One reaps the benefit of having people say things to him or her without hesitancy, saying what others who know the person may feel, one after the other, but do not wish to say for fear of jeopardizing the relationship.

Interestingly, because of the private therapist's objective, to create an atmosphere of full acceptance, he must take pause before telling the patient what he sees and considers important for the patient to know. In this respect, the private therapist weighs his words—especially if the patient is self-attacking or fragile. There are patients so sensitive to having even the slightest fault brought to light that they suffer what to them feels like a near-death blow. These people are, as Viola said of herself in Shakespeare's *Twelfth Night,* "sensitive to the least sinister usage."

Some such people will object strenuously and fight back. "How dare you say that I dismissed you when you were trying to say something? You're no better than my husband." At least these expressions of open indignation have the virtue of being visible. They provide grist for the therapy process. The ensuing dialogue between therapist and patient may uncover the patient's excessive sensitivity to having any imperfection noted.

It may turn out that indignation is at the very heart of the patient's problem—perhaps a parent punished him for his every mistake. Whatever the outcome, investigating the patient's reaction to "being crossed" may prove invaluable and be worth the days or months spent in the study of this reaction. At best, the patient comes to see the need for psychic robustness, resolves his fear of disapproval, and develops that robustness.

Harder to deal with are those patients who, hearing any hint of dissatisfaction from their therapist, feel instantly hopeless and retreat inside their shell. The therapist may never know how his well-intended but poorly aimed intervention has misfired. Or he may have to endure a protracted, sterile period of treatment before he finds out.

Accordingly, the seasoned private practitioner, when he or she suspects such "sensitivity," determines to go very slowly. He collects for himself a ledger of ways in which his patient may be offending others, or offending him in the hour, but largely keeps that ledger to himself.

The therapist's need to establish the relationship, to secure it, holds her back from saying what she would like to say, from citing ways in which the patient is alienating others and isolating himself. She will, of course, get to this material some day. Eventually she will let the patient know how callous certain of his comments are, how critical, how narcissistic, how petty or vengeful or indifferent. But not now. She must wait until she feels she can confront the patient without risking her own status and value to him.

Now let's switch venue to the group arena. There the other members in responding to a person's criticality or pettiness have no such need to be discreet, to wait for a relationship to strengthen so that it can accommodate their complaints. "So what if this irritating woman, who cuts me off constantly, flares up, or even hates me. She is selfish and I'm going to tell her."

Maybe the critic's reaction to this purportedly selfish soul is excessive. In that case, the critic has a lot to learn, about himself and about women. Or, conceivably, he's right about her. In any event, he is right about her reaction to his comment. She does flare up, and in subsequent sessions she appears to nurse a rancor toward him that shows no sign of ending.

Had her individual therapist made such a comment, right or wrong, the woman might have gone into a shell—or quit. However, here all is not lost, and in fact much may be gained. Our woman, though she disqualifies this particular man as a critic, and maybe even as existent, still has reason to go on. She has friends in court. She has the analyst, who may not have defended her but at least did not join the enemy. Moreover, she has the rudiments of an idea, she has that part of what the man said to her that has penetrated her adamancy. She has witnessed herself reacting wildly, and has time to reconsider both the criticism and her own behavior.

The next time someone in group or in her outside life implies that she has dismissed him, she is closer to considering that the comment may not be a rampant assault but a genuine attempt to reach her.

What she hears in different settings and repeatedly, will get through, sooner or later. And as for her critic, he can live a little longer in the shadow of her scorn. Perhaps being in such a shadow is a familiar experience for him, one he is just beginning to see that he brings on himself. Or possibly, he has long feared to say his mind, dreading a woman's scorn. If so, he too has friends in court. The reality will likely be far more endurable for him than his apprehensions.

Whatever the outcome, someone in the group has had the freedom to confront this woman. Whether he has been paranoid or keenly observant and courageous, his doing so has inaugurated an adventure that hurtles both individuals and the group itself forward.

*Providing Patients with Diverse Views of Their
Behavior and Diverse Responses to It*

The most apparent benefit of group treatment is that the patient, having engaged in his or her characteristic pattern, has not one person but *many* observing him. He has not one person reasoning about him but many reacting to him and evaluating what he does. There was a saying in the early 1900s that "forty million Frenchmen can't be wrong." Perhaps they can. But if they are wrong and of a mind about us, such a collective error is very important to know about.

Even the group's irrational responses to a person's behavior are highly significant and useful.

Arthur has the unconscious habit of dismissing certain women when he disapproves of anything they say to him. Especially when he feels touched by a criticism or a demand, he obliterates the female speaker by twisting away from her physically, as if to say, "I can't be bothered with you. You don't exist."

Arthur has been going to a top-notch individual therapist, a man whom Arthur idealizes. But when this therapist even suggests that Arthur may be harsh with a woman in his life, Arthur considers it his bias. Arthur likes the therapist, appreciates what he has gained in therapy, but has concluded simply that the therapist favors women, and hasn't met the kind of women that Arthur himself has met all throughout his own life.

Arthur goes on moaning to the therapist that his wife, his secretary, and the other women in his life are oversensitive and difficult. And the therapist remains unable even to get Arthur to consider that he treats women with sovereign finality, and that he is the architect of his own defeats and of women's perennial anger toward him.

In my group, Arthur is quite adept at dealing with women so long as they remain urbane and pleasant. However, when a woman says nearly anything to him that he finds painful, he simply cuts her off, acting as if she isn't there.

He does this so surreptitiously that for a time no one notices—that is, no one except one particular woman, Dianne, who feels mortified when he does this to her.

After a few weeks, Dianne shouts at him, "You bastard! You're doing it again. I talk to you and you turn away as if you're shutting a door on me, as if I don't exist. You think I'm dirt. You don't even listen to me. How dare you!"

She addresses Arthur with such vehemence, with such a seemingly exaggerated sense of insult, that the whole group is startled.

Further discussion over a series of sessions reveals that Dianne, though supersensitive to Arthur's kind of rebuff, is on to something real and important. Other women in the group soon recognize that Arthur's respect for them is brittle; it rests entirely on their agreeing with him—and more than that, on their respecting him at every moment. They too have felt uncomfortable with him, a fact that they are only beginning to identify. Arthur, they all concur after a while, will accept nothing less than piety toward him as the price for his treating them decently.

What began as an acrimonious criticism of Arthur by a single woman, a diatribe that Arthur could dismiss because it contained irrational elements, has in the group been converted into a considered judgment by not one, but many people. And not just women describe Arthur as sexist and unfair to women—most of the men in the group, including some who are a little like Arthur, see Arthur that way, and tell him repeatedly that he is very callous toward women.

Arthur, who was forever able to discount what any individual said to him, finds it impossible to discount the collective judgment of the group.

At first, he tries to tell himself that the whole group is irrational, that they have misperceived him, they don't really understand him. But even this falls short as a rationalization. Even if he evokes the same irrational response in all women, he had better take stock of how he does this. How does he manage to be repeatedly misunderstood by women?

In the end, Arthur cannot escape the consensual opinion of the group; he cannot evade it. Whereas a highly trained analyst could not convince Arthur to reconsider a longstanding trait of his, the group has prevailed.

In this case, the group's subsequent investigation of Arthur and Dianne's interaction over many sessions was invaluable to Arthur. Doubtless, there was a component of excessive and irrational response to Arthur in at least some of the women whom he neglected. But as often occurs, the irrationality was only the beginning. The real components of Arthur's behavior and of people's reactions to it surfaced before long, and were clearly delineated for all to see.

Thus group has not only the virtue of many observers, each with his or her own vantage point. In group therapy, the patient has the curious benefit of having the other members see him or her from their special biases. When the other members concur in some opinion, despite those biases, the person they concur about is very likely to take stock.

In polite society, those who react adversely to us typically walk away, seldom telling us how we alienated them. When this happens, we go without the benefit of what they responded to. In group treatment, those very people whose responses are most acute, and who could inform us best about ourselves, whose very exaggerations are necessary to help us see our flaws, will bestow on us this gift of response so that we can profit.

And I say "us" because this honing instrument of irrational perception, as well as rational, benefits therapists too. Thanks to our patients' irrationalities and rationalities, our biases and excesses become trimmed over time, along with our other bad habits. As the multitudinous perceptions of the group are brought to bear on us, session after session, we too profit.

Yielding On-the-Spot Experience

Group treatment offers the member an opportunity for *on-the-spot emotional awareness* of himself. The involved member doesn't just store away the observations that other people make of him. Rather, the member is often led to ask, "What am I feeling right now, even as I act this way?" The result is that he can often make remarkable discoveries about himself. He is seeing himself in motion and can trap the feelings that actuate him in the instant.

This is a subtle value of group treatment—and certainly one that I did not myself see or appreciate for years. It is that people can make instantaneous readings of themselves, catching and labeling momentary feelings that are important in their psyches, but that in daily existence are typically gone before they can be captured.

The power of group to do this kind of *in vivo* work is sweeping.

There are people, perhaps the majority, who go through life with only subsensible, unconscious intimations of what they are really feeling; they sense the existence of crucial, activating emotions. If only they were to stop themselves at pivotal instants, to "freeze-frame" their emotional life, so to speak, at the proper moment, then they could pinpoint these dynamic actuating forces within them—these feelings that motivate them and color their whole existence.

However, this is ordinarily very difficult. The moments when these lurking feelings are at maximum strength and most susceptible to being caught and labeled, *come when the person is busily engaged in interchanges*—and are gone by the time these interchanges are being recalled in solitude.

Because group treatment both provides the arena and offers the members an opportunity for spontaneous introspection, it enables people to label and capture their truly actuating feelings and motives. Time and time again, group members are stunned to realize that they have all their lives been doing things for reasons utterly different from those they conjectured were their motives.

For example, Dick has long complained to his private analyst that women all want something from him, that they lean on him, borrow money, exploit his generosity—that they take but they don't give. For a long time in group, Dick does come across as extraordinarily generous. He offers supportive statements to the women; he tutors them as best he can. The members are awed by his liberality, his freedom to give of himself.

Then, in one session, a violent interchange occurs between two people in Dick's group. After observing it awhile, Dick enters, displaying his usual magnanimity. The dispute is between Elaine, a tough but earthy and honest woman, and Hal. Elaine has been accusing Hal of not appreciating her. She charges Hal with pouring his heart out to Magda, a narcissist who gives him nothing, while she, Elaine, with the best of intentions, has been unable to reach him.

Enter Dick, with one of his generous, avuncular gifts. Elaine and Hal both seem distraught, and Dick will now ameliorate the situation.

In as soft a tone as he can summon, Dick assures Elaine that she is every bit as attractive as narcissistic Magda.

"Your difficulty is that you're giving something to Hal while he's trying to reach for somebody else," says Dick. "You can't expect him to stop what he's doing and turn to you. If you picked your own time, a time that's only yours, instead of competing with Magda, I guarantee that you would get as much as Magda does and more."

No one ever spoke more sweetly, and the group marvels at Dick's dulcet accuracy.

That is, everyone except Elaine herself. Far from being appreciative, she vents her anger on Dick, who is the nearest to her. "Listen, Dick, I don't really need your pity. What I'd like to know is where are *you* in all this? What the hell are you getting out of helping me?"

Dick is speechless. No one has ever caught him in the midst of one of these gestures of largesse, or demanded to know what he was up to. "Where am I in all this?" he asks himself before he can put Elaine's question out of his mind.

And a feeling surges up in him—of *envy.* He realizes what he really wants from Elaine, and it is painfully simple—he has been craving affection from her, nothing less than appreciative, loving affection. Hal was his competition. For the first time, Dick sees unavoidably that he has been trying to top Hal and to win Elaine by showing himself as the nearest thing to a saint on Earth, as a creature halfway to heaven.

Two things had to happen for Dick to appreciate this. One was for Elaine herself not to respond as he wanted her to. The second was for Elaine—or at least for someone—to question Dick about his motive on the spot. Someone had to challenge Dick's action with enough feeling and genuine involvement to help Dick see that his generosity in this case was really a ruse to purchase another person's love.

True, Dick might have rationalized even this. One can rationalize anything, theoretically. But the very fact that he genuinely cared for Elaine, that he *wanted* her, and that she questioned his motive at the very instant of his using his generosity-ploy, shocked him into seeing it, into realizing what he was really doing.

All his life, Dick had used this device of helping people as a way of stifling any incipient dissatisfaction with him that they might have. He had, indeed, accomplished something; people, especially women, felt indebted to him. There were even some women who slept with him because they felt that he was a good person. To those women, he was the model of the good man, the one they had always dreamed of, the kind of man they wished their lover was.

Dick's insight into this aspect of his behavior, and into several other of his actions, opened the doors to a spate of memories. He realized that in the past he had sought to purchase women's affections through pseudo-generosity, one after the other. And that this mode of his had proved his downfall with one woman after another.

Twice, women Dick was married to had built up enormous anger toward him—an anger at first incomprehensible to them, he seemed so kind—but an anger that stopped natural communication. His first wife went out and had affairs with more feeling and less noble men, and his second, afraid to express herself freely to such a paragon, had simply succumbed to deep depression and embraced it until Dick left.

It had been crucial for Dick to get to the heart of his beneficence, for Dick himself to realize that his largesse was a device to secure love, which in the end obviated the chance for a truly loving relationship.

Dick's private analyst had seen the same pattern of pseudo-generosity and had asked Dick about certain of his acts of largesse. However, these were actions toward people that Dick had only reported, *past actions,* such as lending money to a woman who had already rejected him. Because they were over and done with, and Dick had obscured his motive for them at the time, it was very hard for Dick to appreciate what truly underlay the acts. Moreover, his private analyst had been impeded by his need not to press Dick too hard for fear of disturbing Dick's growing transference to him.

Group treatment not only evoked Dick's false generosity: certain members seemed desperately in need of what he could give them. It freeze-framed his unconscious motive, and held it up to the light. It both evoked the motive and made demands on Dick to stop and examine it, in those very instants when he could examine it. Indeed, having to muzzle his usual impulses once he had started to express them gave Dick his best chance of seeing what they were.

Often, as with Dick, people find immediate rewards in everyday life for behavior that is truly self-defeating. Because they seem to fare so well with others, this behavior goes unexamined. However, the group experience, in depriving those people of their accustomed rewards, and in questioning that very behavior, holds up their behavior and its motive to the light.

Our ability to pinpoint people's behavior and track it while they are engaging in it often leads us to truths that patients find unacceptable at first. Such *in vivo* scrutiny is especially useful in penetrating reaction-formations.

For example, Arthur, a man somewhat like Dick, would constantly worry aloud in group about his wife's health; he would tell us at length that it pained him to stand by helplessly while she took chances. Arthur worried about her dieting, her jogging in the early morning, her not getting enough sleep, all of which, she maintained, were in an effort to cure her depressions.

One day Arthur went on about the folly of his wife's flying to California to see a guru. He had wanted her, if she insisted on going, to take the Red-Eye, which was cheaper than the morning flight. A slip of the tongue led him to say, "I sure wish she would *die* at night."

Of course, he remonstrated, when this was pointed out. What he really meant was that he had wanted her to "fly" at night. However, certain of the members would not accept things so simply—among them were a few highly independent women whom Arthur had repeatedly disrespected. In fact, these were the very women whom Arthur had said he liked most.

Suddenly they were on to his real motive, which was anger at any woman who made her own decisions. The group kept after him until Arthur recognized this attitude himself. Doubtless, it had contributed to his wife's depression.

There are endless forms of behavior that people engage in but do not ordinarily stop to examine, which group can halt and investigate. If not a slip of the tongue, it might be a facial expression such as a tic, a hand gesture, or a body posture that prompts discovery. Even when a private therapist notes these same things, as mentioned, he or she has many restrictions on delving into such a pattern, especially if there is resistance. On the other hand, one's group members have no such restrictions.

Sometimes a whole subgroup and not just an individual is engaging in a pattern driven by an unidentified motive.

For instance, three people in a group take it upon themselves to police the rest, using the group rules to bully miscreants. When someone comes late, the triumvirate demands that he justify his or her behavior. They loudly disbelieve his explanations, cut him off, cite previous crimes of his, and make him feel utterly unwanted—all in the ostensible service of group cohesion. Individually, these people are dictatorial in their private lives, all sanctimonious, passing themselves off as the last law-abiding citizens in a decaying world.

Finally, a woman, one of the victims of their inquisition, rebels and lets them have it. She asserts that far from sympathizing with her or trying to understand her, the triumvirate is using her "deviancy" as an excuse to browbeat her. She holds to her position.

Others join her, and the cabal is caught in the act. Their true motives come to the fore; once again, having been exposed, the members of the triumvirate profit by deepening their own self-understanding and by becoming more lenient.

What I call "the immediacy principle" also operates to keep the therapists themselves conscious of what they are doing. In the group, we are led repeatedly to identify and study our own behavior. This may or may not lead us to change an approach. However, our deepened recognition of our own motives gives us our fullest options.

Consider an example in which the group therapist, in this case I myself, was able to profit by the very immediacy that group provides.

One day, a group member accused me of favoring Andre, a young pianist. Several other members said my critic was right, that I bypassed people when Andre spoke and ignored them entirely if Andre seemed upset. I heard them out, but nothing registered. It seemed to me that I was treating Andre no differently from the way I treated others.

Nor did I discover anything later when I tried to do some soul searching. Two of my critics had read hostile motives into my behavior, which seemed false; a third was constantly given to complaining; and the last, I concluded, had merely jumped on the bandwagon. Three of the four had problems with sibling rivalry. No, I concluded, there was no validity in what they had said.

Back in the group, I began looking for signs of that sibling rivalry in those three members. I could see that certain of the things they said and did were "rivalrous," but could not go beyond that. By this time, the group was feeling quite stymied. Besides feeling misunderstood by me, they felt helpless to get me to see my preference for Andre.

Then one man observed shrewdly, "Joan was quiet for an hour and you didn't talk to her. Andre's been quiet for five minutes and you ask him if anything's wrong." They dogged me until I could not help but see that I was, indeed, favoring him.

When I finally saw what I was doing, I asked myself why. Andre had reminded me of myself, or at least my ideal-self, and I was treating him the way I had wanted my father to treat me—to give me the close and intimate attention I had always yearned for.

By cuing me in to the truth, they had helped themselves. The group, by catching me *in vivo*, had freed me to treat Andre and the rest of them more even-handedly.

The values of this on-the-spot emotional awareness that group affords accrue to the leader himself no less than to the individual members. Indeed, many of the techniques to be discussed in this book derive their power from the immediacy of the group experience.

Giving the Patient a Chance to Practice New Behavior

Finally, the group affords "life situations" in which the patient can try out new aspects of behavior, rehearse and revamp new approaches to people. The step from group to the world is a much shorter one than the step from the private therapist's office to the world.

There are various reasons, some of them obvious, why patients typically find it easier to make personality changes in a group than in the outside world. For one thing, the well-run group tolerates changes and actually encourages them. The members feel free to experiment with new behavior, realizing that ultimately they have nothing to lose. Early efforts to change are apt to be awkward, and the group reactions are critical. For instance, a timid patient may be clumsy in his incipient assertiveness.

Inevitably, some members will encourage changes, while others will oppose those same revisions of behavior. Still others go along as if utterly oblivious that someone has made a major leap—for example, gone from silent to talkative, from violating people to being respectful of them, from expressing contempt to expressing concern.

The member who does break a personal barrier is very likely to get instant appreciation, or at least recognition, of his achievement in group. He will also meet with opposition in some quarters from those who preferred him as his old self-defeating self. And he will have to face the fact that certain people care so little about him that they don't even notice what for him is an earth-shattering change of behavior. Once again, this variety of on-the-spot responses to the patient, this time to his new behavior instead of his old style, proves invaluable.

And there are members who see involuntary changes in a person, even though she herself has not noticed them, and call them to the person's attention.

"Susan, what's different today about you is that you started speaking at the beginning of the session, instead of waiting till the last two minutes and then acting desperate, as if you didn't have enough time. That's the first time I've ever seen you do that."

Or "Rachel, this is the second time you didn't just complain about the way people are treating you. You told them what you wanted. That's great!"

In still other cases, no one comments explicitly. However, what is

new even then is that *the group reacts* in a novel way to the person
who has begun behaving differently.

For instance, in group Frances talks about her sexual feelings for the
first time in her life. She has lived in fear that any mention of a sexual
desire would incite men to make sexual approaches to her. That
seemed humiliating beyond imagination. In actuality, her venturing to
disclose sexual feelings brings another kind of response altogether.
Timo responds to Frances, not by propositioning her as she had feared
he would, but with very genuine warmth. He thanks her for confiding
in him.

After that, Timo talks more respectfully to Frances—not less respectfully. Frances in turn feels genuinely accepted and discloses still
other sexual longings, which she had hidden. She comes across as a
much more sympathetic person.

Before long, she has won over the group, she is one of them. They
no longer regard her as haughty or distant. She has, by trusting the
group, allowed them to accept her and nurture her, and they have
played their supporting role. This would have been much harder for
her to accomplish in the world at large.

Because the group members are so various, they afford a whole range
of responses to a person trying out new behavior. No private therapist, or any single person for that matter, can possibly do this.

Such variety and not simply encouragement is essential. One person
needs the opportunity to confront people who infantilize him as his
parents did. Another must confront people who want her to be sub-
missive. Another has as his bugaboo those who manipulate him using
compliments. Whatever the form of one's "personal monster," the
patient must practice jousting with that monster, and must practice
over and over again until his or her new behavior becomes effortless
and feels thoroughly natural.

And, of course, in any diverse group the patient is very likely
to find people who, perhaps because they have made similar changes
to his, will cheer him on, more than anyone in his outside life
will.

In fact, there are likely to be some who, having identified with the
patient in his difficulty—shyness, for example, or the inability to
control his temper—and who, having his problem themselves, will

especially appreciate his achievement and underscore it. These partisan onlookers will be inspired as they see him take chances.

As a result, the person who has taken these chances is succeeding not just for himself but for a community. Realizing that his journey is path-breaking for them may spur him on.

The degree to which group treatment affords these five main benefits to patients depends on the special needs of our patients, on the problems they present, and on their readiness to profit by group therapy. And, it need hardly be said that it depends on the proficiency of the therapist in utilizing the power of the group process. Much more will be said about these functions of group treatment as we go along.

Therapists differ in how they stress these various functions of group, and in the degree to which they exploit its various possibilities.

For instance, some lay special stress on the value of the group arena as a place for patients to practice new techniques. They encourage practice. These specialists at rehearsal see the group as essentially a center for trying out new behavior in every session—as if the group were a simulated diminutive world and the patients were there almost exclusively to rehearse their new identities.

Other therapists simply allow practice and say nothing about it. Relying on the technique as heavily as they do, they are sometimes oblivious to certain hazards of this technique.

Of all the special uses of group, one—namely that of the group as a place to do *role-playing*—most often becomes the dominant theme of group treatment by those who believe in it.

Role-Playing in Group—Pros and Cons

Role-playing is in essence a game played by the patient and someone else, the analyst or another group member. By the usual set of rules, the patient plays himself while the other person plays the role of someone in his life giving him trouble—say a husband or wife or boss or friend.

The particular form of role-playing used is designed to simulate difficult challenges and give the patient repeated chances to practice coping with them, to develop and refine a new and successful style.

At first, when confronted by some basic life challenge, the patient nearly always acts in his characteristic ways, which do not acquit him well—he brags when it isn't necessary or loses his temper or becomes tongue-tied or gets flirtatious, instead of confronting someone.

Not only can the group members point out to him the "right" and "wrong" of his behavior; he has ample opportunity to practice his new and more effective mode. Some therapists who emphasize this method of practicing use role-playing extensively. So far, so good.

However, while such role-playing can have real value, it runs the risk of superficiality and insufficiency. In itself, role-playing does not give the patient insight into *why* he or she has gone astray in the first place—or awareness of the underlying feeling that he has been trying to avoid by his self-defeating style. When people repeat harmful patterns, it is always because they harbor apprehensions or have unconscious fantasies; these do not come to the surface when their only method of remedy is learning new behavior. As a result, patients treated solely by this technique remain as they were characterologically; they have succeeded merely in developing a few serviceable coping devices.

For instance, Kurt was applying for a job as an editor with a big publishing house. He was poor at interviews, and clumsy in many of his personal relationships. In recent months, Kurt's group had made him painfully aware that he said yes to people when he had no idea what to say. He would accept other people's givens too readily, in effect promising too much and then finding himself unable to deliver.

The interview that now loomed before him was especially frightening to Kurt. One of the three interviewers, the president of the publishing house, was known to be tough. The president would think up job crises that no one could handle. For instance, he would tell an interviewee that irreparable damage had already been done and then demand to know what the interviewee would do to repair it. He would fire questions at job applicants, more than once leaving a sensitive applicant in tears.

In terror, Kurt told his group therapist that he had no idea what to do. That therapist, a student of mine, decided to use the technique of role-playing, choosing three members from Kurt's group to serve as interviewers while Kurt played himself.

The interviewers did their job—they shot questions at Kurt, including many unanswerable ones, and when Kurt faltered or promised too much, they told him to be honest.

Kurt practiced saying such things as, "I don't know the answer to that, sir, I'd need more information."

"I think we'd have to take the loss on that one, sir."

And even, "Sir, you're asking me to close the barn door after the cow has gotten out."

Kurt felt better about himself. He went off, knowing that he would be unable to answer at least some questions and feeling free to admit it. He would imply, in one form or another, "I can do a lot, I'm top-notch, but I have no instantaneous answer to that one."

On the actual interview, Kurt conducted himself well enough to get the job, though at a slightly reduced salary. Before long, he mastered the art of admitting his imperfections.

However, the real problem remained that Kurt harbored unconscious fantasies of being annihilated for revealing that he didn't know things. Both of his parents, high achievers themselves, had brought Kurt up expecting him to have answers without being told. His sense of his own worthlessness was not abated by his mastering a few devices for particular situations. That feeling continued to gnaw at him, and blocked him.

Though Kurt had mastered a technique, he went on feeling fraudulent, and as a result continued to need detailed rehearsal before any new confrontation. His therapist concluded that though role-playing had helped him perform better, it had not done the real job. Eventually Kurt had to confront his underlying fear, and to resolve it, so as to produce the inner change that made his new behavior truly natural for him. His therapist continued to use role-playing, but only to provide the finishing touches, and never without real analysis of his patients' underlying personality structure.

Other therapists use role-playing by getting the patient to act the part of the person giving them trouble, while someone else in the group plays the patient himself. The troubled patient sees his substitute deal with the problem that has baffled him, and can learn by example.

A further value is that by playing the role of his own father or son or neighbor, the patient can gain new insight into how those people feel and why they act as they do. Used this way too, role-playing has indisputable benefits.

But though the technique has these values, because role-playing stays on the surface, addressing people's coping devices only, it runs the risk of leaving the personality core unchanged.

A major argument against too-ready reliance on role-playing is that it tends to *stop the flow of a group*. Ordinarily, relationships between members are in constant flux. Every minute holds prospects that it is up to the members to fulfill. With role-playing, the majority in the room are blocked from playing any part whatsoever.

The following situation would not be unusual. Theodore, a group member, feels hurt. He has held back his feelings for a week, waiting for the days to pass while anticipating himself rebuking another man in the group for insulting him.

Theodore's actually speaking up will be a major breakthrough for him. As a child, he had needed to stay silent in his home, and only recently realized how necessary it is for him to confront people, especially those he likes. His moment has come.

During this same week, someone else in the group is on the brink of saying something warm to the therapist, whom he has never granted an inch to. And so on. In any group that has healthy pace, most if not all of the members are on the verge of some form of communication; they are in motion.

Now imagine the impact on these people if the therapist were to announce, "Okay, Charlotte, why don't you play the part of that mother of yours, who's so difficult to talk to. And you, Theodore, you be Charlotte, and show her what you would do."

Theodore, who has all week anticipated telling someone off in group, but was in conflict, now has a good reason not to. Indeed, with the role-playing in progress, it would be breaking the rules for him to say anything. He may smoulder, or welcome the excuse not to talk. "Maybe next week," Theodore consoles himself.

The same holds for Charlotte and for others. With role-playing going on, confrontations must be delayed, breakthroughs postponed: momentum is lost. The role-playing itself dominates, it gobbles up the time, it provides good excuses not to act for those who need them, and it heightens the frustration of those who are genuinely ready to work.

What role-playing yields is more extrinsic than what would come out of spontaneous flow. And since the primary aims of a group are flow and communication, role-playing techniques have much to be said against them. There are even times when the participants in role-playing, though they got something, would have gotten *more* if they had interacted freely and learned from their experiences.

Even granting that the participants might get something out of the experience, they are thrown off course. For the others, it is as if a visiting theater company arrived, and they were asked to quit what they were doing and join the audience.

The benefits of group treatment are best imparted in the least conspicuous, the least visible ways. The analyst achieves his effect—elicits a range of behavior from his members.

And he does this as much by what he doesn't say as by what he says.

For instance, he refrains from overprotecting people who need to take care of themselves. He frees people to respond without reservation and is glad when they do, setting limits only when behavior seems injurious, or potentially so. He encourages on-the-spot self-definition and the discovery of feelings and motives. He recognizes that people are constantly rehearsing the new and discarding the old, often even when they are silent in the group, and the ideal therapist is satisfied with that.

CHAPTER FIVE

WHAT THE THERAPIST FEELS

Can a robot ever do group therapy? Why not? We've seen inanimate creatures do all kinds of things. In the medical field, computers are already being used not just to test and evaluate our blood and bones and sinews, but to put all the information together and arrive at diagnoses. Between the nurse who admits us and the doctor at the end of the line, we may go through untouched by human hands.

Obviously, this analogy is to focus on what the group therapist has that can never be replaced—that is, our feelings. It need hardly be said that our feelings are the essential part of what we bring to every group: they are our humanity, our instruments of diagnosis and cure. Not just our feelings, of course, but the feelings of the group members, individually and collectively, are the stuff of which all interactions are made.

For a robot to successfully work with a group (or with an individual for that matter), the robot would need a capacity for despair at being misunderstood, for joy at seeing people flourish, for rage at being interrupted, for guilt over having neglected someone in the group. It would need to make mistakes at times and not notice them; it would need on occasion to fall into other people's manipulative traps. It would need the capacity for misplaced loyalty stemming from false identification with someone; it would need occasional vulnerability to flattery; it would need excessive and self-destructive remorse over mistakes made, and so on. What's best in us and what's worst in

51

us all go into our performance—our humanity is our instrument of treatment. And our feelings are our humanity.

It may truthfully be said that the worst therapists are those out of touch with their feelings, or in bondage to them to the degree that their feelings dictate their performance. The patients of these therapists remain misunderstood, and either leave or stay out of desperate need, doubting whether they themselves can ever be helped.

On the other hand, the best therapists experience a great range of feelings. They let themselves feel nearly everything. This takes courage, but after a while they come to trust that whatever they feel, they remain in command of what they do. Their own feelings are an ultimate source of their power as therapists.

In between the most and the least effective therapists are those who are open to some of their feelings but are frightened of others, and who suppress them. And those who do not know how to utilize their feelings even when they have identified them.

Much of our work as therapists consists of identifying our feelings and understanding where they come from and what they mean. In this chapter, I want to talk about the kinds of feelings we have and how we should process them so that we can use them for a wide variety of purposes.

Before going on, it needs to be said that in the domain of the therapist's reactions, whatever terms we take from the literature prove remarkably controversial. "Transference," "countertransference"—there are so many and such varied acceptations of these two common words that before using either, we must be as clear as possible as to what definition we mean to use. Even then, there are borderline cases; considerable subjectivity remains. And this becomes even more the case whenever we talk about a "reality reaction." So saying, let's plunge ahead.

Most familiar in analytic literature is the idea of the patient's *transference*—the sum total of perceptions, reactions, ideas, and feelings from the patient's past that he brings to the present.

A man repeatedly betrayed by a silent father expects his silent therapist to betray him. And by the same token, if the man himself becomes a therapist and works with groups, he may expect his groups to betray him, even before he learns anything about their composition.

Before he opens the door and introduces himself, this man may be terrified, as when as a boy, his hand touching the knob of his father's study brought terror. Back then, his mother would report on his miscreant behavior during the day, after which his father welcomed the chance to slap him around, using his study as a punishment chamber.

No specific act of the group is needed to evoke a transference; the mere existence of the group is enough. Transferences, where they occur, appear independently of what the group does.

And the therapist also has what we call *countertransferences*—reactions to his or her patients and what they do that are colored, if not fully determined, by the therapist's own past. Countertransference is the therapist's unconscious reaction to the patient's unconscious feeling. While countertransference is a reaction based on the therapist's history, which may or may not contaminate the interactions by the group members, the group analyst's transference is superimposed directly on the group members without any stimulation from them.

For instance, a group member might look like the analyst's uncle. He has always been distrustful of the uncle. The therapist now distrusts the group member for no viable reason. The group member has done nothing to warrant it. This is the group therapist's transference, a direct replay of his past, which has no basis on any stimuli offered by the member. Therefore, it is clear: countertransference is a reaction while transference is a preconceived superimposition.

This needs to be distinguished from the therapist's transference. For instance, a woman running a group feels constantly on edge, uncertain of herself and guilty whenever her group seems out of control, when the members argue, or even when they all talk at once.

Her own parents were typically contained and formal and did everything by the book. Only when they were upset by what one of their children had done, did they lose their composure and then become unpredictable and punitive. No one knew what was coming next. This therapist recalls being slapped and sent to her room, deprived of privileges, her only warning signals being the sight of her mother slightly elevating her voice or interrupting her husband.

With such a history of all-or-nothingness, the woman came to dread any incipient sign of chaos, and she would reconcile people almost by instinct, the way a forest ranger puts out brush fires the instant they start. In fact, when she could not quell disturbances, she felt paralyzed by guilt, as if she herself had done something to incur them.

Her countertransference to all groups was such that when her groups were polite, she felt successful as a therapist, but when even one or two members seemed irrational to her, or uninhibited, she felt at a loss and even guilty, as if she had done something wrong that would lead to chaos and unpredictability.

Like transferences, every countertransference operates with almost infinite subtlety. For instance, in her effort to prevent members from too free a flow of expression, our therapist might impulsively do things to avert silences. She entertains the members, demands that they talk, creates intellectual controversy, and so forth. All transferences and countertransferences make their appearance not just in what therapists neglect, but in what they actually do.

In some sense, all our reactions bespeak our own histories; and in practice our constant aim is to reduce our being governed by transference and countertransference feelings. Ideally, our feelings are critical instruments of understanding, but only to the degree that we keep them uncluttered. We need to be guided as much as we can by "reality reactions" and not distortions resulting from our own particular personal history.

Granting that reality reactions in pure form are only an ideal, since one cannot live without any subjectivity, let's look at an instance of that ideal for the sake of contrast.

A group member pulls a knife on another member. We are frightened. The danger is real and present. Whatever we import from our own histories is secondary.

This distinction between "transferential," "countertransferential," and "reality" reactions is the simplest that we can possibly make. Psychoanalytic literature on these topics is full of discussion, some brilliant but much of it highly abstruse, and even obsessive. (In certain psychoanalytic literature, what we are calling "reality reactions," even if they are almost universal, have sometimes been called "objective countertransference.") Indeed, even with our simplification of theory, we find that in practice the identification and uses of the therapist's feelings afford subject matter for a lifetime of introspection and work.

The therapist who doesn't know what he's feeling will err in understanding, in interpretation, in timing—in all aspects of technique. The one in touch with his or her feelings is empowered in these respects, or at least potentially so. Ideally, our feelings "know" what we ourselves may not.

For instance, the members of a group are talking cheerily about their futures; one man chirps about an upcoming job interview, another about a woman he's about to meet, a third about a stock market venture. A fourth comments that they are all lucky to be with such a wonderful therapist. They congratulate each other over their prospects, and the mood is ostensibly happy, uplifting.

But the therapist, a sensitive soul, does not share their merriment. In front of her, the group members seem to be saying, "If we only had champagne and glasses, we would drink to our leader, to each other, and to the future." But that is the last thing this therapist feels like doing.

She smiles along with them, but experiences a deathly feeling, an emptiness. The image that comes to her is that of mourners attending a wedding.

Another compliment is paid by one group member to another. But now she has the image of someone trying to manufacture spring in the midst of winter.

A terrible sense of incongruity prompts the therapist to heed not merely what the group is saying, but what is going on inside of her. Her own intimations of sorrow are tainting her appreciation of their happiness. Or *is* it happiness?

The question speeds her to look at her own feelings more carefully. Now she studies her own stirrings. More and more, she realizes that she is feeling sad. Questions flood her mind. Is she competitive with the group, resentful of their happiness? Does she want to protect them against disappointment, which she feels always follows optimism— the notion that all pleasure must be paid for, that all great hopes are foolish and unwarranted? No, this line of inquiry produces nothing of value. That can't be it. Then why does she feel so sad?

Suddenly it comes to her that the group itself is sad! Despite their celebrations, there is tragedy at their core.

A new and powerful wave of sadness overwhelms her. She sees that she has been experiencing the group's real, underlying state, one that they themselves are avoiding. Watching them compliment one another, she realizes that they are engaged in a massive and composite denial; theirs is a hail-fellow-well-met defense, fending off awareness that anything is wrong. They are drowning their sorrows, their sense of helplessness, in compliments and joyous expectations.

Right now she is the only one who sees this hollowness, the only one who feels the rumblings. But soon she will use her knowledge to help the others find solid ground, to help them acknowledge their real fears and misgivings, to help them understand their own characteristic refusals to acknowledge uncertainty and fear.

Though at this moment, the therapist is shaken by the depth of the sorrow that she *and they* are feeling, by the collective yearning in the room and the sense of despair, she is infinitely far ahead of where she was. She *knows* what is happening. No matter that the truth is tragedy for the moment. No matter that she, in T. S. Eliot's words, sees "the skull beneath the skin," she is triumphant! She has the truth.

"It had me, but I had it," said Mersault in Camus's *L'Etranger*, when at last he faced his tragedy, the knowledge of death. Indeed, as she lives with her terrible recognition, it seems less terrible. She feels on solid ground, that of reality.

This group therapist's ability and courage, and readiness to use her feelings to understand her group, is what makes her a master. Her feelings, and only her feelings, put her in control of what is going on. Without them, her work would remain anemic, intellectual, and useless. Without the courage to heed them, to follow them, to cling to them, though her own feelings led her into a maelstrom, she would have remained without the tools to do the job.

Feelings are more than instruments of comprehension, they are instruments of treatment at every level. Only the therapist with the courage to feel and to study his or her feelings can truly do group diagnosis, and without proper diagnosis, there is nothing.

Naturally, our feelings are as continuous as the flow of blood through our veins. Most usually, when our feelings are in tune with what we are doing, we discharge them in some ongoing action, as in a thought or fantasy. We're unlikely to reflect that we had the feeling at all. For instance, being fond of someone, we act kindly toward the person, or if we're frustrated by not knowing something, we ask a question. These acts themselves, prompted by the feeling, discharge it, and we don't ordinarily pay attention to the feeling itself.

It takes a deliberate stepping back from the canvas of our lives to look at ourselves objectively, for us to identify the feeling. Indeed, if someone were to ask us what we were feeling, we might have to stop ourselves from acting, from doing anything in the moment, to give him his answer. "Oh, I like Alice a lot, and I was a little worried about her being out sick last time, which, I guess, is why I told her I was glad to see her."

A therapist can be successful only to the degree that he or she is able to go back and forth between action and reflection—or more precisely, to the degree that the therapist can readily identify his own feelings.

As we have seen, our feelings are the ultimate cues in teaching us what is going on in the group—and in ourselves. Left unidentified, our feelings are too likely to govern our actions. Our own unidentified feelings enslave us to the whims of manipulative group members; they dispose us to believe people's distortions and to lose sight of what is going on. And worst of all, our unidentified feelings are what keep us in the thrall of our own past histories.

For instance, a male therapist, because his mother constantly let him down, regularly expects women to disappoint him. Though he has this bias, at least he is aware of it. There is only one way he can prevent it from causing great problems in his group practice, short of his resolving it entirely: he must stay alert to any inkling of his disappointment in women or anger at them.

At times investigation shows him that a woman is actually doing what he has been led to fear. She has been attempting to manipulate him by acting disappointed in whatever he gives her. She has also been violating others in the group by trying to program them—indeed, all the men in the group are angry with her and feel let down by her.

But in other cases, because this therapist still has an unresolved piece of his past, he will discover that his own intense disappointment in a woman patient has nothing to do with that person. Rather, it stems from his own transference or countertransference bias.

Whatever ensues, having uncovered the feeling, identified its tug on his thoughts and impulses to act, he is in a far better position to go beyond it and do his work.

Such a person is not governed by feelings but is in command of them. He is far from being a robot; without feelings, one can hardly be a friend, and in fact, the most seemingly bloodless and cut-off people are typically governed by unidentified feelings.

The ideal in a friend, and certainly in a therapist, is to have feelings—as wide a range of them as life permits; but it is also to understand them, to have access to knowing what they are, so that one can act in accordance with certain ones and not with others.

Just as an artist might want as many colors as possible on his palette, but would also want the ability to choose from among them, the therapist requires as wide a range of feelings as he can get, and the ability to make enlightened selections.

IDENTIFYING FEELINGS—AND EVALUATING THEM

Gaining access to a feeling is sometimes effortless, in which case little need be said about it. We're angry and we know it, we are infatuated with someone, and the fact is painfully obvious to us. But at other times, especially where we have emotional blocks or where feelings are being subtly induced in us, it takes a deliberate process for us to identify what is going on.

Sometimes this identification needs only seconds. Having recognized an impulse of ours, we are stunned that it may seem unreflective of anything happening in the group-room at the time.

For instance, a man in group is complimenting us, and our foot twitches. As soon as we question this twitch, it reveals itself as a full-fledged impulse to kick the man in the groin. Very possibly, we feel ashamed of this impulse, and we become conscious of an urge to deny its validity or to bury it in solicitude for the man. Indeed, such shame has doubtless been a prime reason why we almost stopped ourselves from spotting the urge.

However, because we did not allow our shame to blind us to this impulse, we are now securely in possession of it. Our impulse is real, and so is the feeling that lies beneath it.

What such impulses tell us about our patient or our whole group or ourselves may prove vital. Right now, the point is that impulses, even fleeting ones, are often a key to understanding ourselves and what we feel. If not our only indication of some lurking truth, they may be all we have at the start, and what they can teach us is irreplaceable.

Nor do the most informative impulses or feelings we spot need be antisocial ones. As therapists, we may be possessed by a profound urge to take care of certain group members or to look good to them or to give a person something. We may feel an impulse to bestow a gift—perhaps a flower, or a book, or a sequence of helpful insights.

Here too, if instead of succumbing to the urge, we can identify it without acting on it, we come into position to search for the feelings beneath it, and those feelings will soon become important guides.

Often our own transference is at work. Even before the same patient spoke, we felt unduly protective of him or her. Without our knowing it, we saw in the patient a figure from our own past life, someone whom we admired. Because we are the ones transferring, this is an instance of a countertransference reaction. For a time, we have, in responding to the member, brought in too much of ourselves.

The penalties for failing to identify our own feelings when they play a role in our treatment are various, and in some cases may even prove fatal to the treatment.

In the following case, not as atypical as it might seem, a therapist's failure to spot a strong feeling of his own in time had dire repercussions. Not only did this failure result in his own humiliation and cause a credibility gap in his group, it also resulted in the instantaneous, and arguably justifiable, quitting of the group by one of his patients.

This therapist was, by nature and by his own development, able to meet virtually any head-on challenge. His tragic flaw, however, was being too readily insulted when he felt that someone was being flippant with him or dismissing him.

He suffered from this liability not just with his patients but with those in his personal life. If a doctor couldn't see him for longer than he thought reasonable, or if a friend neglected to answer a phone call of his at once, he would smart with injury. He was, especially at that time, going through a period of being too accusatory, with the result that even his good friends had become wary of him. Only in recent months had he come to appreciate that he even had this tendency, and that was as a result of his own experiences as a group patient.

As fate would have it, a woman in this therapist's group, who had missed several sessions, called up and left a message on his tape a few hours before the group was to meet. With evident alarm, she said that her physician had found a lump in her breast. "Please tell the group I can't be there. I've got to get a mammography Wednesday afternoon."

Our therapist felt instantly annoyed, but failed to register that fact to himself. Not wanting to see himself as unsympathethic, he denied to himself his own outrage. The phone call disappeared from his mind.

That afternoon when the group met, there was a fleeting mention of the woman's absence. The therapist said nothing, and the members, understandably, took up their own issues.

She came to the next session, expecting those present to rally around her with great concern. But she had good news for them; she had rehearsed how she would let them know the medical results were fine—surely, they would take these tidings as a great source of relief.

On arriving, what she encountered instead was collective annoyance toward her. "Where the hell were you?" asked one person. Only a few others seemed even remotely interested, while presumably the rest regarded her as a miscreant not worth their attention.

The woman was aghast. She asked the therapist, "Didn't you tell them?"

Of course, the answer was no.

She had caught him red-handed. He had no satisfactory explanation. She lambasted him for his callousness, and the group unanimously agreed with her.

That was the last time the therapist or his group ever saw this woman. And for a long time afterward, the members, though they returned session after session, were distrustful. Not surprisingly, they had become less spontaneous in divulging how they felt. If becoming like this unfeeling therapist was to be the crowning result of their efforts, then perhaps it was better to go on living with their various problems and retain their humanity.

Observe that the issue was not the therapist's anger at being slighted—at least not in itself. Acute sensitivity, even overreactivity to injury, has real merits; it can teach us a great deal about our patients, enabling us to recognize slights in the room before others do. At best, we can show our sympathy, as Walt Whitman did, with his assertion that "whoever offends another, offends me."

Rather, this therapist's problem was his failure to identify his annoyance, to recognize his "countertransferential excess," and to remain appropriate and effective, instead of letting the feeling derail him.

The Detection of Feelings Through Other Cues

Sometimes our feelings boom their way into our awareness, and we have no trouble labeling them. They beset us, their onslaught making us feel like victims. For instance, they inform us unmistakably that we like or dislike a member or feel possessive or anxious.

But often those feelings that might prove most instrumental to our work are not so evident. They may lurk in a sense of disquietude or in thoughts that we are not proud of when we first encounter them. It takes time and work to uncover such feelings.

Our first reaction when we do see such signs is likely to be an involuntary mental plea, "Go away. Do not exist. Let me alone."

Every therapist is familiar with rumblings that indicate something more is going on than he wants to see—something inside of him or her or something within the group. There is a sound we half-hear, a sound that we would prefer not to know about, stirrings that would unsettle us.

The sky is placid and yet we hear thunder. This cannot be, we tell ourselves, there must be something wrong with our interpretive mechanism, wrong with us. Our impulse is to reinterpret the thunder in some way consistent with what we can see, since if it were really thunder, we would have to reconstrue the reality as it appears to us.

The most sensitive group therapists are those who insist on listening, rather than using devices to mask information. The storm will come, and we might as well know that it is coming and make provisions. In fact, our very efforts to fend off information make its onset much worse for us—such efforts intensify our unconsidered idea that we have botched the job somewhere along the line.

Despite how we may feel, we must move toward these rumblings, as if they were favorable sounds. They are enormously valuable in prospect. Our very investigation of these unwelcome guests will enable us to see that things are not so bad. Even if we did unwittingly contribute to some difficulty in group, and the problem is real, we must confront it.

Any device to ward off a truth will necessarily paralyze the therapist who employs it—there is a price to pay for every defense. No matter how incongruous a fact seems to be, we must admit it as fact, allow it to intrude, for our own sake as well as the group's.

But how are we to deal with these intimations, at first unwanted? For us to answer this question, it is important to first understand the form that they take, the guises that they appear in. They do not necessarily visit us as pure feelings. Rather they assume many shapes.

Let's look at some of these shapes, and consider the benefits that accrue to us when we have the courage to heed these signals and decipher them.

Among the most prevalent are *fantasies*.

For instance, a therapist reports recurrent fantasies of wanting to choke a certain man in the group. His would-be victim is a man who constantly smiles, who announces how well his life is going, and who even compliments the therapist and the group.

When one day this member announces that he won't be at the next session and, with a gleeful look, describes the Caribbean vacation he is planning, one that will cost a fortune, our therapist has the vivid fantasy of rising from his chair, walking over and wreaking his havoc. In the fantasy, the therapist sees himself as Clint Eastwood annihilating a crooked politician.

Curiously, in this case, the therapist feels no anger toward the member; he has only the fantasy, but the aggression behind it is easily inferred, even though it is not felt.

The therapist's examination of his fantasy, in this case, leads him to discover that he is being treated with contempt. His patient has been saying to him, "You are merely a form of diversion and not my favorite one at that."

Using the knowledge, the therapist finds it effortless to endure future slander of the same kind. He proceeds to help the group become cognizant of what the man is doing, to them as well as to the therapist himself. Everyone profits.

Sometimes, what appears first to a therapist as his own fantasy turns out to be a very subtle insight into a reality.

In another case, a woman therapist suddenly has the fantasy that she is going to a funeral. However, she can see no reason for death to have come into her mind. She very much likes the members of her group, and right now they are chatting amiably.

At first, she tries to put her fantasy out of her mind. But it keeps recurring, and soon she feels forced to pay serious attention to it.

Studying the members, she realizes that one of her patients, Martha, is especially subdued. The therapist has no idea why, but comments on the fact. "Martha, you seem to be silent."

With no more provocation than that, Martha bursts into tears and reports that her sister died that very week. Martha had not wanted to tell the group, suffering as she did from an almost phobic distrust of pity. However, she had told them—or more precisely, she had "told" the therapist.

In this case, the therapist's fantasy opened up a profound discussion, not just of the deceased sister, whom Martha loved, but of

Martha's own difficulty in taking from the group what she needed—namely, their deepest expressions of caring.

We've all had such fantasies as winning a lottery or running off with a patient or announcing, "Group, I've got big news. This is our last session." These fantasies must not be dodged. Though the actions they would give rise to are obviously not indicated, the fantasies themselves contain important information about how we feel, about what a group is doing, and why.

Nearly always, these fantasies indicate that we are angry with our group, or would like to run away from it. Proper interpretation of such a fantasy, even to ourselves, can bring us into touch with our anger or distaste for a group. And that in turn can help us pinpoint exactly what we are responding to.

Closely allied to fantasies are impulses to do something, which when examined can also lead us to feelings. Often the two, fantasy and impulse, accompany one another. The distinction between impulse and fantasy, between the neurology and the phenomenology of behavior, need not concern us; the important thing is that either fantasy or impulse may serve as a cue to what we are feeling when we have no other cue.

Or it may be a *slip of the tongue* that tells us that something more is going on inside of us than we realized. For instance, we call a member in our group by a wrong name, that of our own kid brother. Perhaps no one in the group has noticed, or perhaps we haven't even made the mistake aloud: we only *thought* of the person by the wrong name. But *we* know we made the mistake. And when we look at ourselves objectively and ask why, it takes only an instant for us to see that we've been thinking of the person as our kid brother, in the sense that we have some identical feeling toward both.

From there, it is not hard for us to discover why.

We may recall that throughout our childhood, our brother constantly got into trouble and turned to us for help. Indeed, he still does, and for years we have resented it. In childhood, we felt exploited, especially since dear mother devoted three quarters of her waking hours to worrying about him.

Similarly, our patient seems to have a waiting line of emergencies for the group to handle. The group has worked creatively to save him, and some members have sacrificed precious time that might have been better used. As a result, others have often lost out. But, worst of all, we discover, we ourselves have been remiss.

Beginning with our analysis of our slip of the tongue, we come to realize that we've been overconcerned with rescuing this patient, "our brother," and have done far too little to rescue the group from him. As a result, we have been feeling toward this member as we felt, and still feel, toward our younger brother—we resent him—and we especially resent the fact that he has cajoled us all into giving him so much.

From the simple acknowledgment that we called this person by the wrong name, mislabeled him even to ourselves, we have been led to a discovery about him and us that has profound implications for the group. From this fragment we were able to reconstruct the mosaic.

Even more prevalent slips of ours that we might do well to study are *moments of amnesia.* A young male therapist, seeing his first group, repeatedly forgets the name of a certain woman there. At first, he tries to solve the problem by using mnemonic devices, but to his astonishment he even forgets those.

A minute before she comes into the room, he knows her name, it seems obvious. And he knows it the instant she has vanished through the door. But in group, blank. He breathes a sigh of relief when a group member calls her by name, but even that doesn't stick.

Finally, after repeated embarrassment over his failures, he writes her name down on a piece of paper and sticks it to his mirror while he shaves one morning. He catches himself singing a love song with her name in it. To his astonishment, he realizes that he's in love with her. He has fantasies of telling her and running away with her.

Then he remembers that he's been married less than a year. He berates himself, but at least he has become aware of the feeling and of why he forgot the name, and he never forgets it after that.

As another example, a woman therapist keeps forgetting the name of the one patient in her group, also a woman, who is older than she. At first, her amnesia puzzles her. But she goes after the name doggedly and realizes that she dreads the moment the older woman comes into the room.

From there, she recognizes that she feels incompetent and at a loss whenever that particular group member talks. Indeed, the member is a highly controlling person, who gives clear messages to the therapist concerning what she should and shouldn't do. It becomes clear to this therapist why she forgot her patient's name, and she never forgets it again.

Having discovered our true feeling toward a group member, we may be alarmed at its intensity, but nearly always the discovery puts us in position to deal with the person rationally.

In other cases, *we actually see ourselves in motion*, perhaps acting with an urgency that doesn't become us.

A male therapist finds himself making derisive remarks to a very beautiful woman who is flushed with delight in telling the group how happy she is that her lover has just proposed to her. She thanks the group, and tells the therapist, "You've been a real father to me."

The therapist is astonished at himself once he realizes how caustic he has been toward this woman. Even he can see that this is her moment of triumph. However, he makes still another abusive comment. And another, until a group member asks him bluntly, "What's the matter with you, Tom?"

Only then does it click that he has been repeatedly fending off his own romantic longing for her. He has been making less of her time and again. Not until he has identified his behavior as a defense against his yearning for her does he stop belittling her.

Finally, every therapist has particular *habits of body posture* that have idiosyncratic meaning for the person in question. These habits are rooted in feelings and may express themselves in physical acts so long as the feelings behind them go unnoticed. By spotting the habit and tracking it backward, it often becomes possible to return to the feeling.

For instance, a male therapist has the habit of running his hand through his hair, smoothing it down. He does this especially when his anger is preconscious, not when he is fully aware of it. Recognizing that he does this at such times, he becomes able to infer the next time that he must be angry at his group, though he sees no reason to be.

After identifying his own symbolic attempt to smooth down his own ruffled feelings, he realizes that he feels that many of the people there disrespect him. By his grooming himself, he then sees, he has been trying to compose himself without having to acknowledge to himself what he really felt. With this new insight, he soon gets to the root of what has been going wrong in the group.

In all these cases, we are reasoning backward from our behavioral manifestation to our feeling, and we know we have succeeded when we come into touch with that feeling. Rather than sidetrack us or invite counterproductive behavior, our feelings become our most powerful therapeutic tool, one that we continually utilize.

DISAPPOINTMENT IN A GROUP DUE TO CONGEALING

One of the most usual feelings that comes over us when things aren't going exactly right with a group is disappointment. Our further introspection will usually reveal that it is disappointment at the group for *congealing*—that is, when its emotional quality has become frozen.

Ordinarily, let us say, a particular group shows a wide range of response. However, these days when they address a certain individual, they do so with atypical mildness, or with nastiness not characteristic of them.

Or perhaps our scrupulously considerate group now seems satisfied neglecting a certain member utterly. If he never spoke again, they wouldn't care. The kicker is that we ourselves have recently been responding to the member much as the group has.

Whatever the particulars, the group is acting more of a piece than they were—they have taken on a singular frame of mind, and we have assumed it too. It's as if everyone in the room had gone from being emotionally chromatic to monochromatic.

Obviously, the group has been congealing for a reason. In such cases, quite often, both the group and we ourselves share some reaction toward a particular member—a feeling that we have been taking pains not to own up to. Together, we and the group members are suffering from a motivated ignorance—the desire not to experience whatever feeling the particular member is inducing in us.

This is the scenario, but how are we to recognize it?

Being victims of the willful ignorance that blankets the group, how are we even to know when such a scenario is in progress—more specifically, to discern what we ourselves are truly feeling toward the members? It would seem that being in the dark, along with our group, we could do nothing.

But even here, in what looks superficially like an instance of a shared blind spot, and therefore a hopeless situation, there is a telltale sign that, if we have the courage to pause and examine it, can lead us to the light.

This sign is our own *dissatisfaction* with the group, our disappointment in what has become of it. Beginning with our own frank acknowledgment that we feel disappointed, we can go on to learn the whole truth—first about ourselves and then about whatever the group is doing, or not doing. We may go on to discover exactly why our group has shut down emotionally, why it has collectively denied to itself its real feeling toward the particular member.

As always, our first clue, even before we perceive the group's unnatural behavior, its uniformity, is something amiss within us.

The disappointment we identify in ourselves may range from mild irritation to utter dismay—in any case, at first it seems free-floating and unrelated to anything. Only after we identify this feeling of ours and examine it, do we realize the grand sweep of our annoyance. We harbor it not merely toward one or a few members, but toward the group as whole. They are not their usual selves.

Quite naturally, we may then ask ourselves, "Why are we so bothered? Do we not pride ourselves on our ability to accept any form of group behavior, to ride on the streams of change, to be in the moment, existential?"

All this is so, for which reason it now perturbs us that we are so annoyed at the group. There can be no doubt of it—our discontent with the group represents discontent with ourselves. We appreciate that we have joined our group in denying some facet of reality.

At this point, our discovery is virtually always the same. The group has been twisting itself out of shape to relate to a particular member, and so have we. It has shared a desire not to feel a certain way toward this person, and it has paid the inevitable price of acting on the desire not to feel, not to know—namely the price of uniformity and of dullness. We hadn't pinpointed the process because, all along, we had been engaging in the same self-delusion.

From here, it is usually not difficult to identify the member and to appreciate what the others truly feel toward that person. Having released ourselves from the shared denial, we are free to know what we truly feel, which the group feels too. Eventually we will help the group recognize its self-imposed constriction and free itself. But that is a matter of technique. The important thing here is that we ourselves have finally identified what we truly feel.

There are so many steps in the process that it is worth summarizing.

1. We have begun by identifying what seemed like an unwarranted annoyance of ours toward the group or an unwarranted disappointment in the group.

2. Our next step has been to look at the group squarely, whereupon we noted a loss of richness and energy among the members.

3. Investigating that loss led us to its cause. We see that the group has for a time become emotionally dishonest with a certain member, suppressing a part of themselves in the presence of that member. In so doing, they have lost their stuff. As a "member" of the group, we the therapist have done the same thing. We have lost our stuff.

4. From here, it remains only to ask ourselves what we really feel toward that person.

5. No longer defending ourselves against the truth, as we had over weeks or months, we can answer this question for the first time. We see the group's "spore formation" as just that. For the first time in a while, we can see the group members as quite different from one another. We can see at least three kinds of members: There is the "source person," the patient who evoked the collective denial of the group. There is a collection of members who are still engaging in denial of what they feel. And finally, we have set ourselves apart from these two entities. We are no longer succumbing to personal denial. We know at least what we really feel toward the source member and toward the others.

For example, one afternoon while walking in the park, I had the fantasy of losing the keys to my office so that my group and I couldn't get in. Nor was it an unpleasant daydream.

However, my analysis of that daydream took me by storm. To my surprise, I found that I didn't like them anymore—they had disappointed me.

Only a few months previously, I'd told a colleague how alive this group was, how well the members related to one another. Could it be that any group so recently wide-eyed, playful, curious, and bright, to a degree that made me proud of them, were now behaving in such a way that I was reluctant even to see them?

Sure enough, as I thought about our most recent sessions, I could see changes—and they had not been for the better.

I forced myself to think about individual members, one after the other. Tom and Steve, who'd both been full of life, were now mournfully quiet. Alice, always known for her quips, had nothing to say these days. The brilliant Alan, a geologist who had emerged from the rock of his own harsh childhood, now seemed embedded back in it—he'd become stone silent. Gone was all the group's inventiveness and elation and surprise.

Unwittingly, I had been responding to this loss, and I recalled Shakespeare's lament one day that his art "was barren of variation and quick change." Maybe his wasn't, but mine was. What had so constricted the group, bleaching out their colors and leaving me so unhappy with them?

I asked myself, "Was there anything in particular that the group was afraid of?" "Was there an intimation of frightening aggression?" "Could there be some impending exposure that the members feared?"

One member, Ellen, had been discussing her mother's recent death. Had Ellen's discussion of her private loss touched chords in the others, inducing them to pull back?

I pondered these hypotheses and others about the rest of the group, to see whether they might have induced such a reaction in the members. However, I could see no interchange sufficient to explain the group's retreat into dullness.

Next I asked myself, "Was anyone in particular draining excess time or spirit from the group?" To sharpen that question, I set myself to considering which, if any, member had taken up a preponderance of the group's talking time.

The answer was obvious—Denise. For weeks, Denise would cart out a long list of concerns. Denise's mother had been brutal—she had told us about "the witch" ad nauseam. Poor Denise had suffered such an atrocious start in life as to wring tears from anyone with half a soul. However, always Denise, pure and defenseless, had somehow managed to escape—fairy-tale style. Her scars would always be there, they were badges of her suffering, and she never let the group forget them.

We had all gotten Denise's message—"Never again." That message was clear: Denise was insisting that we place no burden on her whatsoever. Apparently, the group had accepted that message as a rule they could not break.

The next session I watched her. Ellen had quietly begun with some insights about her mother's funeral. Poor Ellen was still in shock, that was obvious. But Denise hardly heard her. She had something important to tell us, and moments later she was proclaiming that her own mother had called her once again with an outrageous request.

"Why should I visit my aunt? She's my mother's sister, and my mother knows I hate sickness. She's never been supportive of me the way my friends are."

The group sympathized with Denise, and when a man there wondered aloud whether she couldn't visit her aunt briefly and then meet her friends, Denise whirled on him. "You're just like her. You're just like her. You don't care about my feelings. You only care about a job to be done. The human element means nothing to you."

The man who'd made the suggestion sank back, and the other members subsided into their chairs. Black clouds of remorse hung over anyone who might have wanted to contradict the sanctimonious Denise.

I realized that this was a prototype experience for the group—for some months now, they had been in fear of distressing her. And that fear had implications far beyond what anyone actually said to Denise. Denise's message to them had implied that their own worst predicaments were not worthy of lament alongside what had befallen her. For instance, it would be wrong for Ellen to express too much sorrow over the death of her own wonderful mother because Denise's mother was such a bitch. Nor did they dare even to talk to one another roughly or frankly. Raising voices against one another might unsettle Denise, who needed tranquility above all.

Over weeks, their inhibition had spread, so that in paying unconscious obeisance to Denise, they had forgone almost all spontaneity. No one wanted to disturb the peace, and they had all paid the price. They had permitted the entry of one person to motivate a collective flight from their own personal expression. They had flattened themselves out so as not to offend Denise.

Once I had a grip on this, it was not difficult for me to take measures. One member, Alice, seemed least under the spell of the group's inhibition, and I decided to use her.

When Ellen next began to talk about her mother and Denise cut her off, causing Ellen to wince, I went into action. Instead of letting the matter go, I asked Alice why Ellen's face had dropped. Alice volunteered her opinion at once, that Ellen had something important to say, had been cut off, and felt helpless and controlled. Denise looked outraged. In her desperately weakened position, how could she possibly control anyone? Where was Alice's humanity?

But this time the group had its say. One by one, the members let Denise know that they too had felt controlled by her and afraid to speak their minds. It took Denise a long while to appreciate her role as stifler of people, though she got a glimmer of it that day. But from that moment on, the group came alive. They had divested the fragile tyrant of her power. But more to the point, they had realized there was no need to censor their own inner lives.

By paying close heed to my own dissatisfaction with the group, my feeling that it had let me down by becoming one-note, I had found the problem, and then had pursued it until I discovered why.

More often than not, a group's congealment represents their unconsidered response to the fragility of a member. In catering to that person unduly, the group loses itself. Our knowing this usual cause can help us spot the member and discover what the group is doing.

However, in other cases, our group has been congealing by joining someone in his or her relentless expression of rage. The other members have been using this individual to express their anger for them, and they have stopped examining their lives.

This time we experience the group as one-note in its relentless rage, as if we were confronting a would-be lynch mob. They are collectively fleeing from subtle issues in their own lives, from variations that would enrich the room if they were discussed, burying all this variety under what masquerades as simple outrage.

Here, too, repetition is our cue. The rage of at least some of the individual members may be warranted, but our clue is "rage and nothing more." Once again, we must look for the catalyst member—in this case, someone good at giving people hell. The group is using this person as their mouthpiece for an anger that truly tells only a small part of their story. Again our disappointment or dismay has led us to the discovery of too much uniformity, which in turn has led us to pinpoint the reason and free the group to go forward.

Just as every individual has what humanist psychologist Abraham Maslow called a "self-actualizing" power, a surge to express his or her own individuality, every group has some tendency to cohere, to become monolithic. Since our purpose as therapists is to bring out individual differences and we measure ourselves by how effective we are at doing this, it stands to reason that when a group goes in the opposite direction—that is, congeals, we will feel disappointment or annoyance at the group. And since our feelings are often even more reliable indicators than our perceptions—especially if we too are motivated not to see or identify something that is going on—this often puts us in the position of feeling annoyance or disappointment, even before we appreciate why.

It takes courage for us as therapists to acknowledge to ourselves that we are dismayed by any group. After all, are we not guided by the precept "Nothing human is alien to us"? It might seem that we are refusing our own role when we feel disappointment, when we catch ourselves refusing to accept a group as it is. But our own disappointment is the critical cue, and, indeed, is sometimes the only one we have, that a group is constricting itself unnaturally. Only by studying our own internal state, and pursuing our inquiry, can we see what is really going on in the group and why.

DECODING ANY DISCORDANT REACTION

Every reaction of ours is ultimately a response to something real, or the resultant force of different vectors brought into play, some within us and some out in the world. That is, every feeling of ours may be parsed into components some of which are inherent in the therapist's character and some of which are pure responses to what the group is doing.

More often than not, our feelings are virtually self-explanatory. The feeling makes sense on the face of it. A patient is repeatedly late—we feel irritated or dismayed. Our group fights to help a member arrive at a discovery—we feel proud of the group, successful, happy. But, interestingly, even more informative than these reactions of ours, the measurement of which psychologists would describe as having "face validity," are the very experiences that at first seem to us to be inappropriate, unwarranted, and "wrong."

I've already mentioned examples in which a therapist's reactions that seemed discordant with what was going on proved to be quite the contrary. Far from proving groundless, those reactions upon examination led the therapist to major insights. This is the rule more often than the exception—so much so that we are led to ask, "Why is it that our reactions that seem most groundless at first so often lead us to the most significant truths?"

The special importance of the therapist's seemingly inappropriate feelings derives from a single fact. More often than not, they are an indication of the kind of character pattern that ordinarily goes undetected, and thus uncorrected, over a lifetime. The less obvious it is that a patient is inducing a reaction in us, the more likely he is to have been affecting others the same way for years without their knowing it—and without his knowing it. Toxic traits survive in proportion to the difficulty of seeing them.

The reason for this is worth spelling out. If everyone became easily aware of a harmful trait in an individual, then almost surely someone would have made him aware of it, and he would have amended it. For instance, a boy brags openly. His parents, other kids, *someone* is taken aback, and tells him, "Stop showing off." The boy, if he does not stop outright, continues covertly, developing much subtler ways of strutting his stuff.

Now as a grown-up, he is a master of the subtle brag. Because it is subtle, others pull back from him without knowing why, and as a man he pays the repeated price of losing intimacy and trust, even from those he cares for most. In group, his fellow members react as outsiders do. They feel demeaned and somewhat uncomfortable in his presence, and so do we.

At first, we may experience our own discomfort in this man's presence as groundless. He is mannerly, honest, and successful. Only by our being big enough to acknowledge our own malaise in his presence, which we may even suspect has been prompted by jealousy of him or by some other unresolved problem of our own, may we discover what is really going on. We discover that he has been making us feel this way by his subtle self-aggrandizement, and in subsequent sessions we learn to see plainly what he is doing and how he has made us feel as we did. Indeed, he has affected everyone in the room the same way. All the members keep him at arm's length.

At last, having identified and researched our own seemingly groundless feeling, we have doped out how he is evoking it and why it is not groundless at all. Our possession of this feeling and our understanding of why we have it is precious for us and for him. From here, it becomes easy for us to imagine why his coworkers and why his fellow group members right in front of us have recoiled from him. When later he tells us that his own children keep him at a distance, we understand that, too.

We have found a trait of his that has been highly significant in determining the course of his life. The very subtlety of his effect on people, which accounted for our difficulty in seeing what he was doing, is what made the trait so important and what gave the trait its longevity.

As a general rule, feelings that seem *discordant* with events in a group deserve special attention. Our very impulse to banish any reaction of ours to a group member, or to a whole group, should serve as an alarm to do the opposite—that is, to investigate the feeling. Rather than dismiss our reactions for their seeming inappropriateness, we should embrace them.

A patient of mine kept failing key job interviews and would lament to the group about how unlucky he was. More than once, he had passed two or three interviews, felt sure he would land a job, only to find at the last minute that he didn't qualify for some reason or other. Sometimes it turned out that though nearly all the bigwigs wanted him, the last interviewer, the top executive, was vociferous against him and prevailed. In any event, the ball never seemed to bounce his way.

The group came across as remarkably unsympathetic. A few members told him outright that he was a loser. One shouted coarsely, "Stop bleeding all over us, will you." Some paid no attention to him, and were quick to change the subject.

For a time, I was angry with them for what seemed like their callousness, until I detected in myself a stunning lack of compassion for this poor soul. I had no more sympathy for him than they did. Why not? He went dutifully to his job interviews. He seemed to be doing everything he could. Yet I felt myself strangely detached, as if a voice within me were saying, "Who cares what happens to you?"

I then realized that this reaction of mine, my own share of the group's disdain for him, sprang from a feeling of helplessness. I couldn't reach him.

And my feeling of helplessness was exactly what the man had felt in his home. When as a boy, my patient would bring home a reasonably good report card and expect praise, his father would denounce him for having fallen short of perfection. When he hurt himself physically, his father called him clumsy. Whatever went wrong in his life, his father construed as the boy's fault.

Amazing as it seemed to me at first, the group and I myself were feeling toward this patient exactly what *he* had felt when with his father. The collective disdain of the group, I realized, sprang from our collective despair over being unable to contact him emotionally. We had been as helpless to get his attention as he had been to get his father's.

He had induced this demoralization in the group, I saw, by doing with us the very things his father had done with him. Examining his presentation with this in mind, I could see without great difficulty how he was unconsciously playing his father in the room with us. He was disdainful of us whenever we tried to reach him, to please him, to show that we cared.

Whenever a member reached out to try to help this man, he would treat that person as if that member were his own unloved son. Employing his father's brusqueness, he might say simply, "That doesn't fit." Or "That wouldn't work."

This man seemed programmed never to let us feel that we had the right insight or advice, as his father had never let him feel that he was the possessor of real knowledge or worth. By these and other "fatherly" practices, he had been subjecting the whole group, including me, to a powerful force, making us a roomful of unloved sons and daughters.

With this knowledge, derived through a study of my own reactions, my path became clearer. Among my other insights was that he was doubtless doing the same thing with interviewers, treating them also as his father had treated him, making them feel unimportant and himself getting rejected as a consequence.

However, the details of my treatment of this patient are less important here than the insight that opened up the vista. In a great many cases, what seems like an inappropriate reaction on our part, what we might term an "ostensibly discordant reaction," leads us to powerful historical insights.

How are we to explain such patterns?

The topographical psychic map that charts what we see in action seems helpful here. We are, almost surely, dealing with what psychoanalyst Eduardo Weiss, back in 1932, first called an "introject." An *introject* is a part object, a piece of some significant figure of the person's past, that remains incorporated in the psyche but has never been assimilated into the person's adult ego. It operates as a feeling, an attitude, a *voice* urging the person to act as the significant figure did. By implication, it urges others to act in the role of the patient himself.

In some sense, the person remains a victim of this voice, which lives by its own rules. It is the voice—or more technically, the introject— that induces in us and in the group members what feel to be dissonant reactions. However, they seem this way only because we are responding to the voice and not to the rest of the person.

The study of these dissonant reactions enables us to spot this voice, to hear what it is saying. Invariably, when we are able to do this, we discover that our reactions are consonant with the voice, and ultimately not dissonant at all.

Discordant reactions, by their very nature, bespeak countertransference in a group or in us. When a group shares our still-unidentified reaction to a member, it is highly unlikely that we are all experiencing an identical transference to that person. Nor are we feeling a simple reality reaction. Our very difficulty in identifying the nature of what we feel and why we feel as we do toward a member suggests a blockage with us, one with antecedent roots in our own personal history.

If we simply liked or disliked someone for his behavior, and that was all there was to it, we would have no trouble in considering our response appropriate. The seeming inappropriateness of what we are feeling in these cases always attests to an unworked-out part of our own history.

USING THE GROUP TO LEARN ABOUT OURSELVES

In studying groups, the obvious aim is to acquire as much knowledge as possible about them, as if the group were like a patient lying on the couch. The more we know about the patient, the more effectively we can set down our purposes and choose our interventions. This model of thinking, simply stated, likens us to the hematologist, who examines a patient's blood to know what, if anything, must be done for the patient.

However, implicit is the notion that the doctor is a fixed, invariant being, who needs only to learn about the patient to carry out his procedures. With us, nothing could be further from the truth. The robot image, mentioned earlier, simply does not apply to us because the therapist must use his or her own feelings at every stage of treatment, and in this sense we, too, are variables, needing continuous emotional alignment and realignment.

Startling as it may seem to newcomers to the field, the group itself must serve as a primary instrument to help the therapist discover what he is feeling at critical moments when he has lost touch with himself. Paradoxically, though our purpose is to help others, we must use those others to help us stay in tune with ourselves so that we can do the job. And we must do this not once or twice, but continuously as we work with our groups.

There are various ways in which we can, and should, use our groups to keep us open and calibrated as we do our work. I want to mention three of them, going from the most to the least obvious.

Learning About Ourselves from the Complaints of Members

If we honor every complaint made about us by any member, we will not only discover many transference distortions in our patients and learn about them, we will discover truths about ourselves—and, most pertinent here, we will be led to uncover feelings of our own that we harbored but were not in touch with.

For instance, a therapist is constantly belabored by the men in his group for showing great tenderness toward the women and bypassing them. One man, very articulate, observes aloud that the therapist stops men from talking whenever a woman seems troubled. Someone else in the group agrees and adds that the therapist always lets the women talk generically about how disappointing the men are, but is quick to protect women from anything that seems like an attack on womankind.

Heeding these comments, the therapist discovers in himself first an exaggerated feeling that women are fragile, and next that he is prone to guilt whenever he sees a woman in distress. With such knowledge, he becomes able to let women express their feelings without his trying to extinguish their reactions.

As therapists, we may face an endless variety of complaints—being called hostile or neglectful or fearful or flippant or too materialistic or too prone to give how-to advice.

It might even be a small complaint—for instance, that we talk too fast or too slow—but if those who make this complaint are right, the complaint may have important implications, not just for them but for us. Our speaking too fast may, upon examination, lead us to discover anxiety of ours that we weren't aware of. Our speaking too slow could mean that we're playing it overly safe to defend against antic-ipated aggression.

Understandably, we may feel an impulse to defend ourselves against the pain of being told that we are less than perfect. But we should actually be glad when members of a group confront us openly with complaints about what we are doing. They are giving us a chance to examine ourselves for a particular feeling or tendency.

Though complaints about us may express only a single patient's perceptions and biases, we must honor each in turn. Doing so will, more than occasionally, lead us to important discoveries about what we really feel and why.

Nor need we decide on the spot whether a complaint leveled at us is transferential or manipulative or valid. We will have ample chance to cross-validate in future sessions whatever people in the group say about us.

Discovering Some Feeling of Our Own by Examining Irregular Behavior of a Group Toward Us

In still other cases, our group members sense something about us that they can't put into words. They react to a way we have of treating them that they don't like at all. Doubtless, one or more of those members would willingly tell us what they object to, but they simply can't because they don't know. Without realizing what they are doing or even that they are doing anything different from before, they recoil from us.

For instance, they sense favoritism in us toward certain members and respond by sulking, or they sense our anger toward them and freeze up, or they sense our disdain for them and resort to coming late or to missing sessions or forgetting to pay us. Once again, it would be tempting to lay the blame wholly on their doorstep, to find precedent for their "atrocious" behavior, citing their pathology. Indeed, it would prove even easier to do so in this case, where the members lack the articulation to tell us off in words.

But here, too, it would be a major mistake to exempt ourselves without considering closely that what the group is doing may be a reaction of theirs to some feeling of ours—a feeling that they surmise we hold, though they themselves could not say what it was. From a study of their irregular behavior, we may be led to discover irregular behavior of our own and a previously unsuspected feeling that underlies it.

For example, a male therapist had run three groups with good success for several years. These groups, though differing in the makeup of their members, were all highly motivated, and successful. Within the last few months, however, the members started to seem guarded and even sluggish. They had become less personal, and down-right aloof.

The therapist was slow to see these changes. He had his own prob-lems. He and his wife had recently been divorced, and she was already with another man. In fact, it was evident now that she had been sleeping with that man for some time before the actual end of their marriage. The divorce proceedings were still going on, and he was doing his best to contain his suffering. Ideally, his groups would have provided him with distraction and sanctuary.

Therefore it came as a terrible shock to him when he realized that not one group but all three were becoming repetitive, unemotional, and flat. All three were becoming as unenlivened as his marriage was at the end.

Had a single group reacted this way and not the other two, he might well have directed his whole attention to that one group, as if that group were collectively opposing his efforts. However, his finding that all three groups were behaving similarly led him to realize that he himself must be the common denominator. And he was intrepid and honest enough to turn the spotlight on himself.

What might he be doing differently than he did in the past? Some answers were obvious. He was making many more interpretations and not letting people talk enough. And he was especially not letting people talk about love or sex, as if those subjects were trivial, beside the point, irrelevant to the members' real problems. More than once, he had interpreted a woman's saying she was attracted to a man in a group as a device to manipulate that man.

It was as if the therapist no longer believed in the genuineness of sexuality or intimacy. He even caught himself remarking that sexual-ity is a destroyer of love. He was starting to sound like the cynics at the seventeenth-century French court, who saw all women as prosti-tutes, achieving power by granting sexual favors, as if women didn't really want sex or love for their own sake.

This therapist was shocked at the realization that he had lapsed into this vision of women and that he had been expressing it. Without a doubt, it had been contaminating all his relationships, and in his groups it had been inhibiting the open expression of affection, of love, of sexuality. The very reason the members had come to group—to overcome their inhibitions and learn to drink from the well of love—had lost validity. This therapist had unwittingly made them feel fool-ish when they took even a sip.

Now his own cynical feelings became clear to him. He was a dis-
illusioned and skeptical man these days, and was fobbing off his cynicism and disillusionment on all who would listen. He saw easily why
he had downgraded people's experiences. If women didn't like sex,
then his wife had not really turned to her lover for sex. If women were
all exploitative, then so was his wife, and he had gained, rather than
suffered a grievous loss, by her departure.

Now he saw that in recent months he had assumed a whole collection of attitudes—custom-made to preserve his self-esteem and to dull
his pain in losing his wife.

True, to the extent that he fooled himself, he had perhaps suffered
from the divorce less keenly. But the tradeoff would be disastrous unless he came to his senses. As an unconsidered cost of his denouncing
sexuality and love, of his allowing himself universal cynicism about
women, he was pushing all women, and indeed all people away. What
he had perceived in his groups as a loss of verve, he realized, was actually a response to the change in his own attitude toward the members.

This therapist had begun his own cure by identifying a change in the
group's behavior, and by considering that he himself might be at its
heart. He had looked at himself with a steady gaze, and what he saw
did not please him. Finally, he realized that he had been making an
accommodation to kill pain in his own life, and this accommodation
was blinding him to the essence of his own, unfolding experience.

Every change in a group's behavior may be indicative of a change in
us. Even when this proves not to be the case, no harm is done in our
considering it as a working hypothesis.

Using Group Defaults to Identify Some Lurking
Attitude of Our Own

Finally, let's consider the subtlest mode of discovery about ourselves,
using the group as evidence. This time it is neither the group's complaints nor any overt behavior of theirs that cues us in. It is rather
what a group fails to do.

Especially when more than one group shows the same kind of lack
over a period of time, we should ask whether we have induced that
lack, keeping in mind that group behavior never occurs in a vacuum
but is always part of a reciprocal interaction and that we play a fundamental role in what a group does and doesn't do.

Though, of course, there can be no syllabus for a group's performance or accomplishments, nearly all groups enter a number of basic territories—not necessarily in every session, but over any period as long as a month or so.

For instance, it would be a rare group whose members never alluded to their sexual feelings—desires, fears, concerns. Similarly, having shown that we consider dreams a rich source of information, especially if they seem highly charged or involve other group members, we would be surprised if no one talked about a dream for an extended period. And, if even without our encouragement, no one in a group ever expressed irrational anger toward anyone else, we would wonder why not.

By the same token, we expect our group members to talk about events in the very recent past. Perhaps in our last session with a group, everyone could see that someone's feelings were seriously hurt. But in the next session no one mentions this.

If this kind of thing happens repeatedly, if each session seems a thing in itself, existing as if there are no residues from the past—no unfinished accusations or declarations, no denunciations, no declarations to be completed—then, almost surely, the cause is in us.

In such a case we cannot simply conclude that our group is merely existential to the degree that they never talk about what took place last time. Rather, by some attitude of ours, felt but as yet unrecognized by us, we are stifling their expression.

Noting any of these gaps in presentation, we must ask not merely what is wrong with the group but what may be wrong with us. Their "default" has not been merely an action bespeaking their character-structures. It is something more.

We must therefore ask, "How are we unwittingly contributing to what seems like a lack in our group or groups?"

Every therapist has his or her own mental checklist concerning what is expected of a group. Most of us expect our group members to talk about their early lives, and especially the incidents that prove to have been character forming. We also expect the members to tell us what they think of us, how they feel about us, and how they feel about the group itself. The utter absence of such material implies that we are subduing those comments, one way or another. The point is not the nature of the template that we impose on a group, but that stark defaults are indicative of feelings of our own.

All progress in group treatment parallels the analyst's discovery of his own inner life as prompted by his or her patients. Our discoveries go hand in hand with those of the members, and though we give the talking time to them, we should be prepared to give ample introspection to ourselves. We cannot afford to be robots because our own feelings are important in furthering every group's advancement. By relying on what goes on in group for our own self-understanding, we are best able to help the members.

CHAPTER SIX

ORCHESTRATING A GROUP

William Jennings Bryant once said that two people in a conversation really amount to four people talking. The four are what one person says, what he wanted to say, what his listener heard, and what he thought he heard. Multiply this by ten or so group members, and multiply that product by all the combinations and permutations of members talking in pairs and in trios, and in even larger subsets, and there is so much going on that even the great Indian mathematician Ramanujon, who specialized in such enumerations, could spend a lifetime unable to summarize the number of interactions in a single group, real and imagined.

It is therefore hardly surprising that any group therapist, even an experienced one, can feel overwhelmed when contemplating what is going on in his or her group. How are we even to begin an investigation of so complex a phenomenon as group dynamics?

Only with some vision of what a group is and of what it ought to be can we even begin. Without having specified what we expect of a group, we would be overwhelmed.

Fundamentally, we are observing two phenomena above all others:

1. How the members express new feelings toward one another.
2. How they evolve their emotional relationships.

Does this sound overly simple, set against the background of the traditionally stated goals of group treatment? In a sense it might, at first. But these criteria encompass the aims of a wide variety of group therapists. They represent the requirements of all group therapy, whether the therapist's creed is Freudian, Adlerian, Rogerian, Transactional, or Existential.

Admittedly, we may at times consider ourselves in a triage situation, as when a member threatens violence to himself or others, or when someone has a desperate crisis.

For instance, a woman is planning to leave her husband this week because she found out that he had a gay relationship before their marriage. However, in group, rather than talk about this, she poses some urgent questions about her relationship to other group members, as if they were the only ones that counted in her life.

Here we have an immediate decision to make. Does her marital crisis merit our special attention? Or should we simply let her relationships with the other group members unfold at their own pace, trusting that as she resolves them, she will work out her life?

To do the first, that is, to insist that she talk about her marriage, would stop the interactive flow of group. To do the second, to let her omit all mention of her marriage and outside life, would be to deprive her of other people's perspectives, which might be helpful to her. The decision must, of course, rest with the individual therapist.

In other instances, people try to stop the group by thrusting upon it talk about crises in their outside lives. When they do this, presenting us with mock-triage problems every week, motivated by their demand for our attention, our choice is clearer. Sooner or later—preferably sooner—we must confront them, so that they can see what they are doing and how their seizing center stage using exigency as a pretext has harmed them in the long run.

In general, people's problems in their outside lives are always reflected within the group, and we must be skilled in seeing how these problems are mirrored in the group and in dealing with them there.

But let us return to our two primary criteria when deciding what to investigate. No matter how we conceptualize personality structure and change, we are faced with our patients' need to free their intrapsychic lives and to develop their faculty to form new and enriched relationships.

By virtually every definition, a stagnant group is one that does not enable its members to do this, and the symptoms of a stagnant group are that the participants are mired in the same feelings and unable to act in new ways toward one another.

When people are relating well, are disclosing feelings to each other, we must know it, mainly so that we can honor their progress in action by not interfering with it. We investigate, primarily, the contexts where this is *not* happening—that is, where the group is stagnant by our criterion.

Indications of such sterility are the following deficits. The members do not report their most significant memories; they show neglect or indifference toward one another; they may miss sessions without concern; they forget each other's names, dress in a slovenly way; they are repetitive in such small things as always taking the same seat. One session is like another both in what they say and in how they say it. We can be almost sure that those in such a group are as repetitive in their outside lives as they are with us.

To sum up, we have available a wide variety of questions that we can ask. But, ideally, if someone could read our intentions, he would find that we asked every question with the aim of liberating new emotions in a member *and* enabling the members to relate in some new way.

Perhaps the most obvious kind of question that comes to the minds of inexperienced group therapists, especially those highly capable in their practice with individual patients, is the question to a member about how he or she feels in the moment.

1. "John, why are you so quiet?"
2. "Edward, how do you think this all started in your life?"
3. "Alice, you say you criticize yourself too much. When do you do it?"

These questions, useful or maybe even essential to ask in individual treatment, have serious drawbacks when asked in a group. Even when on occasion they do yield information about someone, they are doing at most half the job. While they bring out the individual, it is at the expense of moving the group ahead as a unit. As a rule, they foster no new emotional relationships between the members, and in putting the spotlight squarely on an individual, they are neglectful of the group.

For instance, while John responds to our question about his undue silence, other members feel bored or they satisfy their intellectual urges to solve John's problem or to guess what he is about to say.

As a result, in asking John about himself, we are either excluding the others, or at best, appealing to what amounts to a crossword-puzzle instinct on their part. Only if we are lucky enough to have someone who identifies with John apply the question to himself will our question have extended value. More often, such questions isolate the members, and they would do better seeing a therapist individually and getting their full time. Recall the discussion about role-playing, which, even while helping one person or a few, does so at the expense of the rest, who become mere observers.

Questions to any individual about him- or herself do very little to help the other group members develop understanding of their own traits. If six members have a tendency in common—for instance, they are women who share disappointment in the men they choose, or men afraid of intimacy—then to help one of those people recognize the trait by a well-posed question of ours may do little to help the others see it in themselves. We are relying utterly on their identification with the person of whom we asked the question, and they may not make this identification for us.

For one thing, it may be unpleasant to see themselves as similar to the person we are addressing. Or for another, they simply don't appreciate that they do the same thing. When we ask Alice why she is so brutally critical of herself, Jeremy, who is also sadistic toward himself for his faults, may get nothing out of her answer. If asked about himself, he would say, "I don't criticize myself too much. I'm just aware of what's wrong with me, and plenty is."

Complicating the picture further and obscuring identifications is the fact that though a set of members may share a problem, they handle it differently. They defend against seeing it in their own individual ways.

For instance, two women feel inferior and are afraid of being judged. One of these women hesitates to give opinions. The other talks incessantly to stave off anticipated assaults. If we ask the quiet woman why she seldom says anything, the other women won't identify with her. If we ask the overly talkative woman about her incessant chatter, even if she explains herself fully, our diffident woman, on the sidelines, will feel that she herself is utterly unlike her.

The two, who actually perceive themselves quite similarly, will remain unconnected and unable to help each other.

Once again, if we were to restrict our questions to asking individuals about themselves, thus depriving the group of its collective power, we would do much better to see the patients individually and give them sustained personal attention. Not surprisingly, the therapist who does limit himself to such questions will soon encounter restlessness among the members. The inevitable question follows, "Don't you think I'd be better off seeing you alone?" Or even worse, the declaration, "Who needs this?"

Recall Reggie, who dealt with the members of his group as if he were seeing them as isolated individuals who happened to be in a room with others. He lost leverage that way, and soon found the members unwilling to share him. Those who wanted to revert to seeing him alone, where they could get more time and attention, had a point. They were not really deriving the benefit of the group experience.

Instead of asking people about themselves, therefore, we should ideally ask people about *others*, knowing that *they are talking about themselves in the process.*

If we ask well-framed questions of people about other people, we simultaneously get them and those others to reveal themselves. Moreover, we invite relationships to form. We develop a "speaking community." Even if one person's answer about another is inapplicable, or only partially true, there is always a spark that takes place when people address each other.

And we can often go further, asking individuals questions about whole sets of people and sometimes about the group as a whole.

The ideal investigative questions are those that involve as many people as possible, both in the adventure of discovery and in the sharing of the spoils of what is revealed.

"DOPPELGANGERS"

Much of our success as investigators lies in our ability to recognize similarities among our group members, especially those not immediately apparent but nonetheless strong.

In virtually any group there are almost sure to be people *similar in behavior*—for instance, there are those who rebut the therapist regularly, or who overstate or who seem overly unrestrained. Less recognizable are people with similar motives who act differently—for instance, who handle their anger differently. And there are those with similar parents or with similar past histories. It is supremely important for the therapist to be able to spot such congruences between patients, especially in those who might not appear similar—that is, for us to recognize what we may loosely call "doppelgangers" of different kinds.

In literature, a *doppelganger* is the supposed ghostly double of someone, the wraith of a person. German culture abounds in accounts of doppelgangers. And Joseph Conrad's *The Secret Agent* is such a story.

My own favorite doppelganger tale is Edgar Allen Poe's "William Wilson." Wilson was a scoundrel, born to a wealthy family, who cheated and misused people from his earliest school days. As a young child, Wilson found himself up against an adversary, who stymied him at every turn, exposing his chicanery. When he reached college, this same adversary destroyed his reputation, revealing that Wilson cheated at cards and forcing him to drop out of school. It was then that William Wilson made the remarkable discovery that this adversary bore his exact name and was born the same day and year.

Over the succeeding two decades, William Wilson lived a nefarious life. Time and again, only his doppelganger somehow figured out what he had done, but exposed him to the world. Wilson's double followed him across Europe, finally causing his downfall. When Wilson, driven to the brink of his sanity, finally stabbed his double through the chest, Wilson himself collapsed and died.

The doppelganger pairs that appear in our groups are, of course, only partially identical—similar in behavior or in motive or in past experience or in attitude, but not in all of these. For this reason, because even "group pairs" are some distance apart, the members retain the objectivity required to help one another and to talk about their likenesses.

We are able to capitalize on these similarities in their variety of forms, when we do our investigations. Indeed, our most effective inquiries are those that utilize doppelgangers in different forms.

INVESTIGATIVE QUESTIONS

Think about the following set of questions, each of which represents a mode of inquiry, as well as a way of starting a group in motion so that it will do investigations way beyond even those we might anticipate when we open the door.

A. "That's your pattern, too, Felice, isn't it? Don't you also avoid men who seem wishy-washy?"

B. "What do you make of George's silence concerning his troubles with his wife?"

C. "Henry, do you know anyone like that?"

D. "Does Peter's treatment remind you of anyone else's in the past?"

These questions have in common that they require a person to talk not simply about himself or his motives, but about someone else. More particularly, in asking the person to consider someone else, all of these questions simultaneously invite the person to discuss himself, either explicitly or implicitly. However, the member is not asked to talk merely about himself. He may make personal discoveries, and sometimes very profound ones, while weaving himself into the group and helping the group go forward as a unit.

Even where a person does not see particular implications of what he says, others may. Even when people misunderstand those implications, that, too, may be progress, because the group may invite the person to think and feel and clarify for himself.

We have seen that one way of bridging is to ask questions that cohere the group, and now we are witnessing the use of bridging as a mode of investigation.

Let's begin with question A, "That's your pattern too, Felice, isn't it? Don't you also avoid men who seem wishy-washy?"

Our asking this presupposes that we've noted a similarity between Felice and the person we're asking her about—let us call that person Mary. We may have in mind a *similarity between how the two people act*. For instance, here we have seen that both Felice and Mary act with deep suspicion and guardedness when asked for intimacy.

Instead of our asking Mary directly about her guardedness, we have chosen to ask Felice about herself for a variety of reasons.

One value of this oblique method of investigation is that it frees the speaker more than if we had put the already defensive-minded person on the carpet. Whereas Mary might have felt put upon, or even paralyzed and unable to respond if asked directly about herself, Felice perhaps has the freedom to acknowledge that she does indeed act like Mary and then go on to tell us exactly how.

Generally, people feel freer to talk about themselves when they can include others in their statements. Ideally, Felice's explanation of why she acts as she does will prove useful to Mary.

Even if Felice vehemently denies any resemblance to Mary in behavior or underlying attitude, we have gained ground. Both women must now scrutinize themselves to refute the comparison. At the very least, we have invited the two of them to consider that they may have something in common that is worth looking at.

Often others join in at this stage. Such questions engender and renew a group's collective curiosity.

Had we simply asked Felice about her own behavior, which resembled Mary's, we would have made her more defensive and also stopped the flow of the group by shutting out the rest of the members—in effect, reducing them to bystanders.

Next consider investigative question B, "What do you make of George's silence concerning his troubles with his wife?"

Once again we are going to choose a second member to help us deal with an initial one, except that this time we will be going after an existing *similarity between their underlying feelings,* one that often exists between people even when they act quite differently.

Though in every case on this list the members may share underlying attitudes, this time we don't require that our chosen respondent behave exactly like the person he's talking about. It is enough that we pose our question to someone who we think shares an underlying attitude with the person in the eye of the group's consciousness. Indeed, as we shall see, there is an actual benefit if the two people express their shared underlying attitude differently.

We must not ask bluntly about the similarity, but inquire only what our second person infers about the first. Then, if we were right in suspecting the similarity, the person we address will almost surely say something that enlarges our understanding of both people.

In the actual case I've been alluding to, when I asked Philip how he felt about George's silence concerning his wife's troubles, it was because I felt convinced that both men imagined themselves frequently humiliated by women. I was going after their shared experience.

Outwardly, the two men behaved very differently. Philip was caustic toward women; he had become known in the group for accusing the women there of being flirtatious and of cutting him out. George, on the other hand, was typically courteous and never accused women of any misdoing. However, George's aura was that of a man repeatedly wounded by women. He would wince and withdraw into himself as if to escape their fury.

One day George was bemoaning what he took to be his wife's avoidance of him. He spoke about her in a way that might easily imply that his wife was having an extramarital affair. In fact, it was hard not to believe that even as he spoke, George had conclusive proof that she was.

The group felt as if it had that proof too. George's wife was simply away from home for too long stretches; she would snap at him when he asked her for any explanation of where she was. However, understandably, as George went on about her, no one in the group felt like accusing her of infidelity to George. Nor was it in my province to draw George's obvious conclusion for him.

It *was* in my province to bring to the surface for George how he was actually feeling while he spoke. And also to help George see that he fended off recognition of something painful. There was something that George didn't want to see, and he was doing his best not to see it—that much appeared sure.

In the past, George had rebutted all attempts by the group to suggest what he might be feeling. He would blast the group, telling them in no uncertain terms that he knew his own mind and that he didn't need them to tell him. He went so far as to assure them that his wife's behavior didn't bother him in the slightest, insisting, time and time again, that her business was her own business.

More than once, he lambasted a particular member, Philip, for being cynical about women.

By then, George's suffering over his wife had become a recurrent group theme. However, rather than confront him directly, asking him to spell out what he felt, I called upon his "feeling-double," Philip. "What do you make of all this stuff that George says about his wife?"

Philip surprised everyone by responding coarsely. "The way George kisses her ass just kills me. He's a jerk. Why don't we face it, his wife is mopping up the floor with him."

Then, before I could even say anything, Philip switched over to himself.

"When *my* wife flirts with a guy in a restaurant, I want to kill her." Before we could catch up with him, Philip was talking about himself, full-steam ahead, telling the group how humiliated *he* felt by the way his own wife treated him.

Then, as Philip went on about himself and his marriage, George broke down and wept.

For five full minutes, Philip kept going. He was speaking, in effect, for the two of them, bemoaning his isolation and George's, his help-lessness and George's, his sense of being betrayed by the woman he loved—and George's.

And a deep truth that Philip was giving words to slowly became apparent also—"The more you show you love a woman, the worse it hurts when she doesn't love you back."

Then, as quickly as Philip's outpouring had begun, it stopped. The group was silent, except for George's continuous sobbing, as he sat, his hands over his face, in abject shame.

After that, George could talk about his humiliation, and within a few months he became able to confront his wife and face the fact that she no longer loved him and that he would have to make a life without her.

This was a more dramatic instance than one has a right to expect, but it was not atypical.

I had begun by identifying a member in the group who felt like another, though the two behaved differently. Then I had asked the more expressive member what he made of the other's experience, and my doing that opened up the truth for both.

Ideally, we choose as spokesperson the member of the pair with greater access to the commonly held feeling.

Note once again that we do not ask that person to speak for the other person, but to tell us *what he or she makes of the other person's feeling.*

From giving us his own reaction to his "group double," it is a short step to his telling us how he resembles that person and how he feels about his own attitude.

In so doing. as often as not, he will express what the other person has not dared say—he will, in effect, articulate it for both of them, and with more passion and precision than we ever could. Then, almost inevitably, he reveals new truths about himself and about the other person, articulating insights more personally than we would have been able to.

It is worth underscoring the benefit of the method to the person being talked about. He—George in this case—is never put on the carpet. Instead he is being given a chance to see himself in another person. He can laugh or weep or feel furious without being in the spotlight.

In this case, unlike example A, the very fact that the two people ordinarily handle the same feeling differently becomes an asset. The more expressive person speaks for the less expressive one.

Here again, we see the special benefit of our investigating indirectly, rather than confronting an individual about himself. Even if we turn out to be wrong, if the two people we have likened in our minds are in reality fundamentally different, we have lost nothing. We have made no accusation or misguided interpretation—nor even an explicit speculation to be rebutted.

And sometimes, though we have addressed one person, another will volunteer an answer to our question. Again the group profits. After all, our inviting anyone to say how he or she feels is a simultaneous invitation to everyone in the group to search for their own feelings too.

As with all these methods, there is no manipulation involved. We can never know the outcome exactly. If we have correctly surmised what underlay our members' behavior, we will have struck a vein of insight and feeling. But even if we have miscalculated, we have not threatened individual members, or even wasted their time.

Now consider question C, "Henry, do you know anyone like that?" With this question, as opposed to the first two, we are asking *the person to find someone else's doppelganger.*

This time our approach must necessarily be more open-ended. People know less about others than they know about themselves, and this is especially true on the unconscious level, because our self-knowledge is so much greater than is readily apparent.

In this case, we may have ideas about whom our respondent will single out, but we aren't sure, and therefore we should restrict ourselves to an open-ended question rather than ask one that points to a particular other person in the group.

We are best advised to take this less-charted route when we feel quite sure about someone's reaction in the moment. We would bet that he or she is identifying with someone in the room and has spotted something and would talk about it with little provocation. We may even have an idea what the member will say. The one thing we don't know is whom the person will single out in the room as his doppelganger of the moment. Our question is an invitation offering the member a full chance to tell us.

For instance, a whole subset is acting in a certain way that we would like to identify and study. We feel almost sure that someone who is not sharing this behavior sees it and could comment about it—not about the subset, of course, but about someone in it; we don't know whom.

Our surmise comes either from knowing this person's previous history or, more likely, from our observing some reaction of his right now. Not knowing exactly what he will say, but alerted by this reaction, a wince or a gesture, we ask him our general question, allowing him to go as far as he can.

He—let's call him Henry in the case to be described—becomes our interlocutor for this very general question because of his unique vantage point.

Sitting next to Henry is Marianne—a woman who has always been insistently polite in our sessions. Marianne constantly describes the men in her life as detached and self-preoccupied. The man she is going with, she says, lives in a world of his own. He's a good man, according to her, but like her previous lover, he can't seem to connect emotionally and may not even want to. Interestingly, though Marianne typically describes her lovers as overly self-preoccupied, she has never confronted any of these men on their being lost in their own thoughts.

Actually, there are several men in the group who seem remarkably removed from those around them. They talk about abstract things, and sound dead even about their own relationships. From what they say, one gets no sense of their involvement with anyone. They are quintessentially dedicated to their own thoughts, rather than to the person they're with.

It occurs to us that Marianne might have been talking about any one of these men. But despite their remoteness, these men have one quality that Marianne's boyfriend does not. They are here in the room with us, and Marianne's lovers are remote geographically as well as personally.

While repeatedly deploring her boyfriend's abstractedness to these very men, Marianne has never accused them of being like him. She has never alluded to their own self-preoccupation. Today, she goes on to these men about her boyfriend, using them as her sounding board, as if—unlike her own boyfriend—they were her utterly committed listeners, and were rising and falling with her.

Obviously, unless Marianne develops the ability to see and deal with such detachment, in person and on the spot, she will go on suffering its consequences in her private life.

Therefore I hoped that Marianne would experience these men's detachment *in their presence,* and deal with it. Of course, I was also concerned with the men themselves, and with what their own detachment was costing them.

Enter my need for Henry—my need and the group's need and Marianne's need and Henry's need for Henry.

Henry, enthusiastic, concerned, was someone whom Marianne genuinely admired. He was clearly outside the subset of abstracted gentlemen, and I could see him yawn and squirm in his chair regularly when they spoke. He was closer to knowing what Marianne was experiencing than either of them realized. Not surprisingly, Marianne liked him, and had even had intimate dreams about him.

Marianne had just finished another lament about her too-abstracted boyfriend. I turned to Henry, knowing that he saw at least certain of the men in the group as precisely like these abstracted individuals, but I wasn't sure which of the men in the group he saw that way at the time.

I asked Henry, just after Marianne had once again bemoaned her boyfriend's deadness, "Henry, do you know anyone like that?"

Instantly, Henry pointed. "Johnnie," he asked whimsically, "wouldn't you agree that you're part of the tired population of America?"

The group laughed.

Johnnie defended himself, but weakly.

With that, Marianne jumped in and described Johnnie to himself in detail. It was the first time in her life that Marianne had ever actually told a man that he was self-preoccupied or removed, though she had experienced the tone of such behavior all her life. Her description brought out her own feelings of neglect, and memories of childhood neglect, which she told us about soon afterward.

Had I asked Henry to respond to a particular member in the group and chosen the wrong one, I might have come up empty-handed. Maybe he saw no relation between Marianne's boyfriend and the particular man who most reminded me of that boyfriend.

By asking my question generally, I was saved having to guess. Observe that in this case, the doppelganger relationship was between a person in the room and someone whom the group at large had never seen.

Next, on to question D, "Does Peter's treatment remind you of any-one else's in the past?"

Unlike the previous questions, this one is primarily aimed at *re-construction*. There are times when we need to bring out more about someone's past life. The person seems mired in a repetitive pattern that began in some early relationship. We have with us in the group a member who resembles the past personage crucial in another mem-ber's misdevelopment.

It's as if the significant figure in the person's past, who was crucial when the problem formed, had been beamed from the past to the present and is sitting with us now. The doppelganger relationship is between someone who existed long ago (who may be dead or have himself changed radically), and someone here with us now. Meta-phorically, in this case, our group member has a "father," "mother," or "sibling," or other right in the group with him.

This time our aim is to utilize this time-spanning doppelganger relationship. We do so by a question best described as "reconstruc-tive."

Reconstructive questions not only bridge time, but pique curiosity so that the members think about their own pasts and about early influences in their own lives.

Once, again, were we merely to ask a person about himself, we would not be inviting the rest of the group to think about themselves or their histories. However, in asking some representative in the group to speculate about someone else in their midst, we are inviting the whole group to think about their own past histories.

Another important advantage of asking reconstructive questions is that they enable members to accept their own actions by seeing those actions in the context of their early lives.

In a sense, we are enabling them to take solace in their history. "If back then you had to fight your way for every step in the streets to survive, it follows that your truculence now has a curious justifica-tion."

The patient who can simultaneously see what he is and *why* finds it less painful to accept an unpleasant truth about himself than the one left to feel that he is simply a bad person. We thus introduce the past to soften the blows of discovery as well as to explain our discoveries.

A man, John, complained in group that people, especially one fellow, Peter, an older man, constantly interrupted him. John couldn't get a word in edgewise because Peter had all the answers.

In reality, John spoke much too fast, deleting details and often assuming that he wouldn't get even the minute he needed to say what he wanted. As a result, many there, and not just Peter, wanted to break in, but Peter was repeatedly the one who did.

Peter would say, "John, you're running your words together. Would you please tell us what you have in mind. I'm going crazy waiting for you to get to the point."

I asked John, "You seem flustered a lot of the time, like now. Is Peter treating you the way anyone in the past did?"

John responded very definitely. "No. Absolutely not. I would never let anyone interrupt me the way Peter does."

But I persisted. "Is that really true? You mean you could always finish your sentences as a kid?"

There was a silence. Then John whispered, "No."

I asked him what he was thinking. Then John told the group a story of how he had won an award in elementary school. He had rushed home to tell his parents about it, but his father kept interrupting him to correct his grammar. "We don't want to hear you talk until you say what you have to say without mistakes. Speak slowly so your mother can hear you."

In despair, John gave up. He never did tell the story. And, now John recalled, there were many other incidents like that one. His father, he told us, just didn't care.

To our collective surprise, Peter himself broke in. "So your father is just like me. Is that the point?"

John nodded.

But that was only the first of many discoveries. It came out before many more sessions had finished that others in the group had also felt like interrupting John. They too had felt annoyed at John's hasty presentation, one that left them guessing what he really wanted to say.

Having begun by our identifying Peter as a doppelganger, John went on to see that he now made people impatient with his presentations, that he fairly invited them to interrupt him. Peter was merely the present culprit. In short, Peter was a doppelganger, but one of John's own creation.

By asking John about his past—in particular, about a possible doppelganger for someone in the present—the door was opened. Rarely would I ask a person about himself and his history so directly. But this time I felt that I was a spokesman for a group response, namely a collective impatience toward John, and therefore that by my question I was not excluding the others.

Obviously, you the reader, if you work with groups, will discover your own brand of investigative questions. Most important is that any question addressed to an individual involve the group—and *engage* the group. Investigation goes on throughout the course of therapy, simultaneously with every other stage of our work. It is, of course, an especially important resource when a group is blocked. The right question asked to the right person may have repercussions for the remainder of the treatment.

CHAPTER SEVEN

STEPPING IN HARD

As in life, there are times when indirect methods, subtle methods, seemingly sophisticated psychological methods, fail or are too slow. We must step in hard, making a decisive statement for the whole group to hear.

Radical as such interventions are, they are sometimes necessary. Were we not to crack the whip, our group, like wild horses, would run so far off course that to recover it, we would need ten times the force necessary now. In as short a time as a few weeks from now, we would have lost certain members for good and crushed others still with us.

We must confront someone, or confront our whole group, and with enough force to make our point. In short, we must stand up as the authorities we truly are. We know what's happening, and it isn't good. At the risk of shocking certain members, we describe what we see, with the obvious intention of alerting others so that they will listen, look—and stop.

For instance, many years ago I was running a group with six men and three women, all highly animated but sharing what might be described as "xenophobia." The nine had been meeting for close to two years, with great eagerness. But though they related beautifully to one another, and seemed freer than ever in the confines of our group meeting room, they were making little progress in the outside world. Interestingly, they would tolerate no newcomer to the group.

Each of these members had a distinct flaw. Several of the men were pathologically stingy, one constantly threatened violence, another drank too much, and the women tended to dislike other women on sight. The members overlooked one another's failings, sometimes even construing them as virtues. They saw the stinginess of the few as desirable cautiousness and good judgment, which had made these members financially rich, and the occasional threats of one as a healthy setting of limits. They overlooked the alcoholism of another. It was as if they had a joint contract not to perceive these traits as flaws.

The members were murder on anyone who tried to join them. When I introduced any newcomer, man or woman, they ignored the person, and if he or she protested, one of them was sure to say, "It's too soon to say anything, you don't know us well enough yet." Or "You don't even know our process, or how we work." If the newcomer persisted, they would tear at him or her like a pride of lions.

Naturally, these newcomers, one after the other, complained to me. A few had quit outright after the first session. The rest I had to put into another group.

Over two years the group had banished six would-be members. And with the departure of each, I had blamed myself for trying to introduce as a member someone better suited to another group. Once they did get rid of a person, they never mentioned him or her again. Out of sight meant out of mind, permanently. Gone was forgotten.

During the time I had gone along with their excluding people, I had completely overlooked their characterological resistance to any newcomer. One way I rationalized was by telling myself that I liked the group for both its zest and its internal intimacy. In any event, I had for too long not even considered that this little knot of people would tolerate no new member, no matter how selectively acquired.

Not until a seventh "guest," a woman, departed in tears, did I fully catch on. It became obvious to me that certain women in the group were keeping her out because they didn't want any competition.

Now as I went over the list of banished would-be members, I saw that each was in some sense a messenger of disquietude to the group. One of the men who had been driven out the previous year, a motivated member of Alcoholics Anonymous, had in his very first session noted drug dependence in one of our people. Another, a woman who had a Ph.D. and was also a happily married mother of two, aroused unrest in several of our women members who claimed that being married and a parent gave them no time to go back to school.

Still another person driven away, a homosexual man who had enjoyed a fulfilling love relationship with a partner for many years, touched off panic in a few of our male members, whose macho stories, which entertained the group, had been attempts to hide their own homosexual fears. These would-be members had no idea that their very existence constituted a threat. Without their knowing it, they were potential bearers of bad news, and the group's banishment of them was a symbolic killing of the messenger.

One might say that the group had preserved its own faulty integrity. The members, collectively, wanted no invasion of their defenses. Yet they could not go forward without information from without. Moreover, I needed their openness to enable new information to penetrate their defenses.

I would have to intervene—and in no uncertain terms.

I decided to tell the group that I was on the brink of disbanding them. "Why do I think that you people don't want anything new, no new ideas? Anyone I put in here you want to destroy. You don't care about the person. You just want to kill the idea that the person bears."

When they asked me what I meant, I pointed out how they got rid of anyone who might teach them something new about themselves. "So that's why I'm going to break this group up."

They rejoined that everyone I'd tried to bring in was flawed and unworthy of them. They told me why, remembering people who'd been there one session—and in one case, less than a whole session. I was amazed at how much detail they recalled.

However, I held fast. "Any one of those people could have brought in some new way of looking at life. But you don't want to look."

Immediately, I gave them some details, knowing that they would blow up at me. I told my drug-dependent man, "You knew that John was on to you. That's why you didn't want him here."

And I told one of the women, "Why did you get rid of Aretha? For only one reason. She was competition for the attention of the men."

On and on I went, explaining how each of the newcomers might have helped them see basic truths about themselves. "So you killed the messenger."

I knew I was being tough, but I had to be. At all costs, I had to confront them. It seemed to me, "Even if they hate me with a vengeance for a while, they'll talk about themselves in a new way. Anything would be better than this eternal status quo, this failure to progress." Actually, I couldn't tell for sure where we were headed. I counted only on the fact that confrontation was necessary.

Then, to my surprise, a wonderful thing happened. Instead of having to suffer their abuse for weeks, as I had anticipated, I was delighted to observe that they suddenly became sharply critical of one another. The group ceased being the homogeneous mass that it had long been, the self-protective body, immune both to harm and to benefit.

All of a sudden, the members were discussing one another's vulnerabilities and pointing out just the things that others needed to see. No longer did the group condone drug dependency or the kind of sibling-hatred that had thwarted progress—or the rationalized self-limitations that certain of the members had placed on themselves.

Within weeks, they were far more curious than they had been, and were uncovering many new truths about one another. A month after that, when I introduced a carefully selected potential member, and someone got caustic with the person, others objected and defended the stranger. My long-belated confrontation had achieved even more than I bargained for.

Confrontation is a technique like any other. As I've mentioned, our usual approach is to have members respond to others in such a way that the whole group participates, including those who seem to be merely observers. Confrontation is reserved mainly for times when this isn't happening—that is, for instances in which the group, or a majority of members, have so congealed that they will not describe one another in ways that are useful.

This was true of the group mentioned. Their conspiracy of silence—"You protect me and I'll protect you"—deprived me of the chance to use my usual methods. Indeed, I myself was temporarily under the spell of this conspiracy.

WHEN TO CONFRONT

There are many indications for our confronting a group directly. As illustrated, we use direct confrontation when a group forms a strong, secret alliance, what amounts to a cabal, so that no subtler method will puncture their invisible wall.

This alliance, which we must penetrate, is sometimes traceable to the subtle workings of a single individual whom the rest dread. We have in our midst someone, a man or woman, quite often worldly, streetwise, tough, who has taken ascendancy, and whom the others have followed without opposition—and, more often than not, unknowingly.

Unless we step in, nothing changes. "Myra, you are dominating this group," we might have to say.

Or "Jack, you cut people off, one after the other, and everybody's afraid of you."

In other cases, the person exerts his or her hold on the group by seeming fragility, conveying explicitly or implicitly, "One wrong word from anyone, and I'll fall apart."

In response, the rest have become gentle to a fault, not only with this "leader" but with one another.

Here, too, we must step forward. "Harry, those tears come across as if you're suffering, but actually they're controlling, aren't they? You're shutting people up, and you're trying it right now on me."

As part of their cover-up, whole groups may conspire not to mention a member's continual lateness, or perhaps the person's self-destructiveness, such as his addiction to alcohol or drugs.

When we bring up the unmentionable, we find ourselves at odds with the whole group and not just the "offender." This is because the secret motivation of the other members in not "casting the first stone" is their desire to avoid retaliation in the form of exposure of their own flaws, real or imagined.

In other cases, a group coalesces in the opposite direction, assaulting some poor member for virtually everything he or she does. When this happens, it becomes taboo in the group to take the victim's side. But this is exactly what we must do. We must support the pariah and confront the group on its lynch-mob mentality and behavior.

Especially delicate are those cases in which the therapist finds himself, or herself, the butt of what might be described as the group's "negative congealment." When this happens, we will almost surely feel tempted to strike back, to confront our oppressors in no uncertain terms. However, we ourselves are robust, or ought to be. Confrontation when attacked should not be our first resort. Rather, we should remain mindful that such assaults on us may be necessary for the group's development. Admittedly, a group's first release of long pent-up anger toward us may be unduly aggressive, but, even so, it would be ill-advised for us to quash a group without allowing it its say.

Nearly always when we do resort to confronting members who

have entered into an implicit agreement not to see something that is going on, we should be using the tactic because other methods have been tried and proved insufficient.

One is reminded of Laura Hobson's *Gentleman's Agreement* or of Galsworthy's *Loyalties*, in each of which there was an implicit pact to ignore the just claims of a minority member. Nothing short of confrontation could make its mark in those cases, or in ours before we opt to confront the members directly.

In short, our only valid reason for confronting a group about some recalcitrant attitude it holds is to free the group itself from the tyranny of that fixed attitude. We should not use confrontation to defend our own image or anyone else's, but only in the service of liberating the members to see themselves in a new perspective and to form new relationships.

How to Confront

Ideally, we should seldom confront a group head-on unless we have already pinpointed for ourselves the group's fixed attitude, and have rehearsed in our minds precisely what we wish to say. More often than not, we have speculated in private about how the group will respond to us, perhaps considering three or four likely scenarios.

Nor should we confront a group or a subset when we are in the throes of any strong emotion. If we are afraid of a member, or overly fond of someone in our group, the whole group may be quick to see that we are speaking from a bias. For instance, if we challenge a group and condemn it for bullying some individual, and the group has come to recognize us as that person's champion, the members will dismiss everything we say. Any confrontation by us that is suspected of bias will breed resentment and be counterproductive.

Healthy detachment, always a requisite for our work, has its highest priority when we confront people directly. With confrontation, our subject matter itself is so strong that it needs an especially light touch. The ancient Romans had a proverb to the effect that anyone can bring good news but that it takes special skill to present bad news, and a group may well experience our confrontation as bad news.

Understandably, when we finally do decide to confront a group or a subset, we may be feeling frustrated by what has already occurred. There's nothing wrong with that. Ours is a reaction to a reality. We feel thwarted by their behavior. However, this means that we must take special pains to acknowledge to ourselves our frustration, to accept it, and not to let it color what we say.

Confrontations are simple, direct statements—"Notice that no matter what John says, no one responds to him."

This means *avoid speculation.* When confronting the group about not paying attention to John, it may undermine our message to explain to them why we think they are avoiding him. Our explanation may be faulty, whereas our description of events is verifiable. Thus interpretations can weaken confrontations or vitiate them entirely.

Consider, too, that interpretations lead the members to turn inward, instead of looking squarely at life, as we want them to.

Ideally, we should never initiate a confrontation with less than fifteen minutes remaining in a session. What we are giving them is strong stuff. They need to experience us in the presence of what we just said, and they deserve time to respond.

Certain group therapists favor doling out what amounts to a few words of wisdom at the end of a session. Even granting that these therapists have a rationale, that of giving their group members something productive to think about, confrontations should never be included among these last-minute disbursements.

To some therapists—especially to those first learning our methods—such confrontations may appear harsh. But the contrary is true. The ultimate betrayal of any group would be for a therapist to take the easy road of allowing the group to evade painful ideas and feelings. Such a group goes along in pseudo-harmony, condemning topics without mentioning them, the way certain prudish parents condemn sex by their silence. The acquiescent therapist in these cases may pass as supportive, warmly protective, "a regular guy," "in the moment." But in reality, he or she is hiding from the group's wrath or disappointment.

Such therapists are purchasing their respectability and status from the members by avoiding the risks necessary to stimulate real consciousness in the group. Mistaken for kindness or "objectivity" is the therapist's fear of becoming unpopular. Not until the therapist comes out of hiding can the members arrive at truly new discoveries or form new relationships.

When confrontation is called for, there can be no successful avoidance of it. Whatever the therapist's motive for not breaking in—fear of the group's rage or disappointment, or fear of having to face an unresolved problem of his own that he shares with the group, or simple ignorance—he inevitably watches the group run down.

As with being a parent, our popularity is far less important than our product. And confrontation when needed is fundamental to our process.

CHAPTER EIGHT

DON'T BE A FIXER

Artisans and artists have a saying, *"Don't fix what isn't broken."*

What they mean is, when you first suspect that something is wrong with your creation, be careful. Scrutinize it before you rush to improve it. Maybe there's nothing really wrong with it, and you're dealing with a variant of something that you simply haven't seen before. A transitional state that needed to be, or even a novel form of excellence in its own right!

Or, as artists learn, maybe something is amiss, but you haven't yet isolated what it is. If you rush in too soon with repairs, you're apt to discover that you've mutilated your painting or statue. Only a slight adjustment was needed, and you've altered the whole thing—for the worse. You fixed what wasn't broken, and left the real flaw intact.

Overzeal in fixing what isn't broken has done harm in virtually every sphere of endeavor. For instance, surgeons used to operate on patients for a problem they called "ptosis," the supposed drooping of organs. More than one patient died on the operating table. Then, further research showed that this "drooping" owed simply to gravity. Their error was in positing the locations of organs from knowledge based on postmortems. The dead were lying horizontally, whereas in the living, who were X-rayed standing up, those same organs were lower. The surgical raising of organs was a supreme instance of trying to fix what wasn't broken. Of course, such surgery was stopped abruptly when this mistake was discovered. But who knows after how much harm?

We group therapists, and psychotherapists in general, have not been immune to the mistake of fixing what isn't broken. In different decades, we've treated people for lifestyles that now seem healthy to us, and normal—for instance, for homosexuality, or for what we regarded as the condition of being "oversexed." In come cases, we mislabeled sexual practices as perversions, behaviors that were commonplace in the animal kingdom; we have treated them as if they were symptoms of deep problems, and have sought to cure them.

In making such mistakes, we were usually acting in good faith. We simply didn't recognize what *was* actually broken, if anything, and succumbed to "repairing" what wasn't. We judged behavior too much on the basis of its social acceptability, forgetting that different lifestyles worked for different people. In many cases, the therapist was literally frightened by the unusual. There was absolutely nothing "broken" about some of the behavioral modes we sought to adjust.

Fortunately, most of us have corrected our own fault of trying to fix what isn't broken. We now accept a far wider range of human behavior than we once did.

However, there is another fault, which, in actuality, is the companion fault of fixing what isn't broken. Paradoxically, this is the fault of "fixing what *is* broken."

For therapists, this takes the form of attempting to make adjustments for our group members that, in reality, these people must make themselves.

Ideally, our role should be merely to bring to the surface our patients' self-destructive activities—to help them see themselves. They will do the rest, if we do this task well. On the other hand, if we do more, they will do less. We must not commit the fault of trying to cure our group members ourselves—as by giving them suggestions or making interpretations before they themselves are ready.

Sometimes the hardest thing for us to do is to wait. When we see how a patient is harming himself, and that patient does not yet see it, we often have the impulse to strut our solutions.

It's as if we had the urge to shout, "I know what's really wrong. This is what you must do. Listen to me, and you'll be glad you came to me."

Only with experience do most therapists learn that we cannot cure our patients. We alone cannot cure *any* patient. To quote Shakespeare, "Therein the patient must minister to itself."

We must not set out to fix a pattern, even if it is broken, for the simple reason that we cannot. The most we can do is to set the stage for the patient to address his or her life in a newly constructive way.

Assume for the moment that we're accurate in what we see. Our group member is doing something self-defeating. We might move in like Sherlock Holmes and point it out, pouncing on the person as if he were a culprit.

In the process, we would perhaps look brilliant to that person and to the group. We noticed a pattern that went undetected by everyone else there—ergo, *we* are the true professionals.

However, when we pinpoint any activity too soon, even if the patient sees it and stops, we have not given him the time to appreciate exactly what he has been doing.

True, our jumping in with our comment may prompt a quick change of behavior. Our patient may doubly resolve not to do the thing. However, he does not achieve any depth-understanding of what he has been doing or why.

If anything, our prompting him to stop on a dime has made it *harder* for him to appreciate the pattern in question. We may actually induce what the early psychoanalysts called a "flight into health." Because our patient hasn't truly grasped what he was doing, or appreciated its roots, his abandonment of the behavior will prove temporary. His psyche and underlying impulses will remain unchanged, and he will surely repeat his pattern or some subtler variant of it before long.

What we want to achieve is precisely this understanding. We want the group member to see his behavior over and over again, so often that he evolves intimate familiarity with it. For this, he must repeatedly see himself in action. He's been doing a thing, feeling a certain way, perhaps since childhood. We want him to *continue* doing the same thing, and feeling the same way, long enough to experience himself in the role, repeatedly.

Only after he has come to appreciate what he does *at the instant he does it,* can he truly assimilate the pattern that did so much harm. Finally, he can appreciate how he routinely creates his own stumbling blocks, and he can develop his own alternatives. Almost surely, when he arrives at all this, he will find himself changing his pattern without exhortations from us or the group.

For instance, our helping a member to experience himself as withholding or hypercritical or vengeful or unforgiving is vital if he is to change. The more sharply he sees a pattern and appreciates that it pervades his life and is harmful to him, the more eager he will be to change, without our prompting.

In some cases, he will make the decision to change quite consciously. "I don't want to be like my father."

In others, he will change unconsciously, perhaps in response to people's facial expressions in the group, which cue him that he is offending them.

Either way, his very observing the pattern over and over again has given him a degree of detachment from it that we ourselves could not have imposed from outside. And with that detachment he is freer to explore his reasons for acting and his alternatives than he would be if put under fire.

The following cases illustrate the potential harm of overzeal on the part of the group therapist.

In our group is a man named Jeff, who talks compulsively when he feels threatened. Jeff interrupts people, makes it even harder than usual for a shy member to come forth. Jeff is well meaning enough, but, let us say, he galls us because he impedes natural communication among the members and he instills dissatisfaction in the group. He makes us feel like a failure.

Suppose we give in to our impulse to correct him on the spot. After bracing ourselves, we tell Jeff calmly, "Jeff, why don't you stop talking until Jane has finished. You keep breaking in."

Or we ask the group, "What can we do to stop Jeff from interrupting all the time?"

Observe that in correcting Jeff this way, or chastening him, we have referred only to his behavior. Moreover, we have done so primarily because Jeff is annoying us. As a result, we can expect Jeff to give us at most behavioral change—he may indeed stop talking for a while, or for a long time. And we can expect him to feel hurt. He sits on his hands, obviously smarting. However, there has been no true psychic change. Jeff is no closer to resolving the problem of his impulse to break in, or to working through the feelings that motivate it.

Or take Helene, who blushes and turns her face away when someone compliments her. Were we ourselves to try to amend this behavior, as by telling Helene not to do that, or even by pointing out that she does, we would simply drive the problem underground. Even if Helene subsequently forces herself to look squarely at the next person who compliments her, we have merely inhibited a pattern. We have not enabled Helene to investigate it or ultimately to resolve it.

We have accomplished nothing lasting if we try to fix people's problems ourselves. On the contrary, we nearly always succeed only in putting greater distance between the patient and the kind of understanding that would free the person from the pattern in the long run.

This fault, of fixing what we consider to be broken, has even less justification in the group context than in individual therapy. One reason is that in a group, a whole array of patients are commenting on the person's behavior anyhow. Almost surely, some have already tried to fix the person's problem and have not succeeded.

For instance, it would seem certain that at least some in Jeff's group have warned him to keep quiet when they talk. They have gotten nowhere, or Jeff would have stopped interrupting people already. In any group, we nearly always have precedent for any corrective measure that we might think of, and we have precedent for people's not heeding it. It can hardly serve us to duplicate an approach that has already been tried and has failed.

Indeed, the very richness of a group, with its multiplicity of observers, makes it extremely likely that whatever egregious thing one does will be picked up and duly noted by someone. Group members see a lot more than we would alone, and, collectively, they offer a variety of vantage points from which to describe what they see.

And consider Helene's rejection of compliments, her inability to digest them. Almost surely, someone else in the room, perhaps another woman likewise trying to overcome shyness, has spotted Helene's pattern. If so, our seeking to amend Helene's behavior by pointing it out would add nothing.

Consider now our alternative, which is to *oppose* blunt attempts by people to change harmful patterns. In a sense, we are saying:

"Let people go on doing what they have always done, but this time *consciously.* By their engaging in the pattern now, they can watch it and understand it, as they never could before. They can see when they act, why they act, and perhaps how they got started doing the thing that they now perceive as harmful to them. And for the first time, they can see clearly how their particular behavior affects other people."

In fact, the more clearly they see all this, the more urgently they will want to quit the behavior. However, paradoxically, now, with our approach of helping them steep themselves in that behavior, we would rather that they continue a while longer than that they stop. Indeed, instead of hurrying them, our approach is to be as patient with the self-destructive behavior as if they had infinite time to continue it. They themselves will undoubtedly quit the behavior, and when they do, it will be with a rich understanding of why they are giving it up.

To return to the Jeff example, we don't only desist from shutting Jeff up. If it occurs that a group member criticizes him, and we see Jeff disposed to unnatural silence—that is, a silence unaccustomed for Jeff—we regard this as an *unfortunate* outcome, not as a favorable one. Rather than join the would-be suppressor of Jeff, if anything, we make space for Jeff and his right to act as he wishes. Of course, Jeff interrupts and infuriates more than one person in the room, but Jeff has a right to do this, just as the others have a right to object to what Jeff does.

In short, a suppression of harmful patterns can actually *increase* our distance from the ultimate goal, which is quite different from that of having the person amend his behavior.

This ultimate goal is to have the person:

1. Become aware that he is repeating some activity that miscarries, depriving him of certain fruits of life—or that it is exerting an undesired impact on at least some other people;
2. Recognize clearly what he is doing, and experience himself doing it in the moment;
3. Ultimately discover why he is doing the thing; and
4. Finally achieve mastery over it.

This is why our allowing the group to diagnose and stifle a member's pattern before it is truly resolved can result in the same failure as if we made the mistake ourselves.

Consider this somewhat more complex instance in which we should ideally encourage a member's self-destructive behavior rather than stifle it.

John is one of those who take refuge in "depth psychology" because he is frightened of real talk and the intimacy that might be required of him in a genuine relationship. Fearfully, John hides in the land of psychobabble, talking mainly about what he imagines is the unconscious of other people. So long as John stays there, who can touch him, or even argue with him?

Typical of his assertions was his comment to Phyllis, who is suffering over her inability to get pregnant. Phyllis speaks touchingly, and everyone in the room is moved, including John. However, while others in the group sympathize or offer advice, John offers his characteristic depth interpretations, and in his usual deadpan way. "Phyllis, the reason you can't have a baby is that you have an inverse Oedipal Complex; you still want to sleep with your father."

Not surprisingly, Phyllis can't make head or tail of this, and reels from it. The group is alarmed, and not a few of the members are revolted by it. These members lead a growing chorus beseeching John to "cut it out."

At first, they don't see precisely what John is doing. Some tell him to let people finish. But John does let them finish, and the group comes to see that his interruptiveness isn't the real hazard of his presence among them.

The real problem, they discover, is that John talks cryptically, addressing people's underlying motives, real or imagined, rather than talking to people warmly and directly. John, they see, seeks to live on the fantasy level of the members, and as a result, makes no real contact.

Once the members catch on to John, they get furious, and more than ever they want to shut him up. They tell him that they don't want to hear his deep insights or his incomprehensible truths.

"Can't you just ever say hello or good-bye?" one member asks John wryly.

Another tells him, "Keep out of people's unconscious. You don't belong there."

They accuse him of not being in the room, but of being in his own world, and they are, obviously, not wrong.

If uncontested, the group's attempts to suppress John's psychobabble would succeed in the sense that John would stop talking that way. However, the real problem would remain, namely that John would go on dwelling in the realm of the unconscious, failing to see the reality of his interactions with others. Unless John could have the freedom to go on doing the thing, he could never come to see exactly when he was doing it, or why.

In this sense, the group's stifling of John would merely push him deeper onto his "invisible world." They would make things worse for him, in cutting off the only way he could yet see of reaching them— namely, by his trying to talk to them in his particular vernacular. They would consign him to an even lonelier and more isolated world than he had been living in.

Rather than force him down toward a life spent utterly in his private catacomb, away from all humankind, we ideally would have John *continue* making his "depth" statements, offering his pseudo-analytical surmises, until he could recognize their function and improve upon them.

Accordingly, we let the group know what *they* are doing—namely, disallowing John his only available expression at this time.

Instead of addressing John, we might address the group in an attempt to afford John the space he needs for self-discovery.

For instance, we might confront them with, "Look, you people are trying to stifle this man instead of letting him be what he is. You people don't want to accept the feelings that *you* experience when John talks that way.

"Sure, John makes you anxious. But you seem to be muzzling him, instead of talking about how you react to him."

Above all, our purpose is to have the group do nothing to attempt to fix John, to change his behavior. John will change it, when he is ready. What we want, solely, is the creation of space so that John can see what he does and how others experience him.

Our aim, we might say, is to enable John to go on living in both worlds, above and below, for as long as he needs to. Only when he sees the light for himself will John emerge and accomplish real change. Curiously, our hazard in this and in many similar cases, is the group's attempt to solve the problem prematurely.

A group's method of trying to stifle a member can sometimes assume an extremely subtle form. But, even here, unless we keep space open for the person to do his own self-defeating thing, he or she will never resolve it.

For instance, a "sophisticated" group, fed up with certain behavior, can offer what seem like perceptive insights into a member's motives for acting. Those insights may be attempts to shame the person out of the behavior.

If, not seeing the deterrent impulse of the group's insight, we mistakenly give the group free rein, they may succeed and stifle the person's behavior before he gets a chance to examine it.

For instance, in one group of mine, a patient, Kevin, would constantly bring in photographs of gorgeous women, describing each as the woman he had been looking for all his life, and announcing his hopes of marrying her.

Each week, Kevin would extol the woman's physical beauty, her intelligence, her background, you name it—and he would imply that his future with her was a sure thing.

But, as the group learned to anticipate, Kevin would soon replace each photo with a new one—the photo of someone else. Kevin would do this, not even mentioning the last love of his life.

In fact, when on occasion someone asked Kevin a question like, "What happened to the last one?" he would repulse the person with, "Oh, that didn't work out."

One might expect anyone treated to those ups and downs to feel stymied, or to get furious. But in this group the members weren't always very sure what they felt, and they were especially slow to recognize their own anger when they felt it.

Rather than turn on Kevin for the way he treated them, and have to acknowledge this anger, the members sought to stifle him as quietly as possible. They took turns politely attempting to construe for Kevin why he was bringing in the pictures. Apparently, their intention was to discourage the activity without ever openly damning him or even raising their voices in protest.

One member whispered benignly, "Kevin, I noticed that in all those pictures of the women you were with, the women had black hair. Did your mother have black hair?"

"Yes, in fact, she did."

And another: "Kevin, those women all disappointed you, and I feel *terrible* about that. Who else in your life disappointed you, I mean much earlier?"

And so on.

Not surprisingly, Kevin stopped bringing in his pictures, and gave up talking about his latest masterpiece of a woman. His travails with women had been "analyzed" out of the group consciousness, and Kevin became conformist, steady and mildly depressed.

Gone was that wonderful exuberance that had accompanied every picture. And more important for our purposes, gone was our chance to see Kevin's pattern, to discover its meaning and its generality in his life.

Actually, Kevin would start not just love affairs but all enterprises with great enthusiasm, and trail off fast. However, the group's premature closure, their attempts to shield themselves from their own feelings by fixing Kevin, had precluded any chance they might have given him to air his real problem and examine it.

Once I caught on to this, it became my paramount purpose to help the group see that, in the guise of making therapeutic analyses, they were controlling Kevin. Naturally, I couldn't simply tell them this, or that their real motive was to protect themselves from their own anger or envy of Kevin for his parade of gorgeous women. I would have to do it not by fiat but in a way that involved them all.

And as often occurs, it was a way that would, predictably, incur the group's disfavor of me, at least for a time.

It took a few sessions for Kevin to venture so little as a comment about his next escapade. Predictably, when he did, a group member began talking about Kevin's "unresolved problem" with his mother. Others started to chime in, adding details to their pseudo-reconstruction of Kevin's past, and Kevin shoved the pictures back into his pocket.

Then, to the astonishment of everyone in the room, I asked Kevin to show me those photos.

Kevin handed them to me, and after scrutinizing them, I said something to the effect that the woman was quite pretty, which indeed she was. I asked Kevin to keep us apprised of how this latest relationship was going.

He smiled and said he would.

I was not manufacturing anything, but rather keeping a pattern alive. That is, I was not setting a scene but giving one space and room to develop.

I had scarcely handed the pictures back to Kevin when the group whirled on me as one. Their accusations were instantaneous. I was playing into his sickness, what one member called Kevin's "repetition compulsion."

Gone was the group's politeness, their collective diplomacy. They were furious at me. Didn't I know that Kevin was only a voyeur, who brought in his pictures and reports simply to get attention and to one-up them? Hadn't I seen that Kevin would tire of these women almost as fast as he'd involved the group in each of his affairs?

Finally one man confronted me outright. "You're supposed to be the one person equipped to help Kevin get over this problem, so why are you encouraging him?"

I seized the occasion to make my point. "You people want Kevin to conform. Maybe you don't like the way his behavior makes you feel. But we're not here to fix a pattern by simply 'analyzing' it out of existence."

Perhaps unwittingly, I was just vague enough for them to have to do some heavy thinking. In any event, the members began to talk about themselves, and in particular about the way Kevin's reports of liaisons caused them to feel.

A few of the men admitted to jealousy of Kevin. One man complained about his own marriage, full of sexual deprivation. Then a woman told us that, frankly, Kevin's stories and pictures of those beautiful women made her feel unattractive. As the group talked about their reactions to Kevin, it grew clear to them how uncomfortable they all were.

Kevin continued bringing in his pictures. Only after he had done so for several months could he truly see what he was doing, and realize that his activity must have a meaning.

Some time after that, with the help of the group, Kevin recognized that he had been flaunting his sexuality and that in fact he deeply doubted his powers. Indeed, he had even allowed the group to conclude that he'd slept with one of the women, which he hadn't, and he had kept bringing in her pictures for two weeks after she rejected him.

If I had simply gone along with the group's suppression of Kevin's behavior—that is, along with their fixing what was broken rather than exploring it—I doubt that we would ever have helped Kevin get to the real roots of that behavior. Without a true understanding of it, his stopping it would have been counterproductive. He would have hidden the evidence that he sorely needed to understand himself, and we would have been accomplices.

Almost surely, Kevin would have remained the same, perhaps not falsely grandiose but as insecure as ever.

Moreover, had I allowed the group to tamp down that behavior, I would have been depriving them of the chance to see their own tendency to stifle people, and to uncover vitally important feelings that they themselves harbored.

Admittedly, I had allowed some tamping down for a time, before I caught on. During that time, neither Kevin nor the group profited. In retrospect, I think I was fooled by the pseudo-analytic quality of the group's censorship, and sometimes even by the brilliance of particular members who engaged in it. However, it was the encouragement of Kevin's pattern rather than its discouragement that ultimately helped him.

Groups have many and diverse methods of stifling behavior, and in this sense, they are no different from even the most democratic society. The corollary to the rule of our not fixing patterns but understanding them, and allowing the member to evolve his own solutions, is that we must not abet our group in any attempt it makes to suppress behavior. In not going along as one of the crowd, we benefit both the particular member and the group.

We are not fixers. Any attempt of ours to induce a remedy bespeaks a disbelief in the healing power that individuals and groups possess. Whereas the carpenter must fix what's broken or it will remain broken, we cannot do this. On the other hand, when we or the group enable a member to see and experience his pattern, and the member takes action at his own speed, he will do more than repair a broken element. He will do more than return himself to some original state of function. The member, if we have patience and skill enough, will lift his or her own being to a transcendent state, one that we ourselves might never have anticipated. Such is the miracle of what Carl Jung once called "the antiseptic power of consciousness."

CHAPTER NINE

THE GEOGRAPHY OF RESISTANCES

As strong as our impulse is for change, for gain, for novelty, perhaps no one lives without virtually as strong an impulse to hold on to familiar habits and practices, patterns that offered protection, or seemed to. It seems part of our human makeup to resist change—indeed, even those changes that we, in our more enlightened moments, can see as potentially valuable to us.

A man I knew as a child kept two ferocious Dobermans at his side. He'd grown up in a slum, where the family had kept them for protection. Now as an adult he was doing well, lived in a building with doormen, but somehow having two dogs, the descendants of his early protectors, remained important to him. Visitors often found the dogs disconcerting, and would ask him to lock them away in a back room, but he could no more do that than starve them if they whimpered for his company. After all, they were protecting him at other times—at least, so he felt.

However, when he suffered a heart attack at forty, and the emergency medical service rushed to his aid, the snarling Dobermans kept the doctors from him, and the poor man died. These very agents of defense had served him so successfully under adverse conditions that he could not dismiss them. And because he could not, the dogs themselves caused his death at an early age.

By analogy, we all adopt mechanisms to protect us at early stages of life. However, circumstances change, and sometimes those mechanisms become obsolete or even crippling to us. When this happens, we need the ability to discard them and to meet the world in new ways. Those of us who can't get rid of our Dobermans may find the world much the worse for their presence. Devices of ours that we thought we once needed now bar our way to making new and better adaptations. We can't learn the new if we refuse to let go of the old.

For instance, a woman severely punished for mistakes when she was young retains an almost uncontrollable habit of fending off criticism. She smarts at even a hint of disapproval, a style that renders relationships impossible. The group members find her prickly. Her early coping mechanism makes her contentious, and has marred her every attempt to get close to people. As an adult, she is depriving herself of the very things she claims to want most: intimacy and a flowing relationship.

As another example, a man seems to dread praise from the group members and even their warmth. Though he generously extends himself to anyone in trouble, when on occasion another member thanks him warmly, he blushes and falls silent.

For years, as a little boy, he was in the maelstrom of battles between his parents, with each of them lavishing fulsome compliments to lure him over to their side. To ally with one parent, he learned back then, was to lose the other, and so he fled from the blandishments of both, and developed an unconscious habit of resisting all enticements in the form of compliments.

Now in group, he resists all shows of gratitude, even warmth, as if to welcome them from one member would mean to lose all the others. Unconsciously, he responds to all people as jealously competing with one another, and he clings to his neutral status. Here again, an early learned habit expresses itself as the person's "resistance" in the group. It deprives him of his chance to evolve any close relationship and to reap its benefits.

Resistances are mechanisms of repression and sameness, embedded in the character structure. They show themselves as mechanisms that once worked for the person, or seemed to work, but that now stand in the way of emotional growth.

Freud saw resistances as a patient's unconscious defenses against anything that would interfere with analytic progress. "A resistance is a defensive action undertaken by the ego to buttress repression." Resistances, Freud taught us, are an integral part of every person's psychic structure; they are the part of repression that we can actually see in the person sitting in front of us. Resistances are activities whose aim is to keep truths from emerging. (Such truths as that I am afraid, or that I hate you, or that I have sexual feelings for you.)

Later, the interpersonal analysts saw resistances as expressing not just the patient's past but his or her ongoing dealings with others. Harry Stack Sullivan pointed out that resistances are an artifact of the given personal relationship. Someone may invoke resistances with one person, but not with another. For Sullivan, even repression was interpersonal. For instance, if the analyst reminded the person of his father, the patient might become distant and oppositional, by way of resistance. If the analyst seemed reminiscent of the patient's mother, the patient's reaction might be warmth and compliance.

The psychoanalyst Wilhelm Reich pointed out that even people's most seemingly open and compliant behavior can be aimed at concealment and therefore a resistance. ("If I am good, then you won't press me to show you too much.") In short, any activity, if it is in the service of concealment, the neoanalysts maintained, amounts to a resistance.

Group therapists, who see their "multitude" and not themselves as their therapeutic agent, have accordingly enlarged their conception of what a resistance is. Originally, a resistance was an act designed to keep a therapist from penetrating a repression. Then Edrieta Fried, the group analyst, defined a *resistance* as "the forces that curb attachment to the group, that interfere with sharing experiences, and that undermine solidification and consolidation."

And how are we to identify "the forces that curb attachment to the group" and that "interfere with sharing"? We can do so only if we have set stipulations for the members—not arbitrary stipulations, of course, but, ideally, stipulations based on observations that we have made concerning what makes a group go forward. We know what makes a group surge ahead therapeutically, and we set criteria to give each group its best chance.

For instance, over the years we have observed that when people talk about their feelings and reactions to each other, they profit more than when they talk only about themselves or even their problems. When they talk about their reactions to other group members, they do better than when they restrict themselves to reporting outside relationships, that is, to experiences that the rest of group can have only secondhand. They do better when they come to their sessions on time, and when they express themselves in words rather than by actions, as by touching each other or throwing things in the room.

Translating what we have observed to be the requirements for therapeutic movement, the "parameters of progress," into ground rules for the members, we simultaneously afford ourselves guidelines for observing when our patients are "resisting" insight and emotional change.

How to deal with resistances, how to use them for advantage to the group, is a matter we will come to soon. Right now, our aim is to define resistances, to make them readily identifiable in the room, so that we can work with them.

Recall the collective resistance of the group in the case of Reggie, mentioned in Chapter Two. There the individual's resistance was that of rejecting contact with the other group members and seeking alliance with the therapist alone. Reggie, who succumbed to this adulation, failed to appreciate that the group was, indeed, resisting growth, and the resistance eventually defeated him. Suffice it to say for now that had Reggie been clear about his criteria for group communication, he might have recognized the resistance as such and not succumbed.

Naturally, Freud and any analyst working with an individual thinks of resistances as an individual matter. That is, the patient, drawing upon his own history, invokes a particular resistance. He or she responds as if the analyst were an important person from the past, most likely a parent, against whom the patient learned to defend himself in some particular way. During the sessions, the patient invokes his particular defense against intrusion.

In group sessions, we see individuals doing the same thing, invoking familiar defenses against either the therapist or other individuals there.

For instance, a woman in group fends off a sense of being unlovable by fighting to enrapture her therapist and to captivate any man in the group who seems to be drawing attention from other women. Here we see an *individual resistance* in the group setting.

But even more important are *subset resistances*. A set of members join in an effort to keep material from surfacing, ideas or feelings that they conjointly fear and wish to suppress. They may collectively employ a single method above others to accomplish this censorship.

In one very large group of mine, a subset of six members, three men and three women, tended to see women as unduly fragile, and men as ungiving and even brutal. This subset of six construed almost every male-female interaction as an instance of the man's lack of empathy.

The woman in turn was construed as oversensitive, and as unable to consider her own role when things went wrong.

Two of the men suffered by accepting themselves as having Neanderthal sensibilities. They hardly let themselves talk and felt utterly undesirable. The third man in the set played upon this point of view as a way of distinguishing himself. He acted excessively gentle and considerate, as if he alone knew what every woman wants. He constantly condemned men as a species, and wondered how women could put up with them.

The *resistance* of this subset was the shared activity of these six members of opposing men's right to express themselves openly. And they succeeded for a time in shaming the other men there, and in discouraging them from anything resembling robust communication. They stymied the group somewhat by their own inhibition and by their subtle discouragement of others.

However, the man outside the subset was especially vocal in saying that women were as emotionally robust as men. He saw women as capable of interacting vigorously, and not as natural victims. During exchanges in the group, he could recognize when women overstepped or were rude, as readily as he could recognize the same fault in the men. He did not share the systematic bias of the cabal.

The subset, acting in accordance with their shared resistance, condemned this man; they called him a "woman-hater," agreeing wholeheartedly that unless he shut up, no woman would talk to him for long.

In this chapter, I am merely describing patterns of resistance, and so methods of dealing with resistances are not pertinent as yet. However, as we shall see, recognition brings us more than halfway toward resolution. And here was a subset resistance in full bloom. Such resistances become even more important to deal with than individual resistances, since they have more power to set the tone of the group and to limit or destroy it.

With subset resistances, the behavior may be directed toward one or more members outside the subset, or toward the therapist. The result is the same—the resistance limits insight and progress.

The ultimate danger to group progress is a whole group's joining in a resistance, as by refusing to deal with a member's anger or sexuality, or even passivity.

For instance, in one group a young woman reported having terminal cancer. She expressed her helplessness and the feeling that her life was pointless. The group, however, was collectively afraid of their own feelings of helplessness, and refused to acknowledge her statements. Some members gave her advice, and others offered her reasons why she was dying, blaming her implicitly at every turn. They speculated that her cancer had symbolic meaning, and in that sense was deliberate. A few even called her cancer a retaliation—as a device to punish others.

Theirs was an attempt to make her feel impotent, as she obviously did. They were attacking her so as not to experience their own helplessness. This was a group resistance, and had to be recognized as such.

With group resistances, we see the wholesale congealment of an entire group in its effort to avoid a certain truth and the feelings that would accompany it if it were accepted.

More often than not, with such resistances, the person being excluded, the messenger of truth being denied access, is the therapist. After all, who else is left? The therapist is the outsider, the unwelcome guest in the room.

Reggie's case was one of a group resistance to acknowledging feelings of competition and anger. The group resisted by withdrawing and focusing on Reggie. They chose to experience their love of him rather than their resentment of others who might steal him away. Because Reggie himself fell prey to their projection on him of his importance, being flattered by that projection, he failed to observe the resistance as such, and became part of the problem. As a result, the group foundered.

The more people involved in a resistance, the more sweeping it is likely to be, the greater the urge we may have *not* to identify it. We may feel more tempted to let a group resistance pass than a subgroup resistance. Especially if the group seems content with its mode of operating, we may not want to identify that mode as a resistance. To do so, we would have to stand alone, to be unpopular, to cite failure in a context that superficially seems to pass muster.

Finally, it should be said that all resistances are contagious; individual resistances may attract subsets who employ them together, and who ultimately may envelop a whole group.

The resistances are seductive. In one respect or another, all resistances promise peace as a way of avoiding some unpleasant truth or reality. It is as if the member or members were employing the resistance to avoid pain, to avoid moving, to avoid getting on with the journey.

Though the word *resistance* in this psychoanalytic context is already a century old, the recognition that whole groups, and not just individuals, may conspire to keep the peace rather than face the unknown is somewhat new.

I sometimes liken a group of mine in the throes of a resistance to Ulysses's crew—to his men, who beseeched him to give up the journey and leave them in peace on that island where they could eat their lotus leaves and never have to think again. Tennyson imagined that crew saying to Ulysses in unison, "There is no joy but calm. . . . Let us alone. . . . How sweet it were, hearing the downward stream . . . to dream and dream."

Our lexicon of resistances that members may throw at us enlarges every year, as group therapy probes new frontiers. In identifying them, group therapists are following in the footsteps of the pioneer analysts, who noted first a few defense mechanisms in their patients and then slowly found new ones, until the list went to over a hundred. Perhaps a catalog of possible group resistances would be worthwhile for researchers to compose, but the real value of increased experience in knowing what they are lies less in such an extended catalog than in our improved faculty of discernment.

The keys to working with resistances are to recognize the presence of them in action, to describe their precise operation (to ourselves, if not to others), and finally, to resolve them.

If not seen or dealt with, a resistance can cause a group to hobble along pointlessly, or to fall apart. On the other hand, once we identify a resistance, whatever its form, and deal with it therapeutically, we can resolve lifelong problems not amenable to any other approach.

CHAPTER TEN

THE RESISTANCES— THEIR CURIOUS DESIRABILITY

Do we want our members to resist us or not? The first answer that may come to mind is, "Of course not. They had better cooperate, or they're wasting their time and ours."

This answer assumes that therapy is a kind of surgery. Hospital personnel want their surgical patient to be medically ready, to respond perfectly to the anesthetic, and to pull no surprises. The rest will be up to the surgeon and his staff. Indeed, the analogy between therapy and surgery goes back a century.

However, it does not hold.

To see why, suppose a man reports to the group a history of botched relationships. He tells us that several wives have walked out on him, and that recently his girlfriend refused to see him anymore. His kids avoid him, and those at work never invite him out to lunch.

However, in group he seems congenial, balanced in temper, and so concerned with other people that he leans forward when they talk. From all that we can see, this man is faultless.

To the group members and to us, he appears exemplary and desirable. Yet we know that in the real world, he must be causing havoc to himself and others. It is simply too much for us to believe that he's had so much bad luck. Besides, he has come to us for help, so that in spite of his geniality and shows of goodness, we are sure that he feels there is more.

Although he readily informs us of the many problems he has suffered in life, he conceals his role in them by not hinting at anything questionable that he may have done in relationships that have collapsed. Week after week, he passes himself off as congenial, even-tempered, accepting, and of high intention.

Nothing we see suggests any hand he may have had in bringing the roof down on his own head. This is in actuality too bad. As long as he comes across as so free of conflict, we can do *nothing* for him.

Such a facade of geniality is a resistance, one of many kinds. Among other things, it conceals all indication of whatever rage the man has felt, of how he has slighted people.

This man, as we are to learn the following year, has, with each of his wives, felt betrayed when the woman merely asked to be heard. He has become accusatory, gone nearly berserk. Our hero's last divorce was occasioned by his wife wanting to go back to school and his blowing up. "That wasn't in the contract," he let her know flatly.

For us to help this man, what we need more than anything is the chance to see him in action, bullying women. Not until we do can we help him see how he does, why he does, and ultimately help him find a better way.

Now consider this next example, in which the very behavior we need to understand is not forthcoming in the group.

In this second case as well, a man has suffered repeated failures in relationships. Here, too, we feel sure that he has played a crucial part in the way his life has gone. Once again, we may assume this with virtual certainty long before we learn enough to fill in the details.

Still, in our group, this man, like the first, comes across as the perfect catch for some woman—if not for all. Whereas many of the other men are quiet and seem out of touch with their feelings, he loves to talk about his. He especially likes to talk about "sharing" feelings. He "explores" the inner life—his own and that of whatever woman he is with. He discusses books and plays gorgeously. He pours out Shakespeare and Dostoyevski and Heine.

The women in the group adore him, and, in spite of themselves, they wish that their husbands were like him. They are sorry that his last girlfriend refused to marry him, but they are also secretly glad because, at least theoretically, he is still available. This man also seems the perfect group member, aside from his being the ideal catch for a woman.

In contrast with the first fellow, who was genial but quiet, this fellow is talkative and full of response and reaction. There's nothing we can say that he won't reply to richly.

In this second case, we are witnessing a resistance that might be called that of "talking away" real life—this man discusses feelings endlessly as a way of not feeling. He has co-opted the vocabulary of feeling, of warmth, using the standard ways of getting close to people as a method of keeping them away. He is a master of group nomenclature.

But though his behavior is clearly a resistance to the expression of his real attitudes toward the group members, suppose that we don't know as yet. That is, let's consider ourselves at an early stage of treatment, not yet understanding this man's resistance. We sense only that for some reason we aren't getting anywhere with him.

Our impulse with him might be to try to shut him up. And if we fail badly at this, for a time, we may even regret having taken him on as a patient, because he so strives to replace us. This man, whom we once prized as devoted and bright, has become a subtle competitor of ours. Worse yet, we realize that he is stifling others, is an obstacle to their growth.

Slowly we become uneasy with both of these patients—the silent, congenial fellow and the sympathetic, talkative one. Nice as they seem, they aren't evolving. And they are inhibiting others.

Contrast these resistances with more obvious ones, like that of someone who constantly complains or someone who roars when criticized by another group member. To help any patient, we must identify whatever resistance he or she throws up at us, and these more sophisticated resistances make it hard to do this.

Therefore, we *want* our group members to resist us *in the group*—to create stumbling blocks for themselves in front of us in exactly the way that they do in the real world.

No matter how uncomfortable their resistances make us feel, no matter how much they seem to hinder us, the presence of those resistances is desirable, even *necessary,* if we are to do our job.

The paradox of resistances is thus that, though they inhibit progress in one sense, they are vital to progress in another. Though they may sting us when we see them, we *want* to see them—we *need* to see them: without them, we are powerless.

And this is not merely a theoretical or intellectual paradox. We *feel* it with every patient. With virtually every group member, there comes a time, sooner or later, when we feel the brunt of that person's resistance. Predictably, this is to be our experience (no matter how practiced we are at our trade) before we identify the resistance.

In identifying our own discomfort, if only to ourselves, we convert that feeling, which the resistance evoked in us, into new understanding of the resistant patient. By that transaction we move from being off-balance to becoming masters of our craft. Our very identifying a resistance converts us in an instant from befuddled group analyst into expert with knowledge of how to help the individual in the group—or, more often, how to help the set of members who have been evincing either that resistance or an analogous one.

That is why unless we remain open to experiencing the resistances thrown at us, we are lost.

After dealing with these relatively subtle resistances, we can be downright thankful for other resistances that people present that are themselves plain and undisguised.

High on the list of these are those resistances that amount to any clear and present breaking of the group-treatment contract.

For instance, one or more members miss sessions repeatedly for no apparent reason; or they come late habitually, or they enter the group-room drunk or drugged. We've made it clear that we want our members there on time and in possession of their faculties.

This time, immediately upon our feeling the impact of such evident resistances, we can identify precisely what the person, or set of people, is doing. With such apparent resistances, we can see almost at once that the immediate problem is outside of us.

With these blatant resistances, we have a choice of tactics, chief among them to investigate the resistance by asking other group members about it. We may ask others how it makes them feel or ask them to speculate about why the resistant member is behaving in his or her particular way.

Such methods are usually better than asking the individual himself, or herself—and there are various reasons for this.

Always we want to invite exchange, rather than to do individual therapy with a member, especially with someone who has continually resisted us. Moreover, we don't want to reward resistances by giving special attention to those who employ them consciously. And make no mistake—blatant resistances are nearly always conscious. Ideally, when such resistances do arise, other members, especially those who feel neglected, will comment, and we may have the need to say little.

Of course, there are those cases (ideally they are rare) in which a blatant resistance is so treatment-destructive that we may have to warn a person to stop the behavior. We may even find it incumbent on us, for the group's sake, to give him one last chance, or to drop the person outright from our group.

This may be so when a group member systematically talks about private group matters to his friends and neighbors, compromising his fellow members. It is certainly so when a member threatens to physically harm someone there. And in cases of actual physical assault, we may have to expel the person at once.

With conspicuous resistances, the interlude of our being off-balance and possibly feeling like a failure, which comes before we can identify the resistance, is short or nonexistent. In a sense, we have less to do, and there is less challenge to our skill when the resistance is obvious to all.

WHY RESISTANCES BECOME SUBTLE

We are now ready to look at the primary problem that all group analysts face, that of identifying the truly subtle resistances, a couple of which have already been mentioned: the one of "unflagging congeniality" and that of "nonstop pseudo-analytic talk" about feelings.

As resistances, both are designed, perhaps unconsciously by those who use them, to conceal what lies underneath, to camouflage their underlying feelings. Such members are blocking themselves and us from the knowledge that is requisite to helping them. And they are doing this no less than those who throw up very evident resistances.

There are several characteristics of the more subtle resistances that are important to consider, before going on to discuss the challenge of identifying them. As distinguished from the group members who employ the more apparent resistances, the subtle resistor has a *stake in not having his or her resistance seen and identified.*

For instance, take the genial fellow, who salutes every accomplishment by another group member. He wants us to like him, even to admire him, and to regard him as constructive. He is quite different from the outright delinquent or defiant person who resists the world openly.

The genial fellow *conceals his resistance* against our knowing what he really thinks and feels. His approach is unconsciously devious. He is hiding a trait, say, underlying contempt for others, and he is also *hiding his method of hiding it,* by using as his shield a socially acceptable style.

The concealment of a resistance, we may think of as a shield in front of a shield.

Such compoundedness of defenses is commonplace. As personality develops, people who go on trying to conceal truths about themselves often refine their methods, doing what they can to make them invisible. They revamp their resistances continuously, lopping off obvious aspects that would give the resistances away. Since the function of every resistance is to preserve an unacceptable part of the self, it serves these people—who, after all, *care* how they are seen—to have their resistances go unidentified.

For instance, a man in a group of mine recalled that in his twenties he would instantly criticize women whom he felt attracted to. He yearned for intimacy but resisted it, driving away any woman who evoked tender feelings in him. In those days, if a woman was as little as ten minutes late, he would rant at her for being inconsiderate. Not surprisingly, in those days the women that he wanted most withdrew from him. They would refuse to see him after a few dates.

Two women he cared for had made it clear to him that he was tough to take. They had each told him virtually the same thing, in effect, "I simply can't give you what you want." They had dropped him.

Observe that at this stage of the man's life, his resistance was blatant.

Back then, it had never crossed his mind to consider that he might have a deep-seated fear of intimacy—a dread of being devoured by a woman if he got too close. In reality, that was the problem, and his criticality of any woman who elicited loving feelings was an unconsciously chosen mode of protecting himself.

Then when he was thirty, after yet another heartbreaking setback, he did pay painful heed to how he dealt with women and why several relationships had gone sour. After considering the possibility that the various women were at fault, he discarded it and scrutinized himself.

However, at that stage, he did what nearly anyone is liable to do when scouring his life for why things go wrong. He considered only how his behavior affected other people. More precisely, he reconsidered his method of keeping women away from him, *but not the underlying cause*—he gave no thought to why he acted as he did.

He simply improved his packaging of himself, resolving not to carp at women, never to tear them down, but instead to flash geniality at every turn. In short, he added sophistication and subtlety to his resistance. Instead of tearing women down, he would suggest benignly how they could improve themselves. In this way he merely polished his resistance, making it harder for himself and others to recognize.

This man's new, refined identity passed muster for a longer time. Observe that he was every bit as fearful of real intimacy as he had been. However, he ceased being obstreperous.

After that when he began feeling the stirrings of love for a woman, he drove her away as surely as before, but in a much more sophisticated manner. He would lose women by his nonstop correctiveness.

For instance, he might begin an evening praising a woman and saying that he was glad to see her, but sooner or later he would observe that she'd gained some weight or could be working at a better job or could improve the way she dressed. He would tell her what was wrong with her friends, by implication criticizing her judgment of people.

As predictably as when he used to profane women to their face, he was still tearing women down. No woman left his company feeling exhilarated. His relationships lasted longer but eventually foundered just as they had in the past. He had polished his resistance but had not changed in any basic respect.

This man was not unusual in refining a self-destructive pattern so as to make it less visible. Like all who do this, he had made the unconscious assumption that he was improving his approach, whereas he had amended it only cosmetically.

By the time he entered group treatment, he had "learned" from his experience, in the sense that he was harder to figure out. Though he told us about his yearning for a great love, and reported to us his numerous failures, it was far from evident how he was pushing love away.

In the group, he actually passed as helpful for months. But all the while he was unconsciously ruling out any real chance for a close relationship with a woman—by his subtle but compulsive giving of "good advice."

Over time, he had so polished his resistance-to-intimacy that it was hardly visible. What confronted us was a tactic much harder to describe than if he had come to our group in earlier days and simply criticized women to pieces.

Because virtually every bright person "learns from experience," and we work with a lot of bright people, we are going to see a host of very sophisticated resistances—those that have undergone a sequence of refinements. Such resistances will baffle us at first; many are every bit as subtle as the one illustrated.

SHARED RESISTANCES

So far, I've been talking about resistances employed by individuals, methods they use to oppose the treatment process, which they employ with a therapist treating them individually or in a group. However, members, a few or many, are likely to share a resistance.

Group resistances differ from *individual resistances* not just quantitatively but in quality.

The most obvious distinction, what denotes a group resistance, is the quantitative. With group resistances, not just one person but many, in some cases a whole group, are working in consort, resisting an understanding of themselves.

Technically, when two or more people employ a resistance together, it is a form of group resistance (some call it a "subset resistance"). Nearly always, however, when we talk about a *group resistance,* we mean one sustained by a half-dozen members of a group or more.

By definition, a fully shared resistance is one in which all the members do the same thing, or express the same attitude. They all berate us, or come late, or all blanket their true feelings under shows of courtesy and love for one another. In these cases, whether the group resistance is obvious or sophisticated, we are up against a wall of common behavior.

With a group resistance, the members may mirror one another's exact tactic of concealment. Some are doing what they have done as individuals, but the bond among members gives them strength.

In the simplest case, a member starts coming late as a way of minimizing his exposure to us. When we ask him why he is late, he makes a lame excuse, but other members buy it at once. They concur that the traffic has been horrendous these days. A few volunteer that they too were nearly late.

The following week, four or five people come late, especially those who toyed with the idea aloud by suggesting that they almost missed their bus last time. Before long, almost no one is there on time, and the group compounds its avoidance by giving a quarter of their remaining time to discussing whether they should meet an hour later.

Such exact sharing of resistance is infrequent, however. More usually, the members show very *different* faces while conspiring not to talk about some major issue.

For instance, a set of group members, or the whole group, feels disappointed in me, their therapist. This disappointment is characterological—at bottom, they are disappointed in themselves, but as individuals they have made a practice of blaming outside forces for whatever goes wrong. Now they secretly blame me.

Here we have a case of their concealing their resistance itself. Were they to face me with their disappointment, they would have to confront my response, which, they well know, would be to investigate them and their pattern of disappointment. Self-examination on their part might have to ensue, and they fear it. Such self-examination would reveal that they shun responsibility for their own lives, that they are creating their own misery.

Though such a process of discovery is the route they must take, it is painful. And they avoid it by avoiding even the first step, which would be to announce their disappointment in me.

Unlike the previous case, in which the members all did the exact same thing, which was to come late, these members do different things to achieve their common purpose. A few verge on expressing their disappointment in me by admitting to that feeling of disappointment, but attaching it elsewhere.

For instance, one woman constantly expresses disappointment in her husband, whom she describes as a fanatic card-player who spends insufficient time with her. Another woman expresses disappointment in her Oldsmobile, which after twenty thousand miles needs too much service. To hear the members talk, one thing in their lives seems to be falling apart after the other.

Other members show not disappointment but some related emotion, such as anger. For instance, a man in the group says he is furious at his son for refusing to go into business with him. Another man constantly praises me for my sensitivity, as a reaction-formation against his disappointment, and so forth.

Because of the diversity of facades, it is far from obvious for a time that there is a group resistance in progress, that a single theme underlies all these presentations. How we discover that theme and deal with it is not the issue yet. Of importance is to appreciate that group resistances, those shared by many members or by a whole group, may or may not appear as a homogeneous entity.

As therapists, it is our task to *identify* whatever resistances our groups practice.

Our signs are twofold.

First, we can see plainly that one or more features of our contract are being broken. The members refuse to talk, or inform us that they have talked about group matters to their friends or spouses.

Or we simply feel ineffective, not yet knowing what the resistance is. There is an interval during which we feel off-balance but are as yet unable to pinpoint why.

The challenging resistances are those that touch us emotionally but that we cannot identify—sometimes for a long time. We feel dismayed or furious or blank or incompetent, without knowing why. We are at odds with ourselves, and unless we've had good experiences treating groups in the past, we may even come to doubt our ability to work with groups.

Such a feeling of incompetence is analogous to what creative artists often report when they are at an impasse—the sense of having dried up, or of having nothing to say or to write. In such a period, though we may not be able to stay calm, we must go on trusting ourselves. The night will end and we will see the terrain around us.

However, as yet we have only a preconscious sense that something is wrong. Already we may witness ourselves grappling with the problem. We are aware of ourselves squirming in our seat or biting our lip, or indulging in some other nervous habit that tells us infallibly that we have already confronted something amiss.

Naturally, the more subtle a resistance is and the more refined it is, the harder it will be for us to determine its form and to specify to ourselves exactly which of our group members are engaging in it.

Many such resistances suggest their presence at first by only vague rumblings in us. We feel bothered without knowing exactly why. We see something, or think we see it, that makes us uneasy, but we aren't sure what it is. We catch ourselves lingering on our way to a group meeting, perhaps getting there a few minutes late ourselves. Beginning with only these misgivings of our own, we will go on to bring out the resistance and make it a very evident group phenomenon.

By now, it should be clear that our task is not simply to stifle a resistance. Rather it is to get the group to identify any resistance, for our sake as well as theirs, and to confront it. Only by becoming aware of their resistances, by seeing themselves actually engaging in them, not once but again and again, can our group members put their resistances aside if they so wish.

Granted, not all our group members will do this. However, over a period of time, those who find more rewarding ways of adapting in their lives will turn to those better methods. The choice will be theirs. Our task is to give them the freedom to make that choice.

CHAPTER ELEVEN

UNVEILING RESISTANCES

There was the door for which I had no key.
There was the veil through which I could not see.
—*RUBÁIYÁT* OF *OMAR KHAYYÁM*
(Translated by Edward Fitzgerald)

Picture a group in which a set of members assails the leader for what he hasn't done. One man, Fred, accuses the therapist of never confronting him honestly, but of cutting him off.

Fred says, "You never give me the man-to-man attention I need."

Another man, Rob, accuses the therapist of letting him babble on about things he really doesn't want to talk about. "When I bring up my wife or my job, you let me go on. You never stop me and say, 'I want to hear about you.'"

Rachel accuses the therapist of overlooking her utterly. "You wouldn't care if I sat in this chair and never said a word. At least you say something to the others here, you don't even talk to me."

Fred, let us say, has the deep, unconsidered sense that he can't do anything right. He has been told this repeatedly in early life, and now covertly tells it to himself. However, he is resisting the recognition of his "incompetence," and the way he resists it is by demanding that the analyst do for him what he feels he himself cannot do.

Rob is babbling on about irrelevancies because he also feels inadequate. Like Fred, he feels undeserving, but has evolved a slightly different tactic, a different resistance. His babbling protects him from experiencing what he really thinks about himself.

Rachel's berating the analyst for overlooking her is her defense against recognizing her own feeling that she is insignificant and not worth his or anyone's attention.

These three people are employing somewhat different strategies but with a similar intention.

Obviously, these are simplifications, and any seasoned group therapist may imagine a host of complexities that might accompany such resistances. However, even here, one thing is very important to note. For the members to go on with their resistances, those resistances must succeed to at least some measure. This means that these resistances—like *all* resistances—must in some measure be protecting the members from full confrontation of a painful truth about themselves.

Resistances must be carried on in the dark, and, indeed, resistances may be said to manufacture darkness.

Thus we could *not* have a scenario in which Fred was fully aware of his sense of inadequacy and was consciously and deliberately blaming the analyst in an effort to hide this truth from himself. For how can one hide what one already knows only too clearly?

Nor could we have a scenario in which Rob saw unmistakably that he was babbling to cover the chasm inside of himself, while knowing about the chasm and realizing what he was doing.

Or one in which Rachel said to herself each session, with knowledge aforethought, "If I keep blaming my therapist for what I know is wrong with me, I will never have to know what it is."

Since the function of a resistance is to conceal a truth from oneself, *if one knows fully what the truth is and how one conceals it, a resistance itself becomes worthless.* For anyone, clear-cut recognition of one's own resistance converts its manifestation into empty exercises, serving no function.

Therefore, our method of dealing with resistances must center on helping our group members *become aware of their resistances*—that is, aware of their form and function. Once our group members know what they are doing, how they are resisting discoveries, they already have at least some insight, and to the degree that they do, their resistances are no longer serving them as previously.

Resistances lose strength in daylight. They lose purpose when our group members see what they are doing and why.

Ideally, when resistances arise, our purpose is to have a group identify those resistances, in one member or in many. We want *the group* to do this pinpointing *as much on their own as they can.* Fellow members, as they spot someone's resistance, in that instant become more than observers; they put themselves in the other person's place, and must at least consider whether they too are avoiding important truths about themselves. That is, they inevitably ask, "How do my comments about him apply to me?"

Our aim of having resistances revealed is so central to us that we don't just welcome them, as mentioned in the last chapter. We need our group members to play out their resistances in every variation and in every detail. We don't want our group members to spare us a nuance of their defenses.

For instance, take Lauren, who accuses the therapist of not talking to her. She does things in the group to document her case that no one cares about her. One such maneuver is to arrive looking disheveled, as a way of demonstrating that people's lack of interest is breaking her. And when on one occasion, she wears a pretty scarf, Lauren does so not to get attention but in hopes of it *not* being commented upon, so that she can observe politely halfway through the session that no one noticed her fine scarf.

Still another way that Lauren dramatizes her being neglected by the analyst and the rest of the group is to cry inexplicably during a session—or if not that, to simply sit looking crestfallen.

Or more subtly, Lauren might make the case that she has been neglected by whispering deferentially to a speaker, "When you're finished, there's something I would like to say, if there is still time."

The point is that Lauren has a variety of ways of expressing her resistance to making a genuine effort to contact people in the group. And we want her to engage in as diverse an expression of this pattern as possible.

In general, we need our members to show their resistances from every aspect and angle so that the group can see those diverse expressions and help the member see them too. The more facets of a resistance that become conscious, the clearer the nature of the resistance becomes to the person. One might do a single thing for any of a variety of reasons, or even two things. But as the number of expressions of a resistance mounts, the theme becomes obvious and inescapable. And, as just stated, the more often a person sees his resistance and its expressions, the easier it becomes for him to let go of the resistance.

Ultimately, we would like Lauren to see that she presents herself as broken by the world so that others will take care of her. This is her resistance to emerging as a mature being, saying what she thinks and feels and taking responsibility for her actions toward others.

For Lauren to grasp this, she must do more than recognize the theme; she must realize exactly what she does and how, no matter how subtle her expression of that theme. For this, we need Lauren to go through her whole repertory, not once but many times. And this is true for all our group members, no matter what their particular resistances are.

In order to bring resistances to light, we need an environment at least reasonably accepting of all the members. The presence of a highly critical person, for instance, someone who mocks others for their faults, makes it quite hard for people to admit their resistances, especially subtle ones. After all, most resistances were learned in childhood, in the presence of a parent who was seen as critical or punitive. We can hardly expect a group member to face his resistance and withdraw it, in a context as threatening as the childhood one.

If, say, there was a man in Lauren's group who mocked her for whispering or for being tentative, she might either go underground further or oppose him openly. But in either case, we would find it harder to expose Lauren's pattern, which, in most other contexts, is anachronistic, harmful to her, and needless. We need her to express that pattern repeatedly in a context not intrinsically suppressive or threatening.

This tells us a great deal about which resistances to tackle first; it helps us as therapists deal with the problem of priority. We begin with a situation analogous to that of triage. Of primary importance to us is to deal with behavior in the group that would terrify or stifle other group members—behavior that would seem to justify their resistance to exposing themselves.

Most such behavior falls into the category of rampant criticality. When we find wantonly disdainful people in our group, or hostile critics, we consider as our chief priority bringing to their attention, and that of the group, what they are doing and how it affects others. In helping such members see that they demoralize others and inhibit them, and see how they induce other people to withdraw from them, we are, of course, helping such critics to improve their lot outside the group. But though important, our doing that is only incidental to our real purpose, which is to liberate the flow of the group, to create a permissive atmosphere in which the resistances of all the other members can find expression.

SURFACING RESISTANCES OF INDIVIDUAL MEMBERS

Our methodology of revealing the behavior of repressive members is typical of our mode of dealing with resistances. We want the members to play as big a role as they are ready to play.

1. One ideal method is to find a pair of members, one of whom engages in a resistance whereas the other has in some respect *been victimized by the resistance* and is supersensitive to it. We ask the victim to identify the resistance.

Consider such a combination. Harry disparages the other group members. He calls them limited. For instance, Harry lets everyone know that he is wealthy. He has traveled more, met more people, made more money than the others have. Every session, he innocently asks someone a question that puts that person in a bad light.

"Martha, have you ever gone skiing in Vail? No? I'm surprised."

Not surprisingly, Harry has no real friends. Most pertinent to us, he is resisting real, emotional communication in the group and stifling others. How do we bring this resistance to light?

We look for someone who has been a butt of precisely that mode of disparaging behavior, and who has the capacity to react to it and help the rest identify it.

Searching the room, we see Maria bite her lip every time Harry lights into someone. Maria's father ran out on her mother when Maria was five. Her mother was a proud and capable woman, and the family clawed its way to respectability and independence. Maria worked her way through college, but she retains memories of having been humiliated numerous times by neighbor children, and even by a cousin, who was better off.

Maria's input on the subject of what Harry is doing promises to be invaluable.

We address her, "Maria, I notice that you bit your lip just now when Harry said he was sorry to hear that most of the group members never ate at a four-star restaurant. What were you *not* saying by that act?"

Maybe Maria won't respond, but she will *think*. If we try this repeatedly, with Maria and perhaps with another life-victim of Harry's style of behavior, we are likely to hit paydirt. The third time we turn to Maria, she observes dryly that Harry always puts himself up at someone else's expense.

At that, Harry's other victims may join in even more sternly, talking, one after the other, about how bad Harry makes them feel. Soon, whenever Harry advertises himself, the group makes him aware of it.

If the group is successful, Harry becomes excruciatingly conscious that his criticality stops the group's flow and is a resistance to something more. Later, we will help him see that this criticality is a resistance of his own—a resistance to identifying what other people are really feeling.

2. A second method for surfacing an individual's resistance is for us to have it described by *someone who engages in the same resistance,* or who used to engage in it and has gone past it. This time, we are not choosing a victim, but a fellow offender or a former offender.

For instance, a group member, Beverly, employs the resistance of stealing the thunder of whoever would criticize her.

When someone suggests to Beverly that she is crowding another group member by asking him too many questions, instead of considering the idea, Beverly turns furiously against herself, protesting to the group that she's a hopeless case. Tearfully, she announces that she knows that she's ugly and that no one could ever love her.

A mere suggestion that she might wish to reconsider a single act, Beverly has met by heaping abuse on herself. Obviously, at least some of the members decide on the spot that they had better not criticize her.

Beverly's tactic results in her getting a lot of false reassurance, praise, and even apologies from other group members. But the cost of this resistance is that it stops people from telling her things that she might have profited greatly from knowing.

Beverly's self-assault, designed as a shield against her being hurt by other group members, is actually a wall that blocks out important information—in fact, it prevents people from piping through the very material that she needs most urgently. She needs to surrender this resistance, but first to become aware of it, if she is to profit from the group.

To bring Beverly's resistance to her attention, in this case, we might utilize not a member excluded by the resistance but someone who once employed that same resistance and *who is either starting to gain insight into it or who has worked past it.*

A quick survey of our resources within the group reveals to us that we have such a person on hand. Elise, a woman slightly older than Beverly, used to turn on herself ferociously as a way of fending off observations that might hurt her even for a moment.

Over time, and with our help, Elise has come to see that she did this, and to assess the costs of such a blind defensiveness. She examined her own tactic and, being encouraged by the accepting environment in the group, Elise slowly surrendered that tactic.

The next time Beverly assails herself, I ask Elise what she thinks Beverly is doing.

Elise volunteers the understanding at once that Beverly is probably in pain. "I know how she feels. I used to feel that way myself when I thought I was in trouble in the group. I used to attack myself worse than they could ever attack me."

At that, Beverly lights up, and earnestly asks Elise how she has dealt with the problem. After that, though Beverly sustained the resistance in full force for a while, she saw Elise as different from the others, as someone who would not attack her even if the group did.

Beverly watched how Elise dealt with criticism in the group, and slowly Beverly too began to hold her own defensive tactic up to the light. Not long after that, Beverly became much more open to people's comments about her, which she would previously have stifled before they were completed. She became far less assaultive of herself.

By the way, as Elise became aware that she herself was an important model for Beverly, she too felt inspired and more open to self-scrutiny. And presumably so did others in the group, who had shied away, even on occasion, from criticism.

3. A third method for surfacing resistances is to *ask the group as an entity what they think is missing in an individual.*

For instance, we observe week after week that a certain member in our group never addresses a particular person or set of people. John never talks to Richard, who is professedly homosexual. Every week, John sits as far away from Richard as possible, and he never communicates with him.

Rather than push John ourselves, we might ask a particular person in the group if he or she has ever noticed that John avoids addressing Richard. Ideally, in this case we would choose someone who does talk freely to Richard—that is, someone who himself or herself is conflict-free concerning Richard.

This person may tell us outright, "Yes, I did notice that. John does always avoid Richard, and I don't know why. Richard's a nice guy."

Or possibly, our hoped-for interlocutor won't say anything, but someone else will volunteer the observation, and before long the whole group will be looking into John's resistance.

Possibly, it will turn out that John is homophobic, as we thought. Or there may be a very different explanation, and we have exposed a different kind of resistance—one that we never suspected.

4. The fourth and last method of dealing with individual resistances that I want to mention here is that of our *re-creating the situation that evokes the resistances so that they will be easy to identify.*

For instance, five men in a particular group share a curious resistance. These men have all failed in love relationships. They aver in no uncertain terms that they want love from a woman and closeness. Yet, as soon as a woman expresses caring for them, they instantaneously become critical, or even brutal toward her. They all tell us stories of how women fell short.

This time we re-create the situation that evokes the resistance—that of criticality to avoid love—as a way of triggering the resistance itself, so that we can point it out in the group.

We realize that Iris, a woman in the group, has a crush on Mario. Understandably, she is hesitant to mention it, since Mario himself is abusive to women. However, we want to surface the men's "criticality-resistance to love," and also to help Iris raise her self-esteem by learning to identify harsh treatment and quickly move away from it.

We re-create the critical situation sure to evoke the resistance, by asking Iris outright what she thinks of Mario.

Iris tells us at once that she loves him. As always, the instant that Iris praises Mario, he is obviously moved.

But, as always, he pushes her away. Mario snaps at Iris that she said almost the same thing to another man in the room last month. By implication, he has accused her of being fickle.

At once Iris draws back. Mario's resistance, we see, is in full bloom.

Next, having re-created the situation that evoked the resistance, we lift it further into the group's awareness.

Without wasting a moment, we ask someone else in the room to tell us what Mario has done. We choose a man who has often done the same thing but is gaining insight. He points out what we already know, that Mario is brutal when he's fond of someone.

We may let the matter drop, deciding that Mario has had enough exposure for one day.

Or, if we wish to, at this stage, we may go further. We may ask Mario himself whether the analysis is correct. Has he indeed engaged in that resistance? Has he really wanted Iris to feel crushed and to retreat? However he responds, we have surfaced the resistance by creating the context in which it was almost certain to present itself.

And by the way, in such a case, let's not forget Iris, who has expressed love and been rebuffed. She will understandably feel at a loss. However, Iris herself may profit greatly from our articulating the reality and accounting for her experience.

If Iris has repeatedly reached out to men who rebuffed her, and then hated herself, blaming herself for even imagining that she was lovable, we have given her new hope.

SURFACING SHARED RESISTANCES

For simplicity of presentation, so far I have illustrated methods of surfacing a single person's resistance. Even more important, however, are applications of our method to resistances shared by a set of people, or even by a whole group.

It can never be mentioned too often that group work typically presents us with collective phenomena. Resistances shared by many people may be harder to discern, because our potential observers, the other members, are part of the problem. Besides, the members engaging in the resistance are supporting one another. However, collective resistances are what we must deal with most often.

When we confront a shared resistance, instead of asking some individual what he or she thinks, *we might ask a whole group* what they think is lacking not in any one person but in the group itself.

Consider this example, in which the therapist supplies the missing piece and brings a shared resistance to light.

The group this time is one in which, though the members speak freely to one another, no one ever mentions the group leader. Obviously, the participants share some unspoken attitude toward the therapist. But from a mere typescript of what the members say, no one would ever know what that attitude was. This kind of omission is surprisingly common.

We might broach the subject directly, either to the group itself or to an individual. "Why do I get the impression that I don't exist here?" Or "George, why is it that no one ever mentions me?"

The members may respond at first with bewilderment.

"What are you talking about? We assume that you're part of us, and that's enough."

Or with annoyance, "Every time we talk to you, you butt in and stop us from what we really want to say. Doctor, you interfere with the flow."

We are not there to debate with them. We have made our point. At the very least, they now are aware both that we exist and that they have been blocking us out.

This time we have confronted the whole group, and not simply an individual. Our indication for using such an intervention is that many members are involved in the resistance. Also, the fact that we are the brunt of the resistance calls for a generalized approach of this kind.

And there are other techniques that have special value when a large group is resisting in concert.

As an example, when we notice that something is utterly missing in a group, and is therefore, presumably, being avoided by all the group members together, *we may furnish the missing element ourselves in order to call attention to the resistance.*

For instance, a group has been scapegoating one member, Zack. Admittedly, Zack complains a lot, but so do several other people there, and they receive sympathy.

The group is utterly intolerant of Zack, and since they are that way without exception, their disregard for him passes as nothing noteworthy or unusual. We alone, the therapist, recognize their treatment of Zack as a resistance to looking at their own lives creatively.

When on occasion Zack brings up a problem that he has at work, the members fall upon him in rage.

"Zack, why can't you stay with us?"

"Zack, I don't give a damn about that job of yours. It's *boring,* you'll never get anywhere anyhow. Why don't you get a new one?"

Though the group members are responding to something real,

namely Zack's overfocus on himself at their expense, their tactic is abusive. Little by little, they are pushing Zack out of the group. His "crime" is venial, and the group's torrent against him is out of all proportion.

After a while, we begin to realize that the members who assault Zack most vigorously are really furious with *us,* and, beyond that, with themselves for not advancing their own lives.

After identifying to ourselves a whole set of members who are displacing their rage onto Zack for this reason, we make our intervention.

We have for a time noted that they have been, one after the other, tugging at us for solutions of different kinds.

One man has constantly asked the group and us whether he should leave his wife. Another has asked for advice about his daughter who is toying with drugs. Another woman, a therapist, keeps asking us how to build her practice.

These people have all been asking for advice and feeling unsatisfied. They are furious with us, but won't say so, being afraid that we will give them even less if they do. Instead, they have been taking out their fury on Zack, as if they were responding to his every reference by saying to him, "We won't help you, since no one is helping us."

We tell them point blank what's lacking. "You're all angry at me because I'm not telling you how to move straight up. So look at what you're doing. In frustration, you're scapegoating Zack, who has turned to you, the group, for help."

In telling the group what they have been lacking from us, and how they have reacted (in this case, by scapegoating Zack), we have brought their resistance to their attention.

Finally, certain techniques, which we would not use for dealing with an individual's resistance, are superbly applicable when a whole group shares a resistance.

Most notable is that of the therapist's *engaging in the resistant behavior himself.*

For instance, all the members in a particular group come in late, but no one will acknowledge the lateness. They are collectively resisting commitment to the group experience.

After mentioning their lateness a number of times, and getting nowhere, I decided to mimic their behavior, so as to bring it to their attention. The group was on the average three to fifteen minutes late, and therefore I made it a practice to come in roughly when the last member arrived.

I wasn't surprised that the group turned on me in rage. They demanded to know why I was late and accused me of not caring about them.

Next, I mirrored their indignation, with every bit as much outrage as they had showed. "Why is it," I asked, "that when I get here late, it's such a big deal, but when you come here late, no one even mentions it?"

A few of them replied that they were paying me to be on time. What kind of model was I offering them?

Others said I didn't care about them.

At that point, their own resistance of chronic lateness became evident to them, and they began talking about it for the first time, rather than sloughing me off when I broached the subject.

In this chapter, I've discussed various ways of making resistances conscious to the group members, individually and collectively. Those who run groups of any kind can use these methods. In accordance with their particular temperaments, therapists will choose certain of these approaches and rely on them more than others.

For instance, certain therapists might feel that mimicking a resistance is anathema, or is simply unprofessional, and for those therapists that verdict might well apply.

Only when we are sure that we are echoing a member's behavior objectively, that is, with absolutely no disdain for that person, should we even consider doing so. We must never use the technique unless we are sure that we are not using it superciliously.

Nor should any device that could easily turn into a lampoon be used if we have even a vestige of annoyance toward a patient. Ideally, all these methods for surfacing resistances should be considered in detail before they are put into practice.

Virtually every group therapist will arrive at his or her own techniques for revealing resistances, for making them inescapably clear to the members who employ them. The important thing is that the therapist be acutely aware that it is necessary to do so.

Resistances left unconsidered may go on preventing the members from trusting their own emotions and from trusting one another. The highly resistant patient is impeding not only his or her own progress, but that of everyone in the room. Such people may, if not dealt with, stifle a group. Indeed, unconsidered resistances are the chief threat to the coherence and progress of any group.

When surfacing resistances, as when trying to accomplish every other group purpose, our best approaches are those that invite the group itself to do the work. To simply run around the room naming people's resistances would be to forgo the enormous power of the group to discover them itself. Thus, though we are the first to see resistances, we are the last to name them.

Having brought such resistances to the group's awareness, we have put ourselves in position to enable the group to resolve them.

CHAPTER TWELVE

RESOLVING RESISTANCES

It would be a wondrous thing if the saying "A word to the wise is sufficient" applied to the study of resistances. Our groups would need only to point one out and the person would discard it and go on to better things.

Of course, the solution is not so simple. Resistances are adamant, like the rest of personality, and in the long run, this is a good thing, or people would be radically changing their essential makeup every day.

It's a rare patient who can put aside a resistance simply on learning what it is. For people to release themselves from the need to resist what others say to them, they must learn to see how they block out painful information, how they do so habitually.

Moreover, they must see themselves doing this blocking out, not once but many times. They must see themselves engaging in their resistances, on the spot as they are engaging in them, enough times to make the resistance, even the urge for the resistance, starkly conscious.

That is, they must see themselves resisting as another person might see them, and have this experience not just once but many times.

Certain group members require repeated mention of their resistance to be offered to them, *in virtually the same words*, for them to get a grip on what they are doing.

For instance, a man named Henry in a group of mine would instantly apologize whenever someone questioned what he had done. More than once Henry said he was sorry after speaking, because he'd imagined someone scowling or wincing while he was talking.

So humble was Henry that people hesitated even to tell him that he'd interrupted them. Henry's resistance of humility, of being self-abnegating, kept others at bay.

After a while, people pointed this out in various ways—for instance, one or two told him that he was hard to talk to because he apologized so much; another said he felt "wiped out" by those apologies; still another speculated aloud that Henry was frightened of his own aggression and must be feeling guilty about something.

But Henry couldn't seem to hear any of them.

I observed that Henry responded to only one of these interventions, the first—which was the simplest. Henry seemed to hear only those who told him *what he was doing,* and told him without embellishment. If anything, the variety of approaches was confusing Henry and making things worse.

I alerted the group to the fact that its medley of messages wasn't reaching Henry. I told them, in effect, "Notice that you aren't getting through. You keep giving Henry your impressions, but he keeps putting himself down. You're failing so far as Henry is concerned."

When they asked me what I thought they should do, I told them that the only thing Henry heard and responded to was a simple description of his putting himself down. I suggested that plain, blunt words of description had more persuasive power than any elaborations—at least in Henry's case.

The group took this new tack.

Before long, whenever Henry invoked his resistance, they described it. They would tell Henry over and over again what he was doing, exactly how he was putting himself down, the instant he did so.

Once the group had resorted to doing this, in virtually the same words over and over again, it wasn't long before Henry heard them. Finally, owing to this simple repetition, Henry grasped his own resistance and soon discarded it.

More usually, as when working with an individual patient, we have to approach the person in a *variety of ways.* Merely to show the person what he or she is doing, by repetition, gets us nowhere.

For instance, Marty, a patient in a group of mine, had since childhood resisted taking in what women said to him, fearing that if he allowed their message to penetrate, he would have to obey them like a hypnotized subject. As a child, Marty had come to see that when he did not heed his mother's request, when he failed to do what she wanted, then and there, she would cut him off utterly—even to the extent of refusing to talk to him. Especially when she would embrace his brothers and contrast Marty with them, he would become subject to the terrible fear of having lost everything.

Back then, when Marty suspected that his mother was on the verge of making a request, he would do anything he could to divert her attention. He would invent stories, saying he had a stomachache, or that someone needed him for something right away—anything to divert her from what she might ask of him.

Not surprisingly, Marty continued this practice of heading her off, and generalized it to any other woman he cared for. It was not merely requests that Marty disregarded but any statement by a woman that she needed something or was unhappy.

Marty could readily enjoy conversation with a stranger, toward whom he felt no obligation. But let any woman he liked merely show need, and Marty's thinking raced ahead. Her unrest was a command to Marty, and all commands to Marty had to be followed.

From about our third session, Marty started his practice of distracting women by interrupting them the instant it seemed that a woman might look needy. If he could stop a woman from showing any need, then Marty wouldn't have to fulfill that need. He was so tuned in to their needs that he could see trouble ahead even before the woman could. He was a champion interrupter of any woman who showed signs of looking serious.

Over the years, having refined his resistance of distracting women, Marty would never simply shout them down or cut them off. Presumably, he had been scolded for this earlier in life. Over time, Marty had gradually exchanged bluntness for his far more refined tactic of diverting women who wanted to talk about their feelings.

For instance, if a woman in the group began to speak reflectively about a bad experience, Marty was quick to act. With ostensible sympathy, he might ask the woman about something she had brought up the previous week and let pass.

Or he would empathically remind the group and the woman that someone else in the room was being shut out and hadn't spoken yet during the session.

Or he would tell the woman about to speak that she had changed the topic without knowing it.

Marty's resistance—that of diverting women on the verge of talking about themselves—was insidious. His resistance remained for a time much more interruptive and hurtful to the group than anyone recognized. In fact, Marty's resistance would often start a domino effect, evoking other interruptions, which sundered the group, leaving many of the members feeling at odds and dissatisfied.

After feeling the futility that seemed to follow Marty's digressions, I began to pinpoint to myself what Marty was really doing, and to appreciate the degree to which it stymied the group's flow.

I told the group what was going on. But when any member set out to explain to Marty what he was doing, he would stampede that person, to divert him or her in whatever way he could. After all, diverting people—and not merely women—had become Marty's speciality. Marty had far more practice at employing his resistance than others had at recognizing it. He proved himself never at a loss for a rationale for sidetracking his critics.

What had worked best with Henry's resistance, for us to point it out simply and in the same words, got the group nowhere with Marty. Such description, I came to see, simply increased Marty's sense of helplessness, which provoked an even more entrenched refusal to hear us. If anything, by singing our same old song in the same words, we were dulling Marty's ear to its message.

To reach Marty, we would have to approach him in a *variety* of ways, as when picking up a blanket from many sides.

So how was the group to approach Marty?

Let's look at some of the methods we have available to resolve resistance, to see specifically how they applied in Marty's case.

I want to define and illustrate three chief methods of helping group members grasp their resistances well enough to give them up. Observe that each of these methods aims at helping the member see his or her resistance in a different way.

1. Our first method of loosening the grip of a resistance we might loosely call the device of *prognostication*.

With Marty, this meant encouraging the group to talk to him about the likely outcome of his stifling women. To this end, I asked an especially astute woman how she thought Marty's behavior would affect anyone he dated. She replied that if it were her, after a first date, she would never see him again.

Another woman chimed in that Marty was the sort of man she used to find attractive but had learned to avoid. "At least I hope I've learned," she added.

I asked yet another woman, one who was still overly subject to being influenced by men, what she thought. She replied snappily, "As long as a woman knows what she feels toward Marty and his kind, she'll come out okay."

The sum total of these comments impacted quite differently on Marty than he had expected. He was stunned to discover how much he hurt people. He could do what he wished with the universal prognostication that women would find him unpleasant. But at least now he knew.

2. The second method of loosening the grip of a resistance is to reveal *the secret desire that lies behind the resistance.*

Time and again, as Marty's resistance surfaced, I kept asking other members what they thought he really wanted. Why would Marty head off women when they seemed urgent or intense?

The group was baffled, and Marty himself contributed nothing by way of explanation. By that time, he had recognized his resistance and its harmful effects, but there were still some vital parts missing in his understanding of its nature.

Then, one day a new woman came into the group, and Marty regressed to his practice of sidetracking her. He did this especially when she talked about her husband. One time, the woman, who was quite attractive, pulled back in astonishment, and asked Marty in annoyance what the hell he wanted of her. Feeling trapped and embarrassed, Marty replied that he didn't know.

However, someone else in the group *did* know. "Marty," he blurted out, "I think I know what you want. In fact, there's only one thing you really want to hear from any woman. Let's face it, you want her to love you and nobody else."

To everyone's surprise, Marty admitted that the man was right.

Going still further, he confessed to an insatiable yearning to be the loved one in the room—adored, talked about, the subject of everyone's fancy. He couldn't bear it when he wasn't.

Marty's deep-seated wish for unconditional love was one that doubtless many of us share. But Marty had never made peace with it, never reconciled himself to its unattainability. It was a wish, so raw and uncompromising, that made any slight of Marty unbearable and, as a result, fueled his resistance.

After that session, not merely Marty himself but everyone in the group stayed in touch with that wish of Marty's. Afterward, from time to time, when Marty broke in on a woman, a friendly voice might be heard in the group chiding him.

"Why don't you just let her talk. We know you want her to love you, but maybe she has something else to say."

Even without such chiding, however, Marty's recognizing what he really wanted gave him a much better sense of what his resistance meant, and brought him closer to dropping it altogether.

Almost certainly, every resistance has at least one fervent wish underlying it. When that wish is discovered and revealed, the "resistor" gains a much better sense of his own behavior than he would otherwise have.

3. A third method of helping a member reconsider his or her resistance and eventually discard it is to *help that member see its secondary gain*. What are the ill-gotten but hidden advantages of his employing the resistance?

Marty's "benefit," each time he sidetracked a woman from something important that she wanted to say, was a curious sense of pleasure. Over the years, Marty had learned to milk those moments of thwarting his imagined enemy—first his mother and later all women who approached him emotionally. An almost imperceptible smirk would cross his lips when he sidetracked a woman—especially if she stammered or became unhinged.

Having observed Marty's smirk more than once, I asked the group if anyone else saw it. To my surprise, the one man with whom Marty was friendliest in the group, Frank, said that he had, and that he hated it.

Frank told us he had never forgotten his telling the group of his having been mugged in his doorway. The members had all commiserated, even Marty. "But there was something in your smile, Marty, that I never forgot."

Though Marty denied having smiled, Frank said that he'd felt sure that it was a smile of triumph. Soon afterward, other members noted Marty's leaning back and appearing to get pleasure when certain women looked frantic. We helped him appreciate that satisfaction, which Marty later assured us wasn't truly sadism but merely a sense of relief at not being the victim himself.

Virtually every resistance provides some sense of relief. The person resisting anticipates some dire outcome of an ordinary event. We may imagine that we know that outcome, but we can never really be sure until the person tells us.

It might be relief from an anticipated criticism, or relief from rejection, or relief from an irrationally conceived threat of being captured or abused or raped or humiliated. But always the resistance is against some form of perceived calamity.

Of course, we begin by turning to others for their impressions, but in the long run if the person is to be free, he or she must identify the imagined threat and subject it to what Carl Jung called "the antiseptic power of consciousness."

In every case, emotional recognition of the gain inherent in a resistance deepens the person's experience of the pattern, and ultimately helps the person drop it entirely.

Observe that the secondary gain from a resistance is often not its motive. The secondary gain of an illness might be the attention the person gets from others who sympathize with him—not that the person wanted to become ill but once he is, he finds ways of deriving benefits from the illness. With resistances, the relief—as, for instance, the satisfaction afforded by their utilization—is often a factor that holds the behavior in place. By helping the group reveal that benefit to the resistant member, we enable the resistor to see unmistakably that he or she is gaining very little in exchange for the freedom and flexibility that he is surrendering.

Naturally, there is some apprehension behind every resistance. Whenever we talk about a motive or a hidden advantage of a resistance, we are, simultaneously, alluding to that fear—to that imagined danger that the person staves off by the resistance. However, rather than humiliate a member by constantly harping on the fear, it is always preferable to talk about potential gains. A patient would rather talk about his or her desire for love than about a fear of being unloved and unlovable. Or, if a person's resistance is a pretense of knowledge, the person would rather talk about his or her desire to seem smart than a fear of being stupid.

People are far readier to appreciate their own resistances and to deal with them when they can conceptualize them as forms of aspiration rather than as forms of flight.

How important is it for a person, or for a group, to identify the history of a person's resistance? Obviously, group analysis relies less on history than individual classical analysis does. In individual sessions, among other techniques, the analyst uses the person's history to help the patient see the problem from many sides. True, the patient may express the resistance with the analyst himself or herself. But an ongoing review of the patient's history absorbs considerable time when the patient is alone in the room, week after week, year after the year, with one other individual.

Group analysis, because it is done in an interpersonal context, evokes a resistance in its varied forms, and does this quickly. A patient who might never reveal a resistance pattern in his or her relationship with a private analyst is likely to reveal it in a variety of ways with a variety of people present. A well-stocked group is almost sure to contain members who evoke one another's resistances, and careful selection of the members of a group can ensure this.

As a result, group analysis provides a substitute for one of the chief reasons for reviewing an individual's personal history, namely, the opportunity to see a resistance from many sides.

There are other benefits of identifying the history of a resistance, of course. Chief among them is that the person, upon realizing what the original function of the resistance was, may quickly recognize that the resistance no longer works. The person comes to see that the very resistance that once protected him now stands in his way. He sees for the first time that he does better without it.

As often as not, we help members overcome the harmful impact of their personal histories without even mentioning those histories. In every group, there are surrogates for people who were prominent in the members' pasts. These are not identical figures, of course, but people who evoke highly specific memories of key figures in the various members' lives.

Even when the member does not talk about his past life per se, by his employing his early learned resistances with those surrogates, he is reliving that past. In relinquishing his resistances, he is eradicating the harmful impact of those early days.

Some theorists believe that, ideally, a person should recall the early key figures in his life and even the incidents that occurred when he formed his resistance patterns. But even this has been debated in recent years. The important thing is that the person erase whatever deleterious effect his past has had on him.

As we reveal any resistance to a member, as we show its motives and gains but also its drawbacks, we leave it up to that member to decide when he or she will discard the resistance, and in favor of what. Will he revert to another resistance, or opt for the behavior that serves him best? That will be up to the person. However, we still have further contributions to make.

Suppose the person simply resorts to another resistance.

For instance, Peter, a member who formerly resisted intimacy by being silent and cut off, came to see, with the group's help, that he'd been avoiding relationships. For two years, the group worked hard to help Peter appreciate that his own tight-lipped style was a method of keeping others away. Still, Peter remained laconic, telling us simply that he had nothing to say.

As analyst of this group, I wondered how long it would take for Peter to come down from his mountain top; indeed, I wondered if he ever would.

Then one day, a woman, Felice, in that group complained that Peter was like her husband, who loved her but never showed it.

The group was shaken by a terrible noise, and it took a real moment for me to realize that it was Peter bellowing, "How the hell do you know who I love and who I don't?"

So saying, he turned to the group as a whole and kept shouting at the top of his lungs. What the hell did we want from him anyhow, why couldn't we leave him alone?

Peter had finally come roaring down from his mountain top.

For months after that, Peter was either silent or abusively loud, as if he knew no moderate way to talk. His raising his voice was, of course, a resistance, no less a one than his silence had been. However, as is usual when one resistance gives way to another, the new one would not prove so recalcitrant. At least, Peter was communicating with us now, expressing feelings and ideas he had long harbored. True, he would not yet dare to present them to us in a way that we could deal with. But he had taken a crucial first step.

The sight of a member substituting one resistance for another can be disheartening. After all, we've worked hard, both analyst and group, to have the member give up the resistance. It might seem that our labor deserves a better reward when it finally succeeds. Alexander Dumas, in *The Count of Monte Cristo,* described a man who took years to tear down a dungeon wall, only to find himself in another cell. Our member, substituting one resistance for another—who, as a result, is still sealed off—can seem like that hapless prisoner.

But no matter how he appears, we must keep our composure, and help the group approach the next resistance as sedulously as it approached the last.

One positive is that the new resistance is unlikely to be as adamant as the old one. The member is less practiced at it, and the group is more practiced at dealing with that person. Surely, the member will need more time. But the group has already profited. In their revealing that member's resistance to him, they have softened their own resistances.

And there is an additional bonus. To our pleasant surprise, we are likely to learn that the member, who in group merely switched resistances, has elsewhere softened his approach to people. Even as Peter boomed at us for tampering with his mechanisms of remoteness, he became less remote to his loved ones.

Usually, though not invariably, when a member drops one resistance in favor of another, the new one is easier to spot, being more primitive. Whereas the initial resistance was sophisticated, the new one is likely to be crude. The person who constantly changes the subject as a resistance, the one who gets sanctimonious, the one who intellectualizes, may all, when found out, resort to infantile bellowing. Whatever time was needed for the person to see and work through his first resistance, the time required to confront the replacement is likely to be short by comparison.

Finally, the member hits on a new mode of expression that truly serves him. Peter is now talking to us, and expressing real feelings. Or a member who constantly fell asleep in group is now staying awake. Or a member who constantly disparaged homosexuals is now talking sincerely to several gay people in the group. Or a mem-

ber who constantly acted as if he would fall apart when criticized
becomes able at last to listen with equanimity when a fault of his or
hers is pointed out.

However, just as personality faults are not immutable, the member's
newly arrived-at healthy mode of expression comes with no guarantee.
Goethe once said that freedom is something a person must earn every
day, and that certainly applies to freedom from having to engage in a
resistance. For a time, we must continue to serve as sentries over the
newly won territory.

We must stay alert for instances of the new and more direct behavior, and have the group underscore them.

Mindful of the resistance that the member recently shed, we ourselves especially appreciate what that member is doing now. For instance, Peter's talking equably to other members, which would hardly
merit special consideration if we had just met him, we see as a mon-
umental achievement. Ideally, the members would appreciate this too,
and we can help them do so.

For instance, we might turn to a woman, Jane, whom Peter had
interrupted regularly for over a year. Our new Peter has just acknowledged a comment Jane has made. Or beyond that, when several other
members have disregarded a comment of Jane's, Peter has chival-
rously returned the group's attention to it. After our intervention,
Jane thanks him, and the two of them draw closer.

And we may even go further, making an intervention that both
bridges and makes clear to all what Peter has accomplished.

For instance, we might ask Jane, "I notice that you talk more easily
to Peter, why is that?"

If Jane knows, she will probably tell us that Peter is coming across
in a fresh way. She feels more comfortable with him now.

In telling us this, Jane will be enabling Peter to appreciate what he
has accomplished, and possibly this will motivate him to want to
continue in the same vein.

Our working this way also helps Jane realize that her words have
real impact. This would be especially important for Jane if Peter had
served for her as a surrogate of some past figure who indeed refused
to hear her out.

Not that we have the scenario all prepared. We can never be sure
exactly where the group will go, but wherever the group does go, we
will be there with them. If it turns out that Jane, feeling unforgiving
that day, begrudges Peter his due, someone else may extend it. That

person will then derive the benefit of appreciating that his own words have the power to buoy another human being. If this is the case, and Jane is begrudging, then sooner or later, the group may address Jane's tendency to withhold her favors.

One never knows precisely who will profit from the exposure of truth. But no matter who actually makes the comments, we have invited the group to acknowledge what Peter has done.

Only as a last resort, if everyone in group refuses to acknowledge someone's personal accomplishment, should we ourselves acknowledge it. This sometimes happens when the person's behavior has so grated on the group that they simply refuse to forgive him or grant him anything. But that is a rarity. Ideally, we ourselves are not the ones to motivate by praise or punishment. The more the group does, the more the group profits.

Obviously, no matter how firm someone's personal gain appears to be, regression remains a possibility. And the time when people are more likely to regress to employing old patterns of resistance is when they are under extra stress.

Naturally, we can't possibly follow a member through life, observe him under pressure, and remind him not to regress. Nor would we want to. But here, as in many contexts, we can make use of the group as a microcosm, observing the member especially closely when that person is under stress. It is at these times, if ever, that he will resort to his old resistances.

We may ask ourselves explicitly, "Does this person, who only recently emerged from the tyranny of a pattern, revert to it when under siege?" If not, we may feel triumphant, and even elicit the group's recognition of the member's success.

But suppose the member *does* revert.

Once again, our best approach is not that of confronting the person himself, but of enjoining other members to study his or her regressive pattern.

For instance, a woman in a group of mine, who formerly employed the resistance of attacking people rather than acknowledge her own role when things went wrong, had given up that resistance for months. However, one day, unexpectedly, she lit into a man, accusing him of being indifferent to her, as if he hated her.

Rather than confront her directly, I asked the group what was going

on. Two members quickly pointed out to the woman that she herself
had slighted this man several times when he had tried to talk. Once
again, she neither saw nor acknowledged her own role and was blaming someone else. With all the prehistory of working on that resistance, the group identified it fast, and she gave it up, this time for
good.

Even long after a person has resolved a resistance, we may allude to
it. Especially when the person is under the kind of siege that might
have evoked it in the past, we may observe aloud that the person did
not resort to it this time. Or once again, preferably, we invite a group
member to mention the person's gain. "Cynthia, how do you experience Estelle, now that she talks to other people about *them*, instead
of dwelling on *herself?*"

Aside from the support that such a method gives to a person who
has accomplished something, it gives the group members an opportunity to speak well of one another. As people learn to recognize and
discuss nuances of one another's behavior, ideally, we invite them to
use these skills to talk about what they appreciate—and not merely
dislike—about each other.

Resolving resistances is painstaking but rewarding to both the group
members and to the therapist. Even at best, it is a repetitive process:
we must go back to step one over and over again, especially as new
resistances replace old ones. Where we can, we try to have the group
see even the same resistances and describe them from novel angles, as
well as in the old ways.

CHAPTER THIRTEEN

BORROWED ROBES— TRANSFERENCE IN GROUP

Why do you dress me in borrowed robes?
—SHAKESPEARE,
Macbeth

As we all know, our group members see us through the scrim of their own personal histories. We are sure to appear to them more kindly, or trustworthy, or ferocious, or untrustworthy than we really are, in accordance with expectations and ways of perceiving that they have evolved out of their own histories.

And not only do they misperceive us. They misperceive one another; they succumb to predilections to misinterpret one another's behavior, for better and for worse, in accordance with what they learned to expect, usually early in life.

Such misperceptions, formed by bringing past expectations into the present, have come to be known as *transference*. The person is imposing attitudes, feelings, and expectations adopted in the past, on people in the present.

Psychoanalysts have clarified their own perception of transference during the century since the concept was identified. Originally, they imagined that transference was only a neurotic process, and one directed only toward the analyst. Moreover, the early analysts imagined that transference developed only gradually as therapy proceeded.

We now understand that from the very first time a member walks into a group, he distorts in his perception of the therapist and the others there—a distortion consistent with his own history. Indeed, every member misperceives in his very expectations of what the others will be like and how they will treat him, even before he meets them.

For us, transferences upon whole groups are also noteworthy. Our members have expectations of the group itself; each tends to perceive it as he or she goes along, in ways that also reveal the person's unique history.

For instance, someone who regarded his parents as hypercritical, whether or not they truly were, would, logically and psychologically, expect a group to be overly critical too. This person will be liable to mistake the group's honest efforts to help him as hostile incursions. He is in a preconscious state of readiness to construe nearly anything said to him as threatening.

On the other hand, a group member whose parents, or those in their place, were nearly always supportive, may expect the same of the group. This person, whose parents criticized him for his own good if at all, might, analogously, be blind to real hostility toward him, misinterpreting it as well-meant criticism.

Though transference, being essentially a mental and emotional set, occurs from the moment a person considers therapy, as a rule, we allow it to express itself for a long time without tampering with it.

One obvious exception is the kind of destructive transference that would stop the person from continuing his or her participation in a group.

Or it may even be that a person so distrusts us, without cause, that he won't come into our group at all. Whoever works with such a person individually must explore that distrust, and resolve it—at least to the extent that the would-be member becomes willing to gamble on the group. Even then, such a person may not participate actively for a long time. Nor should we do anything special to bring him in. Suspicious people should, in particular, be allowed to advance at their own speed.

The other exception to our rule of letting a transference unfold at its own rate occurs in the case of a member who is likely to do real damage to a group. Obviously, where there is such a danger, we would be wise to postpone bringing the person into our group until he can control his impulses.

This too may be best done in individual treatment. Even here, we may be able to take the sting out of such a transference, if not resolve it, by taking action early. And there are times when we must ask a person to leave our group because he holds a hostile and adamant transference toward the members, which so preoccupies them that the group cannot advance until it is resolved.

The Events That Prompt Transference

Technically, from the very instant a person enters the group —in fact, from the moment the person *contemplates* the group and the therapist—transference begins. The member projects onto the therapist expectations and attitudes, carry-overs from the closest exemplars to the therapist that he has known.

However, certain events in a group both precipitate transference and make it more evident as it becomes more pronounced.

A sense of what some of these are helps in prompting us to look for newly blossomed transferences.

For instance, the very form of any *resistance* we encounter is almost surely an expression of transference. The aloof member may have learned his personal style with a harpy mother—the less she knew about what he felt and what he wanted, the safer he was. He now plays safe with us, as he did with her.

The member who becomes coy and seductive as a device to conceal his or her true feelings toward us, may well be employing a technique begun with a parent from whom this person hid his true feelings. He fears repercussions from us, as he did from that parent.

And apart from the form of the resistance itself, which bespeaks transference, we see transferences whenever a resistance is *resolved.*

For instance, a group member has constantly used the resistance of flippancy and humor to mask deep feelings. Resolution of that resistance results in the member's becoming highly agitated—*he sees us as depressed,* as on the brink of collapsing in front of him.

It turns out that he has been entertaining us to distract us, to keep us laughing, as it were, so that we would not succumb to our own despair and abandon him the way his parents did. This person spent a childhood entertaining one or both parents, who were prone to depression and found his sunny disposition their only distraction. The moment he surrendered his comedic approach to us, he feared that we would collapse the way his parents did—and, as part of that fear, he felt utterly helpless.

Thus inherent in both resistances and in their resolution is vital information concerning the members' past lives: if we are alert we can identify transferences in both.

Paradoxical as it might seem, people also experience sharp transferential reactions when they see themselves able to do things that they could not do over the years. A woman has all her life been unable to talk about sex. When, following the example of another woman in the group, she finally voices some of her sexual feelings toward a man there, she suddenly feels dirty and anticipates that the group members will hold their nose and ask her to leave the room.

She comes to the next session so doused in perfume that the group expresses curiosity about it. She recalls that when she was a little girl, her parents made the same ugly face when sex came up in conversation that they did when she had soiled her pants. She expected the group to be her mother, to recoil, as she had. Her very accomplishment in allowing herself to discuss sex loosed the transference, made it plain for all to see. For the first time, she and the rest of us could experience along with her that early-learned expectation of revulsion.

Of the other prompters of transference in any group, a major one is the *group atmosphere* itself. Members who come to group expecting to be censured, or to have conformity required of them, are astonished at the freedom they actually find. Their very experience of this "brave, new world with so many people in it" is itself a shock—one that, more often than not, evokes a spectrum of transference reactions.

For instance, a man who grew up in a very harsh home, and who himself became so caustic that he lost a sequence of lovers and jobs, vowed that he would curb himself in group. He wanted the as-yet unmet members to appreciate him, to welcome him, to accept him.

During the first three sessions there, he said little and was marvelously discreet in what he did say. However, in the fourth session, before he knew what he was saying, he had scalded another member with words beyond anything he had heard in the group. "You're an idiot. You haven't got a brain in your head," he heard himself say.

A moment later he was terrified, anticipating that my group and I would turn on him and tell him to get the hell out. When I simply asked him, could he put what he had just said in different words, without the name calling, he was stunned.

He did indeed make his objection less objectionably, and when the person he'd called an idiot listened to him without counterpunching, he was surprised. He looked around the room, expecting the others to lambaste him, but no one did.

He burst into tears. It was an acceptance that he had never known previously. From then on, he could accept that his roughness toward all of us was itself a transference, not appropriate but also not punishable by death.

Even more important, he could see that his view of people as waiting to waylay him for a misdeed, which in part had kept him so tough, was also a transference. We were not as tough as his parents were.

Doubtless, most of what our members do that seems unprovoked and inexplicable to us at first, turns out to be transferential. Therefore, as we watch the members interact, we should constantly keep transferential explanations in mind.

RECOGNIZING TRANSFERENCE IN THE GROUP SETTING

As we know if we've ever done therapy with individuals, or even read about the process, transference reactions have certain characteristics by which we can recognize them.

Chief among these are their *pervasiveness*, their *insistence*, their *excessiveness*, and finally, *displacement*.

By *pervasiveness*, I mean that a group member tends to see not just one person in a particular way but everyone too much in that light. Alexander Pope was describing a kind of transference when he wrote:

> All seems infected that th'infected spy.
> All things look yellow to the jaundic'd eye.

Our best indicator of transference in a group member is the discovery that this person has a blanket view, if not of everyone then of all those in a particular category. Such a person will be the first to spot that trait in those who truly possess it, but he will also tend to see it in others who do not.

For instance, a man is quick to spot competitiveness in other men in the group, but he also attributes that same trait of being competitive to men who show no hint of it. He sees not just one man in the group but all the men there as trying to forge ahead of him. The pervasiveness of a trait thus suggests strongly, if not decisively, that it is transferential.

By *insistence*, I mean that no matter what the real facts are, the person with the transference tends to cling to his thesis regarding those about whom he holds his preconception.

For instance, a man sees women as manipulative and as trying to rob him of his freedom. In group, he becomes acutely sensitive when a woman happens to be at all exploitive of men, and he mistakenly sees other women as being the same way.

When told by one woman that he has misheard something she just said to him, he declares that he *knows* what he heard. He feels besieged when others there contend that he did actually mishear her.

But rather than retreat, he defies everyone. He insists on defending his perception. His adamancy derives not from a considered belief that he is right, but from the nature of his perception as transferential. It is for this reason that he finds it extremely hard to let that perception go. Such insistence on a perception is an almost sure indicator of a transferential reaction.

Transferences are every bit as tenacious when they are positive— that is, favorable toward the therapist—as when they are negative. We see group members swear that they love their group analyst, insisting sometimes that they want to marry him or her, have children with that person, and make him happy evermore. And we see the same when one group member forms such a transference toward another member.

In spite of evidence that they can't ever have the analyst in these ways, and that their longing for life with another member of the group is equally as unrealistic, these members may go on cherishing their illusion. It appears to them that if only they could possess the other person, their therapist or the particular member, they would have no further problems.

Quite often, such members experience hatred toward the mate of the therapist or of the other member. This "love-transference," when properly parsed, turns out not to be love at all, but an overweening possessiveness. Its very insistence reveals that it is a transference.

The third classical indicator of a transferential reaction in group is its *excessiveness*.

For instance, take a woman whose transference toward most men is that they will find her unappealing, and will reject her. Shortly after she has said something to a man in the group, and he has responded warmly to her, he excuses himself to go to the bathroom.

Instead of being momentarily disappointed, she feels utterly unim-

portant in his life, and falls prey to a desperate sense that he is rejecting her. Whether or not she accuses him of callousness toward her,
she sees him as having committed an act of violence against her. He
has promised her commitment by his response, and he has walked out
on her.

This woman has overreacted to him grievously, out of all proportion. Such overreactions indicate the presence of transference.

The excessiveness of our group members' reactions, which in some
cases reach the level of hysteria, always indicates that we are confronting a transference and not merely the member's reaction to something that has just taken place.

To understand such excessiveness, think of a member's expression
as not simply a response to a single event—that is, to its proximate
cause—but as a reaction to a thousand such moments that have been
registered and retained. It's as if the member expressing the transference reaction were saying, "This is the story of my life."

For instance, a patient shouts that he distrusts everyone in a group
because they mentioned him before he got there that session. He
accuses them of being disloyal, of not appreciating him. They are
aghast at his reaction, the excessiveness of which bespeaks a transference to them.

We understand, however, that in cursing everyone present, our
member is saying, "My family was lousy to me. People have always
abused me, and I know they always will. I hate you for what you and
all those in my past have done to me."

Finally, because transference consists of reactions originally felt
toward someone else—a parent or sibling, for example—all expressions of transference have *displacement* in them. This may seem self-
evident, and it is when the transference is wholly misguided.
However, where a transference is an exaggerated response to a real
stimulus, the displacement may be subtle.

The person toward whom the transference is expressed may have
done something real to provoke some reaction. But that behavior was
in itself insufficient to elicit the reaction that it actually caused. What
we are seeing, and what explains the seeming excessiveness of the
reaction, is the impact of displacement.

For instance, we, or the group member toward whom the transference is expressed, have done something that seems to us quite
ordinary—but it is reminiscent of what a past figure did to the member. Even if this is so, as the very excessiveness of a transference

suggests, the transference reaction is itself at least in part a displacement from that past figure to the present one.

That is, at least part of the person's reaction is a release of a feeling that he felt toward another person in his past. This remains true whether our member ever expressed that feeling toward the past figure or not.

In certain cases, we or the group member who becomes the object of a displacement may be nothing like the person toward whom the feeling was originally directed. It is not the member, himself or herself, who evokes the displacement.

Rather it is some *characteristic* of the relationship between the person engaging in the transference and some past relationship. This is true of displacement in particular and of transference in general.

For instance, a woman for whom a man has a desperate infatuation in no way resembles that man's mother, whom he loved but could not reach. The man's childhood was spent in vain efforts to spend time with his mother and to impress her. In actuality, his mother was beautiful and highly cultured, and did love him. However, she was sickly and lacked pure physical energy and so she often had to withdraw from him when he wanted to spend time with her. She died when he was quite young.

In group, the woman that he becomes infatuated with is utterly without his mother's virtues or good intentions toward him. The one characteristic that she shares with his mother is a trait of his childhood relationship—namely, that he cannot reach her, that he can no more elicit her involvement with him than he could his mother's.

It is this woman's very remoteness that makes her the object of his transference. He is responding to her remoteness and not to her. What he was unable to achieve with his mother, he also cannot find with this woman; the deprivation itself induces his overblown response.

In some cases, the only way that we know that a reaction is a displacement is that we know something about the person's history. For instance, we might know that a man's mother was remote, for whatever reason, and we see him attracted toward the more remote women in the group. In still other cases, though we don't start out knowing the formative elements of the person's past, we can infer them by the reaction that we come to identify as transferential.

Whenever we observe any of these four indicators—the *pervasiveness* of a reaction, its *insistence,* its *excessiveness,* or its

displacement—we may strongly suspect that the reaction is transferential. The presence of all four is virtually proof positive of a transference.

COLLECTIVE TRANSFERENCES

The big jump from doing individual therapy to working with groups,
one that cannot be mentioned too often, is that virtually every attitude
found in a patient receiving individual treatment may be held in common by a set of members or even by a whole group. This is especially
true of transference.

Consider the following case.

A group of mine was running smoothly, the members were very
helpful to one another and engaging in fruitful exchanges. But all this
stopped abruptly when I brought in a particular member—Doris, a
bright woman, well spoken, a mother and also a successful executive.

Doris herself acted in a way that in retrospect was quite understandable. Feeling nervous during her first session, she addressed most
of her comments to me.

However, as I was soon to hear from the group, I must have responded to her by leaning forward and reacting to her with more than
my usual animation. I recall thinking that she was charismatic, though
I certainly didn't think that I was dazzled by the sight of her.

I did notice that after a half hour of that first session, progress in the
group slowed down. The members, rather than continuing to talk to
one another, began addressing most of their comments to me. And
they also seemed full of complaints and entreaties that I give them
something, or explain something, or do something for them.

I felt tugged at from all sides, and I realized that collectively they
had regressed. Like children, my group members were demanding
more attention from me than I could possibly give them. They were,
to be more precise, like older siblings who'd had a parent to themselves until the arrival of a needy infant.

Their clamoring might have been in part a reaction to the real loss
of a scintilla of my attention, but the fear underlying it was transferential. It was a fear of losing me, and with some of them, a resentment that far outweighed the real loss they had suffered.
Because of this transference, what had been a working unit in a
short time became an array of scattered parts.

That my group members had utterly altered their reactions to me and to one another was not in itself proof of a collective transference. However, the very insistence and excessiveness of their demands were strongly indicative of one. I felt pressured by those demands, and from there my inferring a collective transference was not difficult.

When the criteria that identify an individual transference hold for a collection of people, for a set within a group or for the group itself, we are dealing with a collective transference.

ENABLING THE GROUP TO RECOGNIZE A TRANSFERENCE

Implicit in the very nature of transference is the fact that it is a regressive and insistent perception. We may think of it as a relentless bias of attitude and orientation. Even positive transferences limit the group members' range of perception and variety of feelings. Idolatry is a very evident transference: the person in the grip of idolatry toward us or another member finds it hard to express anger and even to see failings.

Thus every transference reduces independence of thought and action. Therefore, with every transference, the time must come when we help the group discover it, with the ultimate aim of having the person, or a set of people, see it and come to terms with it.

We may use our knowledge of the components of transference not just to identify it ourselves, but to help others identify it.

One way of doing this is to underscore any of the characteristics of the transference response already mentioned—for instance, its pervasiveness or its excessiveness. Once the group members see what they are dealing with, it does not take long for them to see the reaction as a distortion.

For instance, we might enable the group to see the pervasiveness of a reaction. This is very easy to do in the group setting with a member who speaks in broad generalizations. He is practically declaring his transference, and all we need to do is alert the others to this generalization.

Brendan, in berating a certain woman, whom we'll call Edna, for demanding constant attention from him, comments in passing that all women are like that. "Women want you to give them every waking moment."

Such a generalization is an excellent giveaway of a transference. We may interpose ourselves and thus underline the pervasiveness of this perception, as a key to revealing the transference that lies behind it.

For example, we might ask Brendan, "You've just said that Edna wants too much from you. What do the other women in this group want from you?"

Perhaps Brendan will describe many or all of the women present as predatory. Understandably, he will offer variations on the theme—one wants his time, a second wants money, a third wants stock-market advice, a fourth wants sex with him. But we see the leitmotif, and can next address the group.

"What's going on with Brendan?"

Almost surely, such an open-ended question will result in at least someone's identification of Brendan's perceptual bias. From then on, the group will see it as fast as we do.

Although underscoring the pervasiveness of a reaction is our best way of revealing it as a transference, we can't always simply point to the generalization. We may have to bring it out.

For instance, though we have noticed that Brendan's diatribe against Edna is nothing new for Brendan, he has limited himself to talking only about Edna this time. We wish he would generalize, since we're quite sure that the charge he is making against Edna is one that he really levels against all women. It would be easier for us to unmask his transference if he did generalize, but he doesn't—perhaps because he has been criticized for generalizing in the past.

In this case, we must interpose ourselves in order to reveal the generalized nature of Brendan's perception.

A straightforward question will usually do. "Brendan, are you talking about Edna, or are you talking about every woman in the group?"

Or "Brendan, haven't we heard this before?"

It's too much to expect that Brendan will drop his immediate charge against Edna and concede that he is painting her with his usual colors. However, he may. But even if he doesn't, we've alerted the group to the possibility of a transference here.

Other members may support our observation. Perhaps a woman in group whom Brendan has treated much as he is now treating Edna will underscore that he has this tendency. In any event, we have invited the group to consider a transference, and they are more than likely to go on considering it.

As always when doing group therapy, we prefer it if members of the group rather than we ourselves make the decisive observations.

More often than not, to demonstrate generality we can turn to someone who has himself or herself been the object of a transference. That person, smarting over the experience of being misunderstood, will be in a prime position to confirm that there is a perceptual distortion being expressed.

Gregory, a member of one of my groups, had a father who wanted him to become a great athlete. Gregory's father constantly sent him to tennis camps and to baseball schools, and would brutalize him when they played catch in the park. The eternal message from Gregory's father was that Gregory was not doing things in a way that would make his father proud.

Gregory came to group because he constantly got into skirmishes with people at work. In the group, he would often accuse people of trying to control him, and of having arbitrary ideas about how he should live his life. He was sometimes right when he charged a member with wanting him to get married, but he often insisted that people had agendas for him when there was no evidence for this.

In session after session, Gregory would single out a persecutor, more often a man than a woman; he would accuse that person of trying to force him to act in ways that were diametrically opposed to what he wanted for himself. A few weeks earlier, he had battered Stephen, a very gentle soul, accusing Stephen of telling him to give up writing and stick to selling insurance. Though Stephen and the group had sought to refute Gregory, he had remained inconsolable.

This time Gregory lit into Daryl, who was himself a professional writer; he accused Daryl of cutting him to the quick. "Who are you to imply that I don't have a poet's mind?"

Daryl had implied no such thing. He pleaded innocence. But Gregory kept on accusing him relentlessly. "Now you're trying to tell me I'm crazy, that you didn't say what I heard you say. . . ."

The group was silent, perhaps because they were stunned by Gregory's ferocity.

I turned to Stephen, Gregory's previous transference victim. "Stephen," I asked, "does any of this sound familiar to you?"

"Of course," Stephen replied, looking straight at Gregory. "You're doing just what you did with me. You think that everybody has goals for you that you don't have. And nothing we say can convince you that we don't."

The group saw how relentless Gregory was, how insistent he was on maintaining his accusatory position. They saw this even more vividly when they tried to reason with him. Gregory ranted and raged and remained unconvinced.

However, this time, the group as a whole, having come to see the irrational insistence of Gregory's point of view, recognized it as a relic—as a transference.

Still another way of bringing a transference out into the open is to invite the group to consider a commonality between a member's perception of us and the report he has given us about the nature of a parent or some past figure. This time we are inferring the displacement element of the transference.

For instance, Alec, who has been taciturn for a month, suddenly accuses us of trying to bring him out, not for his sake but for our own entertainment.

We ask another member, Arlene, if she shares Alec's view that we have been using him primarily to strut our own stuff.

"Arlene, if I were to point out that you hadn't said anything for a while, how would you feel?"

Arlene tells us instantly that she would feel great if we had said to her what we said to Alec.

"So what script is Alec replaying here? If it doesn't fit me, who does it fit?"

Like all questions asked of an individual, we are directing this at one person but are leaving it open, so that anyone who wishes to can answer it.

Very likely, someone will remember, as we do, that Alec has often portrayed his mother as a social climber, who used her children to make her look good. The group will tell us in chorus that he is seeing us as he saw his mother.

We are glad that Alec has expressed this attitude, that he has enabled us to see its deep-seated nature. And we have used the group to reveal its transferential origin.

Our same techniques apply even when the similarity between us in our therapist's role and the parent is very real and not wholly imagined. For instance, like the member's own father or mother, we may tend to be reserved, slow speaking. Or like the member's parent we are volatile, mercurial. In such a case, the member's observation of us may be quite correct.

When a member can cite something very real and evident about us in making his charge, the group as a whole may be relatively slow to see it as a transference.

In such cases, though we use our same interrogations, we must in the end rely heavily on helping the group recognize the transference as such by its fundamentals—its pervasiveness, its insistence, its excessiveness, and its displacement.

Patterns of Transference

As always, the group members themselves are the chief agents in resolving their own transferences. As therapists, we try to play as small a role as possible—we establish the pitch rather than sing the song. For us to utilize the group members requires both a general knowledge of how transferences interlock, and a specific appreciation of what is going on in front of us.

And more often than not, one transference will evoke others.

For instance, one man calls another a stingy, begrudging person; in reaction, the accused man calls the first a fearful person who can't live without constant attention. There is some truth in what each of these people says about the other, but there is also much misperception based on transference.

Or, more dramatically, a whole set of people may respond transferentially to the behavior of an individual.

For example, a woman in group grew up correcting her brothers and sisters, in a vain effort to become the preferred child. Now in group she constantly corrects other people's behavior in an effort to win the therapist over to her side. A clear case of transference.

However, this woman's "brothers and sisters" in group have come from very different family settings. As a result, they respond idiosyncratically, evincing their own transference reactions, which are very different from the responses to her that she found in the home.

One woman in the group feels violent toward her; a man, whose only love came in the form of tough criticism, delights in her vehemence; and still another man, whose parents were stony and silent, becomes perplexed and falls silent himself, not knowing what to make of this waspish woman.

The patterns of transferences that go on continually in any group might be charted as a kind of sociogram, with vectors going in many directions. And though few of us would find it useful to compose such a chart and set it to paper, we should think constantly about these patterns. Dissecting these patterns is necessary for us to utilize whole groups at a time in resolving the transferences of our members.

Our most efficient interventions can be made where the largest number of members are involved in a transference pattern. Not only are we helping the most people, but the very size of the cluster we choose determines how much energy we can release for the group to go forward. For instance, if one person's transference provokes reactions in six others, then those six are vitally concerned with the behavior of the involuntary provocateur.

As we study the perception of the person impacting on those six others, we see that all six suddenly come alive. They find increasing amounts to say about what is going on in front of them. When we work with the transference of the person at the center of the circle, we are doing much to resolve the transferences of those six at the periphery.

CHAPTER FOURTEEN

RESOLVING TRANSFERENCES

No simple scheme for resolving transferences can truly do justice to the process, and yet some scheme is needed for presentation. In an effort to suggest an order, I have broken down the process into three major stages.

First, we must direct the spotlight of the group's attention to a member's transference. Second, we reveal the unrealistic expectations involved in the transference. Finally, as the transference is beginning to melt away, we help the group discover how the member developed his or her reactions in early life, those reactions that have become a transference in the group.

As always when doing group therapy, we find it repeatedly necessary to go back to redo our work at some earlier phase in the course of our working at a later one.

The group analyst who thinks of these categories partly as mnemonic devices for what has to be done, and not solely as an order of operations, will find it easier to go back and forth between stages than the analyst who expects to proceed in a rigorous stepwise fashion.

Keeping the Spotlight on the Transference

Most important in resolving transferences is to direct the spotlight of the group's awareness on them. Only to the degree that the group members recognize a person's transference and appreciate the effect that it exerts on them can they be useful as "transference solvents."

We want the group members not just to identify a transference, but to see how it impinges on them, and to make known their own responses to it.

Ideally, we want them to approach the transferential behavior from every angle—pinpointing not just the behavior, but why the person acts as he or she does, and what he wants to accomplish, which is quite different from what he is actually accomplishing. With enough repetition of the proper feedback, the transference will dissipate. As the person comes to recognize his own behavior, and as that behavior becomes seen as futile, it will lose its apparent utility and drop out of his repertoire of thinking and acting. Our job is to keep the group constantly aware of the transference so that they can play their part.

For instance, Arthur's transference from his father to the group members was to curry their favor, to praise them as he did his father for special benefits in the home. I was his chief beneficiary; Arthur would compliment me for my formulations even when I said things that were controversial or tough to take.

As is always the case, even after the group identified Arthur's transference as such, he could not let it go. He continued to curry favor as a way of controlling us all.

I needed the group to play an active role in keeping Arthur fully aware of what he was doing with us. To that end, I invoked Robin, a woman I knew to be *repulsed* by such behavior for reasons of her own. Robin saw Arthur as a sychophant much the way he was with his father. She saw through Arthur's every ploy and held it up to the light. When Arthur would brush her off, I had other members give their impressions.

Of paramount importance was not merely their insight but their frank *statements of how they reacted* when Arthur behaved as he did. Observe that our repetition of bringing any transference to light is not repetition of identical comments. We are not stamping in our message, inculcating it. The group members as they make their comments are doing so variously and with novelty, giving their miscellaneous perceptions because the same transference affects them differently.

Ideally, when we start bringing a transference to light by eliciting reactions to the behavior, we play a part in deciding whose responses will best serve—for instance, we call on members who we think resemble those who evoked the attitudes in the home. A grouchy member might be reminiscent of a grouchy mother, a silent member might be reminiscent of an older brother who was taciturn and never rejoiced in our patient's achievements. Not that such a choice is absolutely necessary, but by making it we simplify the recapitulation that prompts the release of affect. The very options we have in this case, not available to the therapist working with a patient individually, are measures of the values of group therapy, and we do our best not to let these latent values escape us.

Revealing the Unrealistic Expectations of the Transference

In Arthur's mind lurked the unarticulated notion that if he praised me enough, I would bestow full attention on him and ignore his siblings. As a boy, he found real moments in which he could cajole his tight-lipped father this way.

Arthur had lived with the sense that if only he could find the perfect series of compliments, showing ideal appreciation of his father, the man would bless him permanently. And Arthur had the same feeling with me. If he could enthrall me, captivate me with the perfect words, I would be caught in his web. I could be his forever. He had some of the same feelings about certain of the other group members and sought to single them out similarly.

Such an expectation was remarkably at variance with the reality. The more Arthur complimented me, the *less* affinity I felt with him. His comments were distracting. And though Arthur gave little thought to how his peers responded when he exalted me, he was making a pack of enemies by his exclusion of them.

As for Arthur's extolling some of the group members, though he did indeed win a few over to his side for a time, he would isolate his "love objects" from the others and would soon make them uncomfortable. Even those who felt lifted by Arthur's praise saw it as cloying.

Characteristic of transferential intentions is that far from emending the faulty script of childhood, the person rewrites it in almost the same words. He incurs the very reactions that were expressed toward him when the transference was formed.

In Arthur's case, I asked the group what effect they thought he was trying to bring about by his currying favor with me. One after the other, the members commented that Arthur was trying to win me over to his side. He wanted to be like biblical Joseph, to have me give him a many-colored coat, which was to be the signal of his supremacy over his brethren.

I pursued the group for their surmises. Why, in their opinion, did

Arthur see me as like his father, as one who could be gulled into giving him anything he wanted?

They didn't know, but Arthur himself gave reasons. He accused me of favoring certain members who did things I liked. He argued, in particular, that I had praised one person highly for an interpretation of a dream and had supported another for an act that Arthur considered petty. Arthur saw in such moments not the team effort, the comradeship, the encouragement that I thought motivated my actions, but the fact that I was susceptible to blandishments.

Over a series of sessions, the group members themselves speculated about my real motives for what Arthur took to be favoritism toward others. Arthur began to see that his perceptions of me were way off.

In this case, certain moments lent themselves readily to my helping the group and Arthur further distinguish between what he sought and what he got. These were times when Arthur would bellow at me for favoring another member over him.

Arthur's vituperativeness sometimes shocked the other members. For instance, in one case I had excitedly brought the group's attention to the fact that a withdrawn member had spoken up and helped another. That was quite a different matter from praising Arthur because he had spoken well of me. Again and again, the group made comments that helped Arthur see that his whole position was fallacious—a transference.

I also sought to build the bridge from the other side. When Arthur would recall an incident in which he thought his father had been unfair to him, I would ask him if I had treated him with similar brutality. Occasionally, he said yes and cited an example, but more often he allowed that I hadn't. Such comparative inquiries of mine became so regular with Arthur (and I also employed the method with others) that the group members would, on their own, contrast me with the antecedent figures of the lives of such people.

As we reveal any member's unrealistic expectations of present figures, whether or not we mention past ones, we loosen the hold on the transference. At this stage, the transference is still there, but at least the member sees it and can experiment with it, trying new behavior. The mere recognition of one's own hidden agenda, assuming that the person truly does not want to live by that agenda, weakens it.

It is important that when we first suspect a transference, we never oppose the logic of what the person thinks he or she sees.

Sometimes, as in the following case, we must actually fight to be sure that the person gets the floor and is able to express his transference fully. Like Voltaire, we may not agree with what the member says, but we dedicate ourselves to being sure that he has the chance to say it.

A man in my group accused the whole group of being mean to him. At first the others sought to rebut him, defending themselves as sympathetic. But indeed, by their very defense of themselves, they were subverting his chance to express his transference. If anything, they were further convincing him that they had ill intentions toward him.

I therefore held the group off and asked him to tell us in detail exactly how the group as a whole was abusing him. He replied that we would disregard him, cut him off, treat him as if he weren't there.

Next I asked him why he thought we were treating him this way. He told us that we all considered him another burden, someone we hadn't wanted from the beginning. Besides, he added, there were too many people in the group—and no matter who came in, he felt like the one too many.

At that, a group member recalled this man's telling them that he had been an unwanted child and that he had never felt wanted in his own family. Could it be that he still felt unwanted because that had been so pronounced an experience? He saw a possible connection.

In this case, only after the group had accepted his transference, enough to get him to enlarge on the perception, could the member and the rest of us truly understand it.

Weeks later, after the member had become highly conversant with this transference, and saw it for what it was, I asked him what we as a group could do to help him see us differently. He replied at once that we would have to give him plenty of time to talk, and that we would have to show interest.

After that, I made sure that the group took special pains to hear him out. The change in how he saw us was truly dramatic. It was not simply that we were treating him differently. It was, rather, that this member had freed himself to see *us* differently.

Helping a Member Recognize the Beginnings of a Transference in His or Her Early Life

Admittedly, our members can recognize their own self-defeating patterns without knowing where those patterns came from. However, their understanding becomes clearest in many cases when they can see precisely *how and why they began the behavior in question.*

Moreover, the changes that the members produce are most apt to be durable when they are made with this understanding.

With insight into where a transference came from, a member can bring his or her own associations of ideas and feelings into play. He can "third-personalize" himself. For instance, he can say about himself, "Look what Joey's doing, he used to do that as a kid." Implicit in this understanding of the past is the notion, "Joey doesn't have to do that anymore."

Therefore the person who understands the sources of a present anachronistic attitude sees that he has real options in his present life, which he did not, or thought he did not, have in the past. Seeing his past lurking in the present frees him to this extent.

Our helping the group enable a person to see the historical roots of his behavior is invaluable, and we set out to do this as systematically as we can.

Even while doing the rest of our work—of spotlighting and identifying the transferential patterns in our members—we have started to ask ourselves where those patterns came from. Once a group has shown us that it recognizes a member's self-defeating pattern, we may begin our inquiry into the origin of that pattern.

Our most basic approach as usual is to enjoin the group to do the work, and we do this by eliciting speculations from the members about the person's past. The member himself may volunteer some of his own relevant memories, either in reaction to his recent discoveries or if they are triggered when others in the group talk about their past histories.

Always, the fact that group members represent, in his mind, past figures alive and interacting with him right now, is important in jogging those memories.

If the member himself has not spontaneously volunteered a conjecture about how he came to act that way—that is, what he thought or felt as a child that started him on his present track, we pose the question to someone else in the group.

"Jim, you're good at reconstructing people's early lives. Why do you think Mary keeps snubbing the other women in this group?"

"Mark, how do you think Marty got started on those head-trips? What happened to him when he was a little boy that sidetracked him from talking from the heart?"

Among our primary candidates when we ask how a person got started on a pattern in childhood are three kinds of members.

One is the person who has shown himself, or herself, to be an *expert at reconstructing people's pasts.* Certain members have that flair, and we draw upon it.

Second, we might pose our question to *someone whose own childhood resembles that of the member under scrutiny.* Such a person may be at present struggling with the same pattern—shyness, or overintellectualism, or snideness. Or the person may have seen its origin in himself and have largly overcome the problem.

Our third, and perhaps ideal, candidate to ask is *someone who is especially allergic to the behavior in question.*

For instance, one woman in a group has come to see that the instant she feels criticized, she resorts to high-handed, sanctimonious statements. When told that she interrupts, she responds arrogantly that she is only trying to set a proper standard; she declares that she knows decorum better than others, being from a fine family. Over a period of time, we have made her aware of the pattern, and she wants to change herself.

Let us say that we also have in this group a member who always winces at sanctimony. This man has had sanctimonious parents, and hates to be lectured. He is hypersensitive to criticism.

Such a man is perhaps our ideal choice of interlocutor for the woman. We ask him, "Hank, whatever do you think got Mary started on telling other people how to live?"

Or if Hank is psychologically sophisticated, we might ask him who he thinks Mary modeled herself after when she was a child.

Hank might not answer our question directly, but refer to his own early life. He might begin talking about his mother, for instance. Even so, we're satisfied, because the issue of how Mary got started remains alive and present. We have loosed Hank's energetic involvement with the subject.

Mary herself, on hearing Hank talk about his own life, might remember facts about her past. Or other members, tuning in, might talk about the role of sanctimony in their lives. Above all, we have established in the room an atmosphere of historicity—of curiosity about the past.

Observe that in the first two cases, in which we called upon people for direct answers, we were perhaps more likely to get them than in the third.

But the third approach, in which person-to-person energy is released and the subject comes alive in the room, is far more beneficial in the long run. The topic of where a pattern came from stays alive and current. When this happens, we are almost sure to keep the whole room involved in the topic of where modes of perceptions come from generally, a subject akin to how to change them.

How to plumb the origins of a transference is a theme that arises over and over again in the work of group therapists.

Paradoxically, we deliberately avoid the shortest route in our inquiry about a member's past. We are not private detectives hired to track down facts about an individual in the briefest possible time. As always, we are working with a whole group, even as we discuss the individual—here, it is his or her past life. Our aim, therefore, must be to involve many people at once in our inquiry, even when it seems directed at the individual.

By getting many members to participate, we are inducing these many to look back over their own histories. Accordingly, what seems like a circuitous approach is really the most time-saving one, so far as the whole group is concerned.

Ideally, virtually everything we do as group therapists involves bridging, and our uncovering the roots of transference is no exception.

Many therapists who work with patients individually believe, as Freud posited, that the resolution of the transference is virtually synonymous with cure. We group therapists share this notion to some degree.

And there is a major difference between our work and that of the individual therapist, which allows us to delve into the past in a way they cannot.

The psychotherapist working with an individual patient becomes the object of a succession of transferences; they typically follow a time sequence as the patient grows up in treatment. This is true whether the patient goes forward, or backward through a series of regressions.

As group analysts, we supply the potential for a *simultaneity* of transferences. Our patient sees not just a father, if we are male and that is his transference, but a father-in-the-presence-of-a-mother, as, for instance, when a man reacts with transference jealousy to our paying prolonged attention to a woman in the group. Without our even being aware that we are doing so, we present complex patterns of experience to our group members.

For example, a man may see three aspects of his real mother in three different women in a group—and, more than that, he experiences these transferences simultaneously.

One woman in the group may represent the loving but judgmental mother who watched him critically in his earliest years.

A second woman he takes to be the mother who needs him and needs his loyalty against a father with whom she often argued, especially during his adolescence.

A third woman in the group arouses in him the feelings he has toward the mother he must deal with now, a woman who, especially since her husband's death, clings to him but often becomes furious at him.

Instead of having to talk about such "mothers"—about how he experienced them and what he did in their presence—he shows by his behavior in group who these mothers were. We learn about these mothers through his transference, even before he is able to tell us.

COUNTERREACTIONS TO TRANSFERENCE EXPRESSIONS

Because transferences are, by their very definition, anachronistic responses—imports from situations other than the present one—it is to be expected that whenever a group member acts transferentially, his or her behavior will trigger transferences in others, reactions as anachronistic as the first person's reaction.

As an example, Beverly, a woman in a group of mine, stopped a man abruptly when he raised his voice. Beverly announced to the group at large that she would acknowledge only people who spoke softly and politely to her. As soon as anyone shouted, she announced, she would treat the person as if he or she weren't there.

A few of the members were amused, as they always were when Beverly spoke from on high; she could hardly moderate the world that way, and it struck them as funny that she thought she could.

However, one man, Jonathan, almost went berserk, lighting into Beverly, calling her "stuck-up and controlling."

Scarcely had Jonathan spoken when another man, Arthur, raised his hand for permission to speak. With undue softness, Arthur sought to assure Jonathan that Beverly had really meant no harm; if she had seemed to control people, her intention was simply to be heard.

It took very little time to establish that there were almost as many perceptions of Beverly's quiet control as there were members in the room.

These reactions prompted Beverly to try to explain herself. She felt overwhelmed, she told us, and went on to remember how her father had terrified the household by his bellowing, which was characteristically followed by long periods of unwelcome silence. Ever since then, Beverly realized, she was virtually phobic about people who raised their voices.

This was a simple recognition of a transference reaction on the part of an individual.

However, I noted that Jonathan seemed stunned when Beverly spoke so revealingly about herself. I had guessed that Jonathan himself was on the verge of some kind of discovery. Rather than turn to Jonathan, I described his reaction and asked if anyone could explain it.

Saintly Arthur recalled that Jonathan had said things suggesting that his own mother was an acid person who controlled people.

That was all the prompting Jonathan needed. He told us at once that he would become terribly hurt at home after his most exuberant moments. Not even listening to what he was so exuberant about, his mother would respond only to his raised voice, cautioning him to be quiet at once.

"Johnny, please. People next door have their own affairs. Just speak softly, the way mother does."

Jonathan told us about an incident when he was eight and his mother took him to a ball game. That was in Cleveland, where he grew up, and he loved the Cleveland Indians. As he remembered it, his team was trailing in a key game in the pennant race, but the Indians loaded the bases in a late inning. Then Jonathan's favorite outfielder hit a single to put Cleveland ahead, and the whole stadium went wild.

"I screamed with delight," Jonathan told us, now on the verge of tears, "and I must have spilled my mother's coffee. She scowled at me and pinched me hard and called me an idiot. She said, 'You don't have to scream in my ear. Look what you did to the coffee.' At that moment I swore to myself that I'd never go to another game with her and I'd move out as soon as I was old enough."

No one even had to sum up why Jonathan hated controlling

women. He was understandably allergic to them and repelled by them because of these experiences with his mother. And women who were not controlling, if they even expressed preferences, he was quite quick to condemn as controlling.

Jonathan, in telling this story, could feel the group's support of him, and was buoyed by it. A conflict inside of him was resolved, and he felt surer of himself, more of one piece.

The next time saintly Arthur sought to subdue him, Jonathan turned on him. "Look, Arthur, I don't need you to tell me how to act. If I want to get upset, I will. You've got a great need to keep peace everywhere, and you better get over it."

The members could see that this was so—Arthur could explain anything away—they realized that he had a compulsive need to induce amity between opposing forces. Arthur would do anything, the group came to see, to reconcile people. In the end, such behavior merely stifled people and thwarted the understanding that was necessary for true reconciliation.

This too proved a transference reaction. A month later, a woman prone to say nearly anything that came to her mind, got furious at Arthur for telling her she should understand someone in the group. "I'm not your mother," she shouted at Arthur, "You don't have to hold your family together. Give us some room, will you."

Three transferences, which had sprung up in minutes, and which had given rise to one another, were on the way to being resolved.

Obviously, no merely written statement can do justice to the complexity of relationships among even these three transferences, which were expressed not just once but repeatedly. The point is that transferences prompt others, and the spirit in which transferences become examined and resolved is also contagious. As a group helps one member trace the roots of his or her own reaction, they are glimpsing the roots of their own.

The discovery of transference reactions and their resolutions is thus a process that occurs simultaneously in many minds. The group therapist's task is to realize this and to keep the process in motion.

The early psychoanalysts, who equated resolution of transference with cure, were in a sense right, but in another sense, optimistic. In this chapter, I've described methods and a process. However, as with all personal change, there is a strong need to confirm it, before it becomes reliable. The philosopher Blaise Pascal's comment that "nature is second habit" applies not merely to behavior but to *habits of mind*—to patterns of thinking and experiencing.

Even as we work with group members, they are confirming their personal discoveries ("stamping them in," to use the language of the behaviorists) in their everyday life.

But there is more that we can do, that we must do, to help our group members experience these changes as comfortable and natural. We have not completed our task until they are able to do this.

CHAPTER FIFTEEN

CONFIRMING NEW IDENTITIES

Of course, people don't change all at once. Traits need time to grow. This is true whether we are talking about openness of mind, or confidence, or the assumption of freedom, or the ability to love. First the seedlings appear. Then, in accordance with Goethe's maxim that what we nourish within ourselves grows, we see a trait blossoming, and finally it blooms.

In group therapy terms, this means that we see a new trait only in moments at the start.

Henry, who constantly cavils and bemoans the fact that no one cares about him, misses a session because of back trouble. He walks stiffly when he returns. Diana tells him that she missed him, and she asks him how his back is now.

"Bad," replies Henry curtly. However, he then adds, chiding the others obliquely, "At least somebody here noticed that I came in here like a cripple. I couldn't get out of bed this morning. It's a miracle that I got here."

At that, Diana, feeling dismissed, waves her hand in front of Henry and chides him lightly. "Hey, Henry, that *someone* is me, Diana. *I* was the one who asked about your back."

Henry smiles, taking her in. He nods almost grudgingly. "Oh, yes, yes," he says, embarrassed. "Oh yes, I thought about you this week."

Progress on the part of a man who never allowed that he'd thought about another group member before?

Yes, it was progress, but only the seedling of the progress in store for Henry.

At this stage, we might almost expect Henry to withdraw, to neglect Diana in the next session, implying that no one notices him—and acting in ways that would ensure such an outcome next time. But even if Henry does withdraw, there has been movement, and we must content ourselves with what we achieved. Henry's having recognized another member even once has changed him, though not significantly as yet.

A few weeks later, Henry tells the group with animation how he just succeeded in a business deal that afternoon. With only slight prompting, he lets us know that he's proud of what he did. Months after this, he begins making more comments about others in the room—he notices them. He takes pains not to be late. He shows interest in how the group is running, and for the first time, when told by another man that he neglected the person, he doesn't recoil.

The following week he surprises us all by asking his last week's critic to tell him exactly how he neglected that person. Apparently, thoughts about the group have come into Henry's mind all week.

When again he expresses curiosity about the charge that he neglected someone in the room, he lets on that his wife has often accused him of being self-absorbed; Henry is beginning to think that there may be something to what she says.

Without being aware of it, Henry is resolving transferences toward other group members; he is behaving differently, he is coming to life. He is developing the traits of caring and of showing-that-he-cares, by repetition. He is changing in a way so fundamental that his whole life may assume a different course.

In this brief account, I have not referred to our techniques of helping him change; the group has made contributions at every stage in many ways described in this book. And there are other contributions we also make as change occurs.

The question before us now is how do we help Henry solidify his change and make it durable? More generally, how may we help any member confirm his gains—feel natural and effortless with what he or she has accomplished? This implies that the person's change must not merely be manifest in the group where it is learned, it must manifest itself more broadly. Ideally, the change is so sweeping that even where the person himself doesn't recognize it, or yet feel natural with his new identity, others point out the change.

For instance, we might expect Henry to be surprised when someone in his office tells him that he looks happy these days.

"Why?" he asks, and the person tells him that he comes across as much warmer, that he isn't moody the way he used to be, that he seems more concerned with other people's interests. Or someone else might tell him he is easier to talk to. Or even if no one characterizes him, Henry finds himself invited to more places, cherished by more people; he feels more at home in the world.

All this may take place possibly without Henry's even recognizing his own agency in bringing this progress about. At this stage, Henry no longer needs the group as prompters for his gain. He may use the group for new insights and advantages, to learn and practice new skills, but there is what the social psychologist Gordon Allport called "a functional autonomy" in what Henry has accomplished. He is not doing anything to impress the group or to create any impact, for that matter. Were he to leave the group tomorrow, Henry's change would be durable.

There are a variety of contributions that the group may make to foster the kind of development just described.

Five salient ones are (1) modeling the new trait, (2) observing even rudiments of the new trait in action and remarking on their presence, (3) using regressions creatively, (4) helping the member see his or her line of progress, and finally, (5) immunizing the member against regression by submitting him to trial under fire.

Modeling the New Trait

By modeling a new trait, we mean the enactment of a trait by others, a trait that a person is learning for the first time, or is seeking to enlarge in his personality. Modeling may be thought of as demonstrating a standard.

Invariably, whatever trait is being replaced has a strong transference component. The member has been operating, at least in part, under an illusion, one that he evolved from prior experience, usually in early life. For instance, it was one thing for Henry to see what he did and how it harmed him, quite another for him to comprehend an alternative—that is, to comprehend an alternative for *him*. Sure, others showed interest in one another, but Henry never had openly accepted people and literally didn't know how.

Lacking precedent in his own experience for what he now wished to do, Henry found it particularly hard to change, even to try out new and warmer modes of expression. To Henry, what he should change *to* remained at least a partial enigma.

At first during his group experience, Henry didn't even recognize how different from him other people were; he didn't see that they addressed one another more warmly than he addressed them. While Henry had been oblivious to people's expressions of genuine warmth and caring, he had suffered an inexplicable sense of being excluded. To Henry, with his "blind spot," it had seemed that people all played favorites with one another at his expense.

As he became aware that he was in fact dealing with others coldly, Henry was in a quandary. He had no alternative behavior with which to replace his lifetime mode.

My having the group model such new behavior became critical for him. They had to demonstrate in their behavior alternatives that Henry would find preferable to his former mode.

For instance, one day Marie, a woman in Henry's group, attacked me for something I'd said. Henry, agreeing with Marie, assailed me also—even more vehemently. Later, when Marie turned on Henry in anger regarding another matter, Henry was stunned and called her an ingrate for the support he had given her. Now it was Marie's turn to be surprised. She had no recollection of Henry's showing her any support or compassion.

When asked, the group attested that it perceived things the way Marie did. If Henry had indeed shown her gallantry or loyalty or kindness, they certainly hadn't seen it.

I turned toward Janice, also in the group, and asked her in effect to model the kind of warm comment that Henry might have made. "Janice, what might Henry have said that would have given Marie a sense that he really cared for her?"

Janice responded at once, "Marie, I loved the way you kept yourself centered while you made your point. You didn't yell like you used to, and you stayed logical."

Marie smiled broadly and thanked Janice, and then turned toward Henry and agreed that such a presentation would have meant a lot to her. Henry listened to the comment with profound interest, especially because he saw Marie so affected by Janice's formulation.

As such modeling was repeated, Henry became slowly able to grasp his real alternative. Being dour and argumentative were sorry substitutes for the modes of expression Henry was now learning firsthand.

I kept inviting the group members to suggest variations on the theme of reaching people through warmth. Henry found more and more phrases that he could use.

The mere comprehension that an old mode is injurious or pointless may mean little until the person finds new, replacement modes. And we use the group to model those modes.

As the member's consciousness of the direction he would like to take is heightened, he begins to see models all around him—people who express themselves in ways that once felt forbidden to him. Having taken the suggestions that were offered by other group members very deliberately to help him, a person in the process of change broadens his perception. First the group and then the world becomes his school. Thus Henry might seize a phrase from one person and a style from another, constructing a trait in the only way that people ever acquire traits—through conscious and unconscious imitation.

Remarking on the New Behavior

As a member evolves any new and more flexible mode of acting with other people, shucking off some past limitation, it's only natural that others in the group will respond differently. Some among the members, especially if invited to do so, will comment on the new behavior and tell the person how it makes them feel.

We welcome such highlighting of favorable changes—indeed, we want members to have the largess to point them out. A sizable benefit of learning in the group setting is that even rudiments of positive change can be seen and appreciated. The person who has struggled for a lifetime, showing occasional sparks of behavior that would afford him huge benefits, becomes enlightened if we do our job instead of lapsing without ever seeing the way.

With our assistance, the group can point out the way, pave the path, and help the member recognize that he has already chosen his direction.

We have various devices to spur a group to do this.

Rick was the oldest son of a rather gross but successful salesman. His father virtually never really listened to people. His idea of a relationship was that of a monologue with the other person. He saw himself as a bon vivant, and would tell one joke after another, not pausing to consider how the person was receiving him. When on rare occasions the other person did talk, Rick's father would respond with a quip or with a comment that he thought was funny. Not surprisingly, he had no real friends.

Rick, in his father's likeness, had many acquaintances but no real friends. However, slowly, with the group's help, he began to appreciate how he had been pushing people away and what his alternative was. After a number of months, he began showing signs of authentic response to people.

Observing that several members who had shunned Rick in the group were beginning to react well to him, I asked one of them, Jerry, how he felt about Rick at that moment.

Jerry answered, "This is the Rick I could see introducing to my friends."

Seeing someone else smile, I turned to that person and asked him what his opinion was. He explained, "Rick, what you said was great. You stayed right on the other person's level."

A few weeks later, I realized that a woman in the group, whom Rick had especially estranged by his heavy-handed disregard of her, was coming around to responding to him. She actually agreed with something he said—a great rarity for her. I knew even before turning to her that she could articulate what Rick needed to hear. I asked her what had occasioned this change in her.

She replied, "Well, first of all, Rick is right. Second, I noticed that he was making a real connection with the other person. I didn't feel he was just showing off."

Another way of helping the group note Rick's new behavior was to draw general attention to the way the members were dealing with him.

I mentioned to a member, "Last month, you didn't seem to notice Rick. Now there seems to be a lot of rich give-and-take between you and him. How come?"

When the member replied that he felt more at ease with Rick, I asked him to explain. He said something to the effect that he no longer felt so defensive with Rick. At that, others chimed in, saying that they too felt more relaxed in talking with Rick. Then, spontaneously, the group volunteered its own observations of how Rick had evolved.

This method of having Rick realize his progress through its impact on the other members is especially strong. Not just the change but the *benefit* of the change to Rick provided special incentive to him to continue changing in the same way.

Even after most of the members could recognize Rick's change and how they were responding to it, I kept bringing it to their attention. At the end of one session, I asked the group if anyone noticed how engaged with the group Rick had been that day. There was a general murmur of agreement.

Observing changes is a ceaseless process for the group therapist. It is not so much that we ourselves point out and underscore changes that benefit the person; if anything, we subdue this tendency in ourselves so that the person will not perceive himself or herself as changing for our benefit, to win our favor. Rather we facilitate the group's noting the member's progress.

Among our best informants concerning changes a member has accomplished are other members who have been previously hurt by that person's old behavior—those who have felt neglected or attacked and now feel welcome.

Also potentially precious as informants are members who have struggled much as this person now is struggling, and who have partially or fully overcome the problem. For instance, a member whose accomplishment is in standing up for himself against opposition may find an appreciative audience in another member who similarly overcame a fear of asserting herself.

There is a more general truth here. Those who have grappled with a problem that is now daunting a member are especially able to appreciate his efforts—both his successes and his failures.

Using Regressions Creatively

Naturally, group members never progress in a straight line, and we must learn to expect any member to revert to behavior that the person seemed to have outgrown. How are we to deal with these moments of regression, which are the rule rather than the exception?

Of course, we can't beleaguer a person whenever he or she acts below his "age level"; however, some monitoring of progress and noting of regressions is in order.

Sarah, who formerly broke into tears when she got angry, has recently come to express that anger in words. At best, she is quite articulate and is able to hold her ground against adversaries. However, especially when the person who confronts Sarah is an older man, she still reverts to tears on occasion.

We have learned from prior discussions that Sarah uses tears to instill guilt in others and that she began doing this with her father in the home. It comes as no surprise that Sarah still melts when she experiences an older man as assailing her. We see Sarah comport herself brilliantly with others, but when Fred, the group's elder statesman, finds fault with Sarah, we find in front of us a little girl sobbing because her father doesn't love her.

However tempted we are to point out the regression, it behooves us not to say anything for a time, so that Sarah herself can compare her present behavior with the pattern she has recently acquired. Ideally, she will stop herself, observing in effect, "There I go again. This is getting me nowhere," in which case, what we witness is a sudden turnaround. After sobbing, she rights herself and warns her adversary to stop attacking her. Sarah has brought her newly acquired awareness into the hardest amphitheater of all, the one most reminiscent of the theater in which her old behavior, the sobbing for mercy, was adopted.

Only when necessary do we intervene, and then, as always, it must be through the group members. We might, for instance, turn to a man who we think is prompting Sarah's regression reaction, and ask him outright, "Are you behaving like Sarah's father?"

When I did exactly this, in one case, the man, whom I've called Fred, replied, "Not at all, I'm behaving like myself." The group agreed—in reality, Fred wasn't really attacking her at all.

"So why is she crying?" I asked another member.

He explained that Sarah was responding not to Fred but to somebody in her mind.

That proved enough for Sarah to banish her tears.

Another way of dealing with regression is to turn to the person doing the regressing or to others in the room.

More than once, I turned directly to Sarah, asking her what she was trying to tell us by her tears, or to Fred himself, or to someone else in the group, asking them the same question about Sarah.

Sooner or later, if we have done our spadework, someone in the group—the regressing person or another member—will observe that a regressive pattern is in evidence.

A variation of this approach is to ask the person regressing or another member what seems to be going on that prompts the regressive behavior. "Is there anything special that Fred said that is causing Sarah to revert to tears?"

And when Rick, the bon vivant, resurrected his practice of telling jokes instead of facing his feelings, I whimsically asked the group, "Do you think I should charge Rick a double fee?"

Rick looked shocked and asked me why.

I posed the question to the group, and, sure enough, someone said, "You mean because Rick is two people."

The group then puzzled out that we had in front of us today the old Rick, who always told jokes especially to mask his fondness for a woman, and the new Rick, who could say openly that he cared for a woman. The image of "split personality" became a temporary label for Rick, who was, after that, better able to spot his own use of humor and to examine it rather than simply give in to it.

Our most obvious, though least dramatic, way of coping with regressions might be described as the brute-force method. We treat the regressive behavior not as a reversion but simply as an instance of the kind of behavior we encountered when we began working with the member. That is, we disregard any concept of a gradient along which the person has moved, and we deal with the behavior existentially—as if it were fresh material.

Whatever we did at the start to resolve the pattern, such as having the group bring it to the person's attention, helping specific members investigate it, helping the person resolve the underlying problem—we do again. We go through the exact same steps.

Predictably, our task will be easier because the member has a history of insight and of progress to draw upon. The member is traversing a somewhat familiar road. However, in this version we make no special reference to the person's history, and even if the member or someone else does, we might choose to let it go. This method has the advantage that we seem to be omni-accepting, we are not making progress reports, we are not disappointed in the regression.

Members will often attack themselves for regressions, as if they expected their own progress to be linear. We know better. We explain to the group in our own words that reversions are the rule, not the exception. In letting them know that all progress consists of taking two steps forward and one back, we are modeling a kind of permissiveness that we hope they will incorporate. In some cases, that very self-acceptance that a member may achieve in our presence is even more important than the person's acquisition of the new pattern.

Helping Members See Their Line of Progress

As mentioned, personal attainments come gradually, are lost and recovered, and at times even those members who advance most directly are apt to feel that they've forfeited everything—that they're worse off than then when they started.

In fact, stark progress is typically accompanied by a feeling of loss. This is because there have been benefits and a sense of the familiar in even the most self-destructive modes of living—there are what we call "secondary gains." Were it not for these "benefits," our group members would hardly need us, they would proceed on their own to what was best for them.

Then too, progress brings new challenges, new awarenesses —and in this sense, new penalties. In short, even when a person has just achieved something he has always wanted, it may feel to that person that he has achieved nothing.

One of our functions is to perceive progress, to retain a sense of what our members were, what they lacked, and what they are attaining. We are like photographers hovering in a hot-air balloon above a battlefield, watching an army march, engage in skirmishes, retreat, and then march forward again. To the foot soldiers, it will surely seem at times that nothing is being accomplished, but we see otherwise, and especially in their darker moments we help the group apprise particular individuals of what they have attained.

Before considering interventions, it must be noted that we need a clear sense of where our members have come from, of what they were at the outset, and of where they are headed.

In our very first screening session, we will surely form certain impressions—for instance, we see melancholy, or a tendency to complain, or a floating sense of disappointment in the member. Or we see strengths not utilized: intelligence or a lyrical gift for words in a person with low self-esteem.

It is useful to make careful notes of what we see in this screening session (surely not by writing them down in front of the member, but by noting them in our own minds), because once we are under way in our efforts to work with the person, we may forget those earlier impressions and the larger picture.

Especially during our first few months of working with the person, we do a lot more observing than confronting. We study who the member is and where he is heading. We watch how the member interacts with others, for better and for worse.

And as we watch, we note his abilities and liabilities with others. We may see congruences between what happens to the person in our group and what he describes happening to him in his life away from us, and if the person doesn't talk about his life outside of the group, we form surmises. Perhaps our single most repeated question to ourselves is, "How does this person get in his own way, and why?"

Our language is that of the group—for instance, we ask, "How does he arrange to have the group overlook him or not take him seriously?" Or "How does he induce resentment in others?"

Such questions will soon serve us as markers, as buoys to which we can refer when the person has dealt with these initial obstacles but feels adrift because he has confronted same brand-new problem. Not until he is dealt with the initial hazards of his own personality was he or she even in a position to face the new problem. New challenges are an eternal cost of progress. But daunted by them, the member may not recognize that he has even accomplished anything, though from our vantage point, we can see that he has.

It becomes important that the group convey that he has, so that even in despair the member may feel solaced by the recognition of what he has already achieved.

Ideally, we formulate the problem in a few words. For instance, Matthew is a man who will do almost anything to avoid disappointing a woman. The group has made him aware that he will promise the moon to assuage a woman's wrath, or to head off even her mild disapproval.

Out of anxiety, Matthew has repeatedly promised too much to women, and in the end has disappointed them all. In our group, we soon spotted this, and thought of him with the mnemonic "Matthew, the calmer of women."

We were careful not to use this phrase aloud, it was for our benefit alone. But we kept it in mind as we watched Matthew week after week, and it reminded us of where he had come from and of how he would have to evolve.

We may use this mnemonic repeatedly to orient ourselves. It will bob up in our minds.

For instance, after eight months, the group has helped Matthew recognize that as the ostensible champion of women, he has typically been dishonest with them. He has curried favor with them and inhibited their freedom. They are on to him, and he has gained glimmerings of insight into what he has done all his life. Partly liberated by this insight, tonight Matthew suddenly lets loose, telling a woman in the group that she is relentless and hard and that he can't stand her. He pulls no punches.

For Matthew, this is progress. However, when the woman wilts and starts to cry, Matthew regresses. He disavows everything he has said and apologizes remorsefully. He feels villainous and guilty. Matthew proclaims to the group that he is getting nowhere. He feels utterly lost, contending that he has made no progress whatsoever and cannot even picture improving.

Suddenly, two women in the group speak up in unison, both telling Matthew that things are quite the opposite, that they like him better now than they ever did. But when I ask them why, they can identify only that he seems somehow more accessible.

My phrase "Matthew, the calmer of women" comes to mind. I realize that for the first time in my recollection, Matthew has forgone his impulse to soothe a woman, and has spoken his mind. It occurs to me that his new expression of freedom represents great progress and that, understandably, he is frightened because he has changed.

However, rather than say this aloud, I turned to the group, and asked of another man in the room, "What do you think Matthew is so afraid of?"

The man responded cryptically, "New terrain."

When I asked this man what he meant, he explained that he thought that because Matthew was used to pleasing women, this was a new land, one in which Matthew felt unsure of himself.

"You mean when he says what he thinks to a woman, he feels scared?" I echoed.

Several other group members agreed that this was the case. In the very moment when "Matthew, the calmer" felt most lost, he was indeed finding himself. The group helped him see this. After that, they could appreciate Matthew's development and more than once reminded him of it when he felt desolate.

Especially when a group member laments aloud that he or she is the same as when he started, when in fact we are clear that the person has progressed, we can invite the group to help him see landmarks that indicate that progress has been made.

In some cases, we may do this by having the group remind the person that he is doing something differently.

Not long ago, a man whom I'll call Richard had temporarily lost sight of excellent progress he had made. Richard had come to the group as a chronic blamer; he would find fault with the other members and with the whole therapy process whenever things went wrong. This mirrored Richard's tendency in life to blame others for his failures.

As he began to recognize his own hand in his life and to see both his successes and failures as due to his own acts, he naturally felt worse in some ways, not better. Richard's very progress of self-awareness at times made him feel that he was going backward. He suffered the near-universal tendency, upon discovering a trait, to see it as ubiquitous in his nature and unalterable.

During one of those thorny moments, Richard moaned to the group, "I can't do anything right. I don't know what I'm doing here."

I turned to a woman in the group and asked her, "What's the difference between what Richard is saying now and what he used to say?"

She replied at once that last year Richard would attack the group whenever he felt bad. "Now he attacks himself."

"You mean that Richard has merely switched targets?" I asked.

At that, the group as a whole chimed in. "No, this is a lot better. Richard is looking at himself, and he just doesn't like what he's starting to see."

From there, it was an easy realization for Richard that this was of fundamental value, that things had changed. Richard's seeing his own part in creating problems was a necessary step toward his averting those problems.

In other cases, when, even after accomplishing something real in group, a member feels tempest-tossed and hopeless, we can help him appreciate his real attainment indirectly. This is to have him appreciate that other people *respond to him more favorably*. The fact that people are regularly more responsive and sympathetic to the member than they used to be is not due to mere familiarity. He has been treating them differently or he would not have evoked these better reactions from them.

We have a very subtle message to convey. "Though right now you don't realize that you are different, proof that you are is the fact that people like you much better than they used to."

To help the group convey this, we can ask another member outright, "What's the difference between the way you feel about Linda now and the way you felt about her during that first year?"

If we have chosen the right member to ask, and have done our job well, we will get an answer.

"I like her a lot better." Or "I'm much less afraid of her anger." Or "At least, I know that she won't hold a grudge for three weeks."

More often than not, our asking one member to note evident change in another brings not merely an answer but an explanation. "I feel different about him because . . ." That explanation is the very thing we want made explicit.

The answers we elicit might be sheer statements of good feeling toward the member, or statements left unexplained, in which case we may follow them up, asking the person why he feels as he does about the member.

Here, as always, consensus is likely to mean a great deal to the member being discussed. For a whole group to aver that it feels more secure with a member carries a highly persuasive charge.

And by the way, on occasion the fact that a group turns against a member who was formerly accepted, may be a marker of that member's changing for the better. The member might, for instance, have discarded a manipulative trick that held people at bay and elicited positive response but was costly to that person himself. He was perhaps too much of a "crowd pleaser" and paid a price by not asking for what he wanted.

Or if the group itself has a bias, perhaps even a brutal one, then their coming to dislike a member who declares himself, or herself, for the first time can be a good sign. A woman, unhappily married for years, gets a divorce to preserve her sanity, and the group, unable to tolerate her new demand for independence, expresses annoyance at her. This time, their change in attitude toward the member is from like to dislike, but that change nonetheless signifies progress by the member.

Finally, we might help the member appreciate that his own perception of others is different, even though he or she doesn't think it is. For instance, he is less afraid of saying things that might pain others than he used to be—ergo, he is less afraid of people. The fact that he behaves differently implies that he must perceive others differently.

Always we evoke our critical insights through the group members rather than merely stating them ourselves. For us to state them outright would be counterproductive in many ways. We would be inviting the member either to change only in order to please us, or to defy us by not changing. We would be reducing the arena of his efforts to change to that of the transference.

On the other hand, to the degree that he perceives himself as changing against the backdrop of the whole group, he is changing himself-in-the-world, and that change will be lasting.

And always our guiding reason obtains for having the group participate in all progress of the individual members. Whatever the other group members do for the individual, they are simultaneously doing for themselves. Here, as they inform a member about unacknowledged progress he has made, they are informing themselves about their own progress.

Our group members are never mere bystanders witnessing an individual's progress, but are agents in their own journey, even as they discuss another person's.

Paradoxically, to the extent that we are truly successful in helping people change, our members may complain about us and our work. The person who has changed for the better will take the position that he hasn't changed at all, and that the whole therapy process is worthless. And if he does, the group or at least a subset will cite evidence that he has changed and will attempt to reassure him that he has.

IMMUNIZATION

As with anyone who has evolved a trait in recent months, our group members remain liable to regressions.

For instance, when subject to more than ordinary stress, the member who has recently learned to take criticism in stride may revert to tears or to vehemence designed to stymie a well-intended critic.

Or, for instance, the person who has recently come to accept his or her aggression may, when becoming acutely annoyed at another group member, go numb as he used to before his gain.

Whatever the gain, even after the member has accomplished it and sees that he has, even after the group sees and appreciates what the person has done, there remains a risk of regression under stress.

Freud once likened personality structure to a crystal, which when hurled to the ground would shatter in what seems like a random way. As Freud put it, just the way a trained jeweler using his loop might have predicted the exact ways the shattering would occur, a trained psychoanalyst might have inferred how personality would shatter, or at least regress under pressure. And the prediction would be that the member would return to behavior and attitudes held prior to his evolution to his higher level of functioning.

Our final task in helping our members confirm their new identities is that of *immunizing* them against such regressions. Not that we can do so infallibly, but there are techniques that the group therapist can use that help the members solidify their gains—techniques of immunization.

Willard, a man in a group of mine, used to become frantic at even the slightest suggestion that he talked down to women. Yet it was obvious that he did. For a long time, Willard would never mention his wife, except to say that she was good in bed. In the group, when a woman made a point, Willard would seem hardly to be listening, and he literally turned his chair at an oblique angle more than once when a woman was talking.

For Willard, being corrected by a woman, having a woman tell him that he was amiss in any way, was the supreme insult. Let this happen, and before the woman finished her second sentence, Willard would berate her in the foulest language he could muster. Several people reminded Willard that he was breaking the group contract by such attacks, but to no avail.

For a time, women kept their distance and didn't criticize Willard (in the process avoiding him altogether), but after a while a few women brooked his wrath in order to raise their own self-esteem.

It took many months for the group to help Willard see how defensively hostile toward women he was. Willard continued to fight the painful insight and the vulnerability to women that it implied. However, Willard gradually did come to appreciate that he was treating women as enemy aliens, that he sharply differentiated between the sexes in favor of men.

Then slowly Willard thawed out. Gradually, the women in the group, who had kept a safe distance from Willard, approached him. They began talking to him as an equal and Willard enjoyed this greatly. He reported better relationships with some women in his outside life.

Still, the question remained. How strong was this change, how robust? Could it stand the pressure of the unexpected? If a new woman in Willard's life, most likely one he encountered in business, proved to be sexist and somewhat unfair to Willard, would he revert to overkill? Would he become the Willard of old, the slayer of women?

It was important for Willard to solidify his change, to insulate himself against panic when criticized by a woman, so that he would no longer lose his composure and make a bad situation worse.

Immunization was called for. The prime function of immunization is to strengthen newly formed patterns, so that the group member who has formed those patterns can count on them. A secondary function of immunization is that we determine for ourselves how general the gain is, and how lasting it is likely to be.

The method of immunization is that of meting out small doses of the very stimulus that previously disabled the person and induced his regression. We *want* women to criticize Willard—not in giant doses but in small ones; and we want this not just for the sake of the women in the group but so that Willard can test his mettle and strengthen it.

Accordingly, we might deliberately select a woman in Willard's group, Clara, who is struggling to speak her mind to men. Moments after Willard has held forth too long on a subject, we turn to Clara. "Clara, how is Willard doing? What's your impression of what he just said?"

Clara tells us, in the process criticizing Willard mildly for going on at too great length.

We watch Willard squirming in his chair. We imagine that he is resisting his old impulse to counter her comments and to assail her, but, it seems to us, that at least this time Willard is aware of his impulse. Perhaps he survives what seems to him like a brutal onslaught.

If he does, we want to have the group underscore this accomplishment. We might turn to another member, and ask that person how Willard fared in listening to Clara's criticism. The person compliments Willard, perhaps adding that he himself could not have held still as long for the same critique. We have immunized Willard just a little by helping him appreciate that he can endure a woman's critique, that even when a woman points out a fault of his he may profit. Willard is a hero.

However, we haven't finished. Suppose the pressure on Willard were even greater. Would he crack, like the crystal?

We have in our group Sarah, who has had great problems with men, in part owing to her sharp intelligence. Sarah has lost more than one relationship after speaking tartly to a man who then felt demeaned by her. Actually, putting a man down was the furthest thing from her intention, but Sarah has long been wary, not being able to distinguish blazons of her own intelligence from true assaults. Sarah has become gun-shy with men, finding it almost impossible to be at ease with a man for fear of saying something abrasive that would devastate him.

The next time we want a critique of Willard we choose Sarah to move the immunization process along.

A few weeks after the last incident, Willard is boasting to the group of how he outwitted a competitor in a business deal. His listeners range from slightly bored to sorely annoyed. Noting a dour look on Sarah's face, I asked her if anything Willard just said had rubbed her the wrong way.

I had created an obvious conflict for Sarah—that between telling the truth, which would possibly trigger Willard's rage, and saying nothing and pandering to Willard's pomposity.

In the actual case, Sarah rose to the challenge of giving her opinion to a man and considering his feelings at the same time. She told Willard carefully that though perhaps he hadn't realized it, he had been going on without taking his audience into account enough.

Sarah finished by saying, "Actually, I'd personally prefer it if you connected with the people right here, in the group."

But even that felt tougher to Willard than anything he'd had to endure in a while.

"Are you criticizing me?" Willard asked flatly.

"I'm not really trying to," Sarah said, and smiled. "I'm sorry if I hurt your feelings, but I do have to speak my mind."

"You didn't hurt my feelings," Willard said, softening. "I just wanted to be sure of what was going on." He laughed with relief.

Both people had reached a milestone. Willard had not regressed, but had showed himself more robust than he had been. He had proven to himself and the group that he could tolerate being criticized by a woman without retaliating. He had endured his moment of immunization without side effects, and was stronger, less likely than ever to regress inside the group or out. Sarah too had progressed: in her case toward freer expression to men.

With immunization, we titrate our dosage as physicians do. We increase the stress by introducing more challenging situations into the members' group experience. If a situation proves too challenging, we reduce the stress—always staying at the member's tolerance level.

When necessary, rather than rebuke the member, we push back the clock, retracing steps already taken. For instance, we may bring the regressive behavior to his attention again, as if we never had; we work it through once more, we again study its history in the member's life, and so forth.

If regression does occur, we content ourselves that in time, inevitably, we will again arrive at the need for immunization. But always we temper communications until they become tolerable to the person. Gradually, having begun communicating with those people most sympathetic, the group member edges out toward those who ordinarily subject him to the most pressure and would induce regression.

All the while, the more nurturing members may be helping the person by appreciating his progress and by construing his motives in the most favorable light. They elicit the member's best behavior; they inspire the member toward still greater change, even as they immunize him against regression.

However, our nonnurturing members perhaps contribute even more in their own way. They are, after all, our on-the-premises representatives of figures who, in the outside world, provoke the member to be at his worst. Thus these members, not fundamentally sympathetic to the person, are the ones who ultimately make the person strong.

On the rare occasion when a group lacks members able to serve as agents of immunization, we ourselves may need to play the part of "adversary." For instance, one woman so held a group in awe that I was the only one who could confront her. She had seemingly overcome her tendency toward bursts of excoriating rage, but I had to be sure.

When I did say something that I thought was true but that she obviously didn't want to hear, I was pleasantly surprised that she did not regress. Instead, she considered what I said and simply disagreed.

Who could be sure of the truth? The important issue was that we could have dialogue. After that, other group members felt able to confront her, and we were all convinced that her new accessibility was real and would withstand stresses.

Because psychic life is organic, continual confirmation of identity occurs over people's lifetimes. Long after our members leave us, they have experiences that recall adventures they had in group. Those experiences confirm discoveries they made ages ago.

Oscar Wilde once said that people pay for a single character flaw a thousand times over. Likewise, they reap the benefit of gains over and over again. And we group therapists are no exception. If we care to, we ourselves keep confirming our identities, adding discoveries and nuances as long as we persevere in our efforts.

CHAPTER SIXTEEN

TERMINATION

The time has come to consider a member's leaving. We have paved the way for his or her progress. We are content that we and the group—essentially "we through the group"—have helped the person profoundly in at least some domain of his life.

Nearly always this means that the member has come to recognize his self-defeating patterns. He has discovered them to be at the heart of his difficulties over a lifetime. By acting in the group in ways that express and manifest these patterns, the member has come to understand his own role in his defeats, and to develop new patterns of feeling and acting.

To this end, we have used the other members not merely as investigators and interpreters but as players in the person's immediate life. The group has served as a stage for reenactment of the critical patterns that needed to be seen and confronted.

"The external world echoes inside of us," wrote the great sociologist Emile Durkheim, as if describing the isomorphic mapping between what goes on inside of an individual and that person's experience of the outside world.

In working well with a member, we have made extensive use of this mapping, but we have gone in the other direction. We have found other group members who represent the person's internal forces, so-called introjects, and our member nearing termination has, little by little, discovered his problems and resolved them by dealing externally with these others in his group. Thus the group has served as an enlargement and reification of the person's inner life.

To the extent that the member has succeeded, he feels differently and perceives himself differently. The member perceives at least certain other people in ways that free him to serve his or her own ends more immediately and richly than before. And this is not narcissistic. He serves other people better too. His character structure is different.

The member may have changed goals and purposes, after enlightened examination of them. But this need not be the case. Nor is it necessary that we, as group therapist, share the person's purposes and aims.

But when has a member reached such a stage? How long any given person remains in group is of course a function of what that person wants for himself.

For instance, we see group members who after a short time come to grips with a single self-defeating pattern. Having triumphed over some formerly crippling trait, they announce their desire to leave us. They let us know that their priorities are elsewhere and then go off into the wide world to use whatever they have cultivated within themselves while they were with us.

We may wish that they remained with us longer, and perhaps we see new ways that we might still help them. However, if we concur with them that they have indeed done what they set out to do, we cannot in good conscience prevail upon them to stay on. We have taken the person as far as he wanted to go. That someone wants to leave us does not in itself imply that the person is "resisting" further growth, which we might have in mind for him.

At the other extreme are those who fall in love with the process of self-discovery—they range from the excessively self-preoccupied to true adventurers of the spirit. These people may wish to stay on and on. And so long as our group serves them, why not?

Of course, there are as many forms of therapeutic failure as there are techniques of helping people. The failure to orchestrate a member into a group, the failure to deal with resistances, a failure at working-through, the failure to immunize a member against regression—any of these may limit our success in helping a group member.

In some cases, we are quite content that a group member whom we have not helped over a period of time stays with us. Especially if the member looks forward to the group sessions, who are we to say that he is getting nothing out of the experience, even though we don't see the progress that we looked for? Conceivably, without our knowing it, we may be providing a vital ingredient that keeps the person able to cope and to like himself as much as he does. In some cases, people don't show real change for years and then progress very rapidly.

On the other hand, an obsessional person who is full of dissatisfaction, and whom we have not helped noticeably, may well demoralize the group as well as himself. We do not throw such people out of our group. However, sooner or later they do leave us. They are clearly among our therapeutic failures.

Admittedly, we have failed to identify a resistance of theirs that stymied us and in the end cost them our help. We have failed to resolve their very obsessing. In some cases, this was because we ourselves suffered from a personal limitation that inhibited our best efforts to help them. If so, quite obviously we need to examine ourselves after such a failure.

And a great many of our therapeutic failures come because we haven't recognized a smoldering resentment on the part of a member. Or if we have sensed the presence of that resentment, we haven't surfaced it or dealt with it properly. The member has come to our group regularly, obeyed the rules externally, but has seen us as an adversary—as someone who would become hostile or even triumphant over him if he told us how he felt.

Whether or not he started out seeing us as an opponent whom he had to defeat, he has arrived at that conclusion. To let on what he really feels, what he is afraid of, would, in his view, be itself a defeat, and so he conforms to the letter of our group requirements but congeals in his refusal to change.

Our failure to surface such a person's agenda will inevitably result in trouble, though in at least some of these cases we never had a real chance. The person's secret agenda may have been to stymie us, to render us impotent, the accomplishment of which gives him a curious sense of victory.

Our best cue that such a failure is in the offing with a member is a sense that the person is detached or uninvolved with us. He keeps a circumspect distance from us. There is a silent, slippery gap between him and us. We get a sense that though he has had ample invitation, he isn't yet ready to talk: he hasn't quite built up enough confidence or trust of us. In such cases, we and our group members usually feel deprived by the person who withholds so much from us. But especially if this kind of member is prone to talk about how other people whom he trusted in the past did him in, we feel hesitant to confront the person head-on.

It's as if we were afraid to do something that the person might construe as harsh—to repeat the sins of his predecessors, whom the member says mistreated him and injured him.

Unless we identify the member through these cues—a hesitance on our part to confront the person, even to acknowledge to ourselves his excessive privacy with us; a tendency on our part toward favoritism; a protectiveness of him that we extend toward few other people—we are in for a big comedown. No matter how careful we are, the person will stun us by announcing his departure and telling us that we gave him nothing.

When he accuses us of not understanding him, he is in a sense right—had we understood him, we would have intervened early. One technique might have been to predict his departure, or at the very least, we would have enabled the other group members to identify this person's "patrician delicacy" and his demand for special treatment. Either they would have reached the member and decoded his secret message before he acted on it, or failing that, at least when the person left the group abruptly, they would not feel so wounded and inept.

In the worst-case scenario, when such a person does leave our group, we have the problem of helping the other members appreciate that they were not all bumbling and incompetent. They have not once again demonstrated a basic lack of the sophistication needed to cultivate so high-minded a person. They would see that this person walked out on them without giving them a fair chance—and, of course, without giving himself or herself a fair chance.

As for the creative people who keep using group profitably, we revel in their expansiveness, in their romanticizing their own lives, which they see as glorious odysseys. We watch them continually use what they learn from others. To them every personal limitation is a challenge. Such people are, as a rule, flexible and adaptable and become more so as they work with us. It is not a failure for them to work with us for years, or even decades, so long as their inner lives keep enlarging.

Granting that there are as many forms of success in life as there are individuals, certain criteria of accomplishment are worth stating.

A successful group member has resolved self-defeating patterns that he or she came into the group with—ways of acting and of perceiving events.

Such a person can identify with others when necessary, can process experience before acting. He can tolerate high frustration even in the area of his presenting problems.

More generally, the successful group member has become able to identify the source of his or her own strong feelings. Such a person doesn't blame others for his own actions, but takes full responsibility for them.

Curiously, though the experience of being a group member, like that of being in therapy generally, heightens self-consciousness and introspection, this self-preoccupation should ease up as the member nears termination. That is, there comes a time when a successful group member must make the transition from his self-referential world to the real world outside.

It is not unusual for a member involved with personal repair to fall prey to excessive self-reference. For instance, another person's growth is seen as threatening, as if it were a designed insult or a reminder of his own failure to change fast enough. Or another person's decision to leave the group may be seen as abandonment. The member so caught up in what Shakespeare called "the pale cast of thought" must again become more object-oriented, learning to see the world for what it really is.

This transition occurs visibly within the group itself. The person approaching termination comes to see the other group members as separate entities, living their own lives, engaged in their own struggles. His interactions with people, rather than heightening his solipsism, take him away from his self-concern. Narcissism, whether the member suffered from it before treatment or as a by-product of treatment, diminishes sharply in the final stages.

The successful group member, whether he becomes more or less outgoing, is at least more sensitive and more a master of his decisions involving other people. If he wants to socialize, he can. If his ambition is to become a recluse, ideally, we have given access to himself to make this more possible too.

Nearly always, the finishing group member has evolved greater empathy and an appreciation of what other people feel. Though he may offend people at times, he comes closer to Aristotle's criterion not to offend other people unknowingly.

Actual Departure

From the moment that a member tells the group that he or she is thinking of leaving, assuming that we concur that this is a good idea, there are steps we must take to help him leave us with minimum obstruction.

In almost every case, certain of the other members will want him to stay, for any of a variety of reasons. Some will resent his progress, some have unresolved business with the person, still others feel acutely abandoned whenever anyone marches out of their life.

Rather than protest his decision openly, such people may seek to undermine that decision. They may imply that he still has serious problems that he is running away from, or they may act superior to him because they themselves are staying on to get more. They inflict a kind of perfectionism on him.

Whatever their tactics, the overriding motive of these protesters is a dislike of the feelings induced in them by the member's decision to leave. Because no one is a hundred percent resolute about even the sagest decisions, whoever would leave a group may fall prey to these machinations designed to weaken his resolve.

Our aim must be to help clear the member's way to leave us, while simultaneously understanding and helping the other members resolve their individual misgivings about letting him or her go. From the time a member announces his intention to leave, assuming that we also consider him ready to go, there is much that we can do to help make his departure itself an enriching experience.

No matter how resolutely a person announces his decision to leave, he almost surely has second thoughts. How could he not? After all, has he not found his new strength in the context of the group and with its encouragement? He has used the group members to play out his doubts and hesitations, to rehearse his plans, in some cases to reassure him that he is rational. Since his newfound gains, he has never had to face the world without the group somewhere in the background.

After even a short time, he may find reasons not to go. His old symptoms may return. A woman who learned to control her temper loses it repeatedly during the week. A man who thought his sexual problems were solved finds himself impotent once more. People find themselves afflicted by the very problems that led them to go to the group in the first place, and these problems would seem to indicate that they are in no way ready to leave.

We may have thought that we immunized them against regression, and we did immunize them in the sense that ordinary stimuli did not set them back. However, the prospect of their leaving the group, the threat of abandonment that the member feels (though, technically, he is doing the leaving), is a stimulus greater than any that we were able to introduce as part of our immunizing drills.

Once again, we rely on the group to do the work. Ideally, we turn to someone in the group who is favorably disposed to the member's leaving. We ask him how he construes the return of these symptoms on the part of the leave-taker.

"Look," said Alfred, in a group of mine. "Pattie, I know why you're scared. From the moment you told us that you'd be stopping group this summer, you've gone backward. You've been yelling at us, and now you tell us you're going berserk with your husband. You're trying to make a case for staying." Pattie seemed to collapse. She immediately attacked herself, "There I go again. You're right. I'm not in control of my life. I don't know what I'm doing."

Pattie had taken Alfred's comment and used it to make a further case for her staying, as if he were warning her that she was not ready to leave. But I sensed that Pattie was not nearly as distressed as she let on, that, if anything, hers was a subtle cry for reassurance.

Just then, another woman in the group, Claire, who was a very nurturing person and who had consistently supported Pattie, looked frustrated. I commented that Claire looked uncomfortable, and she replied instantly that she was. "Yes," she said. "Don't you see, Pattie, it's the same old story. You're not really falling apart. You want us to tell you that you're great, and you are."

Pattie smiled at once. Hers had been a lame attempt to use an old pattern, a device that she herself didn't believe anymore.

The group talked briefly about Pattie's twinges of personal uncertainty and her tendency to turn on others, and then her ensuing feelings of guilt. In the past, she would fall prey to these feelings for weeks, without insight. However, this time Pattie nodded knowingly as the group spoke, and rewarded us by acknowledging, "You're right. I even saw it coming."

I annotated the exchange. "So this isn't really your Achilles' heel, anymore. Is that what you're saying?"

She smiled. "No, it isn't," she told us. "It's only a bit of nostalgia."

Now it was the group's turn to laugh.

Within weeks, Pattie had left us, and we knew that she was forti-
fied, and we felt proud.

Assuming that we have immunized our member and that we are
now seeing only the remnants of the neurosis that once ruled the
person, such last-minute misgivings actually solidify the advances already made. Because leaving the group is itself a decisive act in the
person's life, the members' very preparation to leave is an act of
growth.

Although our emphasis throughout treatment has been on *how* the
member interacts with those in the group, on the assumption that
group is a microcosm of the world, we may find it useful to talk about
the real world more in these last stages. We pay special attention to
any concern that a soon-to-depart member might express about his or
her life to come.

For instance, a man talks about marrying someone or about changing careers—these are topics that have haunted him before. In the
past, we did our best to translate these issues into group issues. His
difficulty in committing himself to marriage expressed itself as a difficulty in speaking intimately to women in the group. During his
two-year stay, whenever we could, we dealt with the group manifestation of his problem.

This time, however, we are readier to talk about his real-life difficulty in the terms that he presents it.

Our discussing the member's outside life in its own terms helps
both the member and the group make the eventual separation. The
member who will be leaving comes to see the others less as fictive
beings, as products of his own inner life, than as real people with real
ideas. He sees them as friends, or if not as friends, then as comrades.
In making this translation to a new way of perceiving the other group
members, he is separating from them psychologically. He is on his
way out. The final leave-taking will be easier.

Moreover, our allowing this quantum of reality into the sessions
tells the others that something fundamentally different is occurring.
They are beginning to contemplate his departure, to accept it as real.
This person is truly leaving. He will be out of their lives. Thus our
greater emphasis on the departing member's outside life makes his
departure easier both for him and for the others. By their helping him

take his step toward the real world, take it in their presence, they are helping themselves adjust to his moving out of their lives.

During the last month or so, some reference should be made in every session to the member's leaving. We want the group members to vent whatever unspoken feelings they might have about not seeing him again. It is at such a time that one person might express frank envy. "I don't think I'll ever be able to do what you did."

But more often, such envy is expressed indirectly. Arthur, a member, says bitterly, "Well, Marie, you always do things fast."

Suspecting possible aggression in such a remark, we might ask another member what he thinks lies behind that comment. The member accuses Arthur of making a put-down statement.

This exchange not only profits Arthur, it helps Marie to leave without being burdened by the inference that she is doing something hasty and ill-advised.

No matter what reactions the other group members have to a person's leaving, we want those other members to put those reactions into words. In so doing, they both resolve their own apprehensions and help the person leave without being burdened by their unexpected feelings toward him.

No matter how often a member has talked about leaving, his final session has its own identity.

Nearly always, the person himself will bring up the fact that this is to be his last time with us. "I've been thinking about this for a long time. And all last week, I've been sensing how much I'll miss you people."

The member may want a chance to speak individually to a number of people in the group. Or he may single out some individual, perhaps thanking that person for his or her support. Or he may simply wish to say to the person, "I'll miss you."

Certain departing members simply wait to be approached, just to be sure that they are loved. Sure enough, someone will bring up the subject of his leaving.

And surprisingly often, we see poignant endings that we didn't expect. For instance, the departing member turns to someone toward whom he feels he has left something unsaid.

"You know, there's something I always wanted to say. When your mother died, I was quiet, and I feel terrible about that. It's always bothered me. I was quiet because my mother died of a tumor also, and I know what you felt. I want you to know that I suffered all the same things, the same way. You're not alone."

Or the "something unsaid" may be to the group as a whole. "I want you all to know that even though I'm doing fine now, I had bad problems in business, pretty bad ones. I folded, and I never mentioned it. I was too embarrassed. But now I don't want to leave like a big shot. And this is very important for me to say."

This impulse on the part of a member to convey something about himself that has been left unsaid is very common. Without making such a disclosure, the person feels that the group never fully knew him. For him to leave cleanly, it is important now that they do. Of course, no one can possibly convey his totality, but people on the brink of leaving may become almost obsessed by the need to convey some particular truth about themselves, which stands, metaphorically, for the rest of them that must remain forever unknowable.

Understanding this, we try to help the person deliver this final message. We may paraphrase this truth to help the others appreciate it, and we may invite responses, getting others to tell us how they feel about the person's ultimate disclosure.

Nearly always, they are glad that the person told them. They sensed that there was something more about him, and now they know what it is. They receive his final statement as an ultimate act of trust, though seldom do they reevaluate him as a result. Such disclosures are typically far more important to the person who makes them than they are to anyone else.

People leaving sometimes want to celebrate. The person tells the group proudly what they have done for him. He will miss the other members, he cares deeply about their lives, but his own has taken on great momentum. He may tell us his future plans.

Ideally, we want from the departing member: (1) some comments about the people in the group and what they contributed; (2) at least a brief statement concerning how he or she feels about leaving; and finally (3) at least some comments about what he or she plans to do in the future.

Some group therapists try to elicit this formally. They ask the person specifically to make a brief comment to each of the remaining members, indicating in particular what the member has contributed to his life. One may think of this as a formal acknowledgment of each of those present.

Or the therapist may ask the members in turn to offer their reactions to the person's leaving and to describe their feelings about him.

These methods, though they have their virtues, have a stifling formality. We are singling out individuals in the group setting, imposing a template on the session itself—in effect, delegating speakers and listeners. The risk is that we suppress the fluidity of the group.

Any act that does this may prove costly later on. The sessions that follow may be marked by a sluggishness, a despondency. The members may think of themselves as in a kind of mourning. But in reality, it is the inevitable result of our imposing any formal ritual on a group—such rituals, whatever seeming benefit they have in the moment, snuff out spontaneity. The members, having been called on, wait to be called on again, which is why the group loses momentum.

Therefore, though we want both the member and those left behind to discuss how they feel, we allow this to occur naturally. If it doesn't, we study why not.

Rather than ask Bill, a good friend of John's in group, "How do you feel about John's leaving today?" we turn to someone else—Mary.

We ask Mary to explain Bill's silence.

"For two years Bill and John have been totally involved with each other in this room. Mary, why do you think Bill hasn't said a single word about John's leaving?"

Such a question, though directed at a third party, soon becomes fair game for anyone else who cares to answer it. It releases discussion of the group's resistance to giving its reactions to the person's leaving. By dealing with this resistance, wherever we find it, we open up the floodgates for expression of many feelings that have been withheld. We will get far more this way than if we had simply gone around the room posing direct questions.

Though therapists differ regarding how long a hiatus members should allow before contacting someone who left, assuming that they want to, I recommend at least six months.

My own experience has given me several reasons for stipulating this. One is that when members meet earlier, they tend to see each other more as group members than as real people. For instance, within the group, one member stood for another's brother or father or lover or boss or adversary. People served as one another's ideal. Too soon a contact with a member who left is likely to leave the members seeing each other almost exclusively through the lens of such transferences.

In short, their perceptions of one another within the group session are beclouded by their symbolic meanings to one another. This has long been recognized in the case of patient and therapist in individual treatment. These same transference clouds distort relationships between group members, with similar unfortunate results.

Paradoxically, the better the group treatment, the more the need for delay. The very nature of group treatment at its best is that transferences among the members are most prolific. The expectations the members hold of one another duplicate expectations they had of people in their early lives.

Time and subsequent experience tend to melt down at least some of these idealizations and other distortions. Even after the six-month period, some of these distortions remain, so that in my opinion six months is a bare minimum for the members to wait.

Indeed, it often occurs that a member who objects to the six-month barrier loses all interest in calling the other person long before that time is reached. Members, after feeling sure that they will become a lifetime friend of someone leaving, lose impetus as time goes by and the person's symbolic meaning to them dissipates. This is especially so when their "transference fondness" for someone has been a too-easy escape from their need to deal with problems at home.

Another reason for a lengthy separation after a group member leaves is to discourage misuses of group. We don't want people to join our groups to make friends or to meet lovers. Social groups serve useful roles in our society, and we have nothing against them. But therapeutic groups, for the reasons already given, cannot also be social in essence. It is not merely that transferential perceptions interfere with social relationships, the opposite is also true. Socializing tends to attenuate the symbolic meanings that people have to one another, and interferes with the therapeutic aims of the group.

Finally, our six-month stipulation discourages people's dropping out simply to extract benefits from the other members. Some members, after discovering and expressing feelings toward one another, mistake this for immediate license to act on what they say. Our six-month stipulation discourages these members from acting on their newly uncovered desires—their desire for love or friendship or to start business dealings with others in the group. These very people, who want to convert ideas into action without delay, need our six-month stipulation for protection against their own impulses and so that they do not pester others.

No matter how gracefully a member leaves, the group is sure to feel a gap when he or she is gone. Although encouraged to express all their feelings while the person was there, the members left behind are likely to have still more feelings about him weeks or months later. We want them to talk about that person. Though gone, he remains important to them, and we want the members to say what he meant to them. This not only helps the members understand themselves better. They can also see that long after they themselves leave the group, they will be remembered and their impact will be felt.

Naturally, when a person leaves, the mosaic changes, with other members taking on some of the roles and functions that the departing person had. At best, we have the sense of a job well done, by us and the group.

However, almost as often, we are left with a sense that we might have done more. We have this sense, even as we recognize that the person has accomplished a great deal. He or she tells us, by letter or in person months later, that his life has opened up as a result of our work. Or he lets us know indirectly by referring someone else to us and virtually insisting that the person come to us.

In these cases, we feel the way a parent often does, whose son or daughter has left unfinished some dream the parent held for him or her. We are gnawed at by the recognition that the person could have given himself more, become more. "If only Mary had gotten in touch with her deeper sense of rage, learned to harness it and use it for her own ends." But Mary says that she has finally found the ability to love, and is enjoying her life. "If only Jonathan had stopped pleasing other people as much . . ." And we could go on and on.

However, like the parent, we are thinking about ourselves and not the other person. Life is full of incompleteness, and we know that. We experience it daily. Our wistfulness for the other person is in the end a longing for perfection. We have done what we could. The rest will be up to the person whose life we have joined for a time. Though our member is no longer in our lives, his journey is not over.

As time goes by, the gap in us will heal. We will recognize a job well done, if indeed that has been the case.

CHAPTER SEVENTEEN

TOWARD EXCELLENCE

Most of the traits that qualify a person to run groups are those that also qualify him or her to treat individuals. These include intelligence, wide-ranging sympathy, compassion (even when insulted or injured by a patient), and that curious combination of detachment and involvement that is the signature of our profession. This last is almost impossible unless the therapist has a sense of humor, which allows him or her to see events lightly and to invite people into the flow of humanity.

Moreover, the attainment of general culture, of a background in history, mythology, literature, and theater that enables us to see people writ large should be our responsibility as long as we remain in this field. After all, we are like detectives looking at details and drawing conclusions from them, and the more we know about all of humankind the better.

Although, in essence, one needs a therapeutic personality to treat groups or individuals, certain abilities seem more at a premium when one works with whole groups. In part, this is because the group therapist is more on display; he or she cannot hide deficits or even defenses. Anything resembling a facade is far more likely to be detected by a group than by an individual coming for help.

Then, too, we are more on the spot in a group because patients see us as less necessary for their survival, their cure. The patient in private treatment may see his therapist as standing between him and chaos, and have a need to overlook the therapist's failings, even obvious ones.

But in a group the members have one another as mainstays in their striving toward health, and they also have one another to verify whatever they see or think they see. Our faults cry out to be mentioned, and once a group member spots one, we can expect others to point their fingers at us too.

Because every group is composed of many sensibilities and vantage points, the therapist himself, or herself, is under scrutiny to a degree that few therapists are when they work with individuals. This being under scrutiny has implications for everything we do. If we are grandiose or self-serving, someone will unmask us and will alert the others. If we favor people of one sex over the other, or one lifestyle over another, there will almost surely be an informant against us in the room—not just in one of our groups but in all of them.

And if we break a rule, even by accident, we will pay a price. For instance, we meet a patient accidentally at a summer resort and chat with him briefly. If we are working with the person individually, though we expect him to have reactions, they are unlikely to reverberate in our work for long. We can talk about them in the very next session, and delve into them.

However, if we meet a group member in exactly the same way, we may not get off so lightly. Back in the group-room, when the person mentions meeting us, even if he or she does not react markedly, it is very likely that others in the room will. We will doubtless have a variety of reactions to cope with, and some will erupt not at the time but months later. Group treatment, in this respect, is full of wild-card factors, and the group therapist needs a special kind of alertness and plasticity to deal with them.

In particular, certain demands of us are much greater with groups than when we work with individuals.

For one thing, though we are fallible, we must beware of facades, of pat ways of doing things, of devices that insulate us from genuine emotional exchanges. Of course, we can make mistakes. But if we deny them, if we overprotect ourselves, we will pay an enormous price. At worst, our group members will lose faith in us. And at the very least, our group will stumble about for a while. What counts above all is that when confronted with our biases in a group, we listen, not defensively but openly. To err is human, but to remain open when our errors are hurled in our face, that is the mark of the true group therapist.

Our willingness to hear our faults cited—indeed, to hear ourselves criticized even when we don't agree with the criticism—without losing composure or distancing ourselves from the speaker is an utmost achievement. We must never punish a critic by removing ourselves emotionally.

As surely as defensiveness on our part will barricade avenues of progress, our readiness to stay open will demonstrate a new way of dealing with unwanted observations; it will free our group members to study themselves, as many never have before. Our openness to comments about us, favorable and unfavorable, is the group members' high-road to health.

Our patterns of thinking, over the years, evolve differently from the individual therapist's. True, we both keep a high premium on knowing what we are feeling, and are continually on the alert to identify sources of what we feel. But the individual therapist mainly distinguishes between feelings that come out of his own history and those induced by the person in front of him. There, the question asked over and over again is, "What is this patient in front of me doing that makes me feel this way?"

The group therapist has a very different question that he or she keeps asking, "Who in the group is making me feel as I do?" And the answer, as often as not, comes back: "It is not a single person making me feel this way, but a whole set of people. There is a shared mood or attitude in the room, and I must identify it for myself before this group can progress."

This brings us to the essence of what qualifies the group therapist, as distinguished from the individual therapist—it is a style of thinking. The group therapist always thinks in terms of sets of people, of groups. Regarding the whole group as his "patient," he or she comes to ask, almost instinctively, as a mother would, "Who is being left out at this moment?" "Who is angry?" "Who is talking too much?"

We work for total effects, and think of wholeness in our group-room.

This is, of course, not out of disregard for the individual—our bottom line is individual change—but because the group is our instrument to accomplish change in individuals. The successful group is one whose members change for the better. And as I hope I have shown, there is no paradox once a certain truth is known. It is that the successful group therapist is the one who creates and sustains a therapeutic environment. The group is the instrument of personal change.

SOME FURTHER READINGS

Ackerman, N. (1949). "Psychoanalysis and Group Therapy." In *Group Therapy,* Vol. 8, Nos. 2–3. Edited by J. C. Moreno, pp. 204–15. Boston: Beacon House.

Agrarian, Y. M. (1989). "Group-as-a-whole: Systems Theory and Practice." *Group* 13(3&4): 131–54.

Aronson, M. (1979). "The Unique Advantages of Analytic Group Therapy in the Middle and Later Phases of the Therapeutic Process." In *Group Therapy.* Edited by L. Wolberg and M. Aronson. New York: Stratton Intercontinental Medical Books.

Bach, G. R. (1954). *Intensive Group Psychotherapy.* New York: Ronald Press.

Bader, L. J. (1984). "From the Private I to the Public Ear: Effective Learning Groups for College-age Students." *Group* 8(1): 48–52.

Battegay, R. (1986). "People in Groups: Dynamic and Therapeutic Aspects." *Group* 10(3):131–48.

Berger, M. (1966). "Group Methods and Human Potentialities." In *Explorations in Human Potentialities.* Edited by Herbert A. Otto. Ann Arbor, Mich.: Books on Demand, UMI.

Berne, E. (1966). *Principles of Group Treatment.* New York: Oxford University Press.

Bion, W. R. (1960). *Experience in Groups and Other Papers.* New York: Basic Books.

Bry, T. (1951). "Varieties of Resistance in Group Psychotherapy." *International Journal of Group Psychotherapy* 1:106–14.

Burrow, T. (1927). "The Group Method of Analysis." *Psychoanalytic Review* 14:268–80.

Corsini, R. J. (1957). *Methods of Group Psychotherapy.* New York: McGraw-Hill.

Day, M. (1981). "Process in Classical Psychodynamic Groups." *International Journal of Group Psychotherapy* 31:153–74.

Denes, M. (1978). *Gestalt Group Therapy in Group Psychotherapy—Theory and Practice.* Edited by Hugh Mullan and Max Rosenbaum. Chicago: The Free Press.

Dies, R. (1986). "Practical, Theoretical and Empirical Foundations for Group Psychotherapy." *The American Psychiatric Association Annual Review* 5:650–77.

Durkin, H. (1964). *The Group in Depth.* New York: International Universities Press.

227

Epstein, L. (1990). "Some Reflections on the Therapeutic Use of the Self." *Group* 14(3):151–56.

Fisher, M. (1977). "The Potential for Authentic Relatedness in Group Psychoanalysis." *Group Process* 7:141–50.

Foulkes, S. H. (1975). *Group Analytic Psychotherapy: Method and Principles.* London: Gordon & Breach.

————— and E. J. Anthony (1965). *Group Psychotherapy: The Psychoanalytic Approach.* 2d ed. Baltimore: Penguin Books.

Freud, S. (1921). *Group Psychology and the Analysis of the Ego.* Standard edition 18:67–144.

Friedman, R. (1977). "An Informal Experiment in a Community College." *Psychoanalysis* 2(1):113–19.

Furgeri, L. (1978). "The Celebration of Death in Group Process." *Clinical Social Work Journal* 6(2):90–99.

Glatzer, H. T. (1978). "The Working Alliance in Analytic Group Psychotherapy." *International Journal of Group Psychotherapy* 28:147–61.

Goodman, M., M. Marks, and H. Rockberger (1964). "Resistance in Group Psychotherapy Enhanced by the Countertransference Reactions of the Therapist." *International Journal of Group Psychotherapy* 14:332–43.

Grotjahn, M. (1950). "The Process of Maturation in Group Psychotherapy in the Group Therapist." *Psychiatry* 13:63–7.

Hadden, S. (1959). "Dynamics of Group." *Diseases of the Nervous System.* 20:258–62.

Hammer, E. (1978–79). "Use of Metaphor in Individual and Group Therapy: Interpretations Couched in the Poetic Style." *International Journal of Psychoanalytic Psychotherapy* 7:240–53.

Hill, W. F. (ed). (1961). *Collected Papers on Group Psychotherapy.* Provo, Utah: Utah State Hospital.

Johnson, J. (1963). *Group Therapy: A Practical Approach.* New York: McGraw-Hill.

Kadis, A. L., J. D. Krasner, C. Winick, and S. H. Foulkes (1963). *A Practicum of Group Psychotherapy.* New York: Harper & Row.

Kotkov, B. (1957). "Common Forms of Resistance in Group Psychotherapy." *Psychoanalytic Review* 44:86–96.

Milman, D. S. (1974). *Group Process Today.* Edited by D. S. Milman and G. D. Goldman. Springfield, Ill.: Charles C. Thomas.

Mullan, H. and Rosenbaum, M. (1962). *Group Psychotherapy.* New York: The Free Press of Glencoe.

Munzer, J. (1967). "Acting Out: Communication or Resistance?" *International Journal of Group Psychotherapy* 16(4):434–41.

Ormont, J. and L. Ormont (1986). *Conjoint Therapy, Psychotherapist's Casebook.* Edited by Alexander Wolf and Irwin Kutash, pp. 424–33. San Francisco: Jossey Bass.

Pines, M. (1981). "The Frame of Reference of Group Psychotherapy." *International Journal of Group Psychotherapy* 31:275–85.

Powdermaker, F. and J. D. Frank (1953). *Group Psychotherapy: Studies in Meth-*

odology of Research and Therapy. Cambridge, Mass.: Harvard University Press.

Rosenbaum, M. and M. Berger (1963). *Group Psychotherapy and Group Function.* New York: Basic Books.

Rosenthal, L. (1985). "A Modern Analytic Approach to Group Resistance." *Journal of Modern Psychoanalysis* 10:165–82.

——— (1987). *Resolving Resistances in Group Psychotherapy.* Northvale, N. J.: Jason Aronson.

Rutan, J. S. and A. Alonso (1978). "Some Guidelines for Group Therapists." *Group* 1:4–13.

——— and W. Stone (1984). *Psychodynamic Group Psychotherapy.* Lexington, Mass.: The Callamore Press.

Sherwood, M. (1964). "Bion's Experiences in Groups: A Critical Evaluation." *Human Relations* 17(2):113–30.

Slavson, S. (1964). *A Textbook in Analytic Group Psychotherapy.* New York: International Universities Press.

Spotnitz, H. (1952). "A Psychoanalytic View of Resistance in Groups." *International Journal of Group Psychotherapy* 2:3–9.

——— (1961). *The Couch and the Circle.* New York: Alfred A. Knopf.

——— (1969). "Resistance Phenomena in Group Psychotherapy." In *Group Therapy Today: Styles, Methods and Techniques.* Edited by H. Ruitenbeck, pp. 203–17. New York: Atherton Press.

——— (1976). *Psychotherapy of Pre-Oedipal Conditions.* New York: Jason Aronson.

Wender, L. (1936). "The Dynamics of Group Psychotherapy and Its Applications." *Journal of Nervous and Mental Disease* 84:54–60.

Whitaker, D. and M. Lieberman (1964). *Psychotherapy Through the Group Process.* New York: Atherton Press.

Wolf, A. (1949–50). "The Psychoanalysis of Groups." *American Journal of Psychotherapy* 3:16–50; 4:525–58.

———, and E. Schwartz (1962). *Psychoanalysis in Groups.* New York: Grune and Stratton.

Yalom, I. (1975). *The Theory and Practice of Group Psychotherapy.* 2d ed. New York: Basic Books.

SELECTED READINGS BY THE AUTHOR

(1962). "Establishing the Analytic Contract in a Newly Formed Therapeutic Group." *British Journal of Medical Psychology* 35:333–37.

(1964). *The Talking Cure*. With Morton Hunt and Rena Corman. New York: Harper and Row.

(1968). "Group Resistance and the Therapeutic Contract." *International Journal of Group Psychotherapy* 18(2):147–54.

(1969). "Acting in and the Therapeutic Contract in Group Psychoanalysis." *International Journal of Group Psychotherapy* 21(4):420–32.

(1970). "The Use of the Objective Countertransference to Resolve Resistance." *Group Process*, pp. 96–111.

(1974). "The Treatment of Pre-Oedipal Resistances in the Group Setting." *Psychoanalytic Review* 16:129–41.

(1981). "Principles and Practice of Conjoint Psychoanalytic Treatment." *American Journal of Psychiatry* 138(1):69–73.

(1984). "The Leader's Role in Dealing with Aggression in Groups." *International Journal of Group Psychotherapy* 34(4):553–72.

(1988). "The Role of the Leader in Resolving Resistances to Intimacy in the Group Setting." *International Journal of Group Psychotherapy* 38:19–46.

(1989). "Role of the Leader in Managing the Pre-Oedipal Personality in the Group Setting." *International Journal of Group Psychotherapy* 39(2):147–71.

(1990). "The Craft of Bridging." *International Journal of Group Psychotherapy* 40(1):5–30.

(1991). "The Use of the Group to Resolve the Subjective Countertransference." *International Journal of Group Therapy.* 41(3): 433–47.

INDEX